Aroused

A Collection of Erotic Writing

Also By Karen Finley

Shock Treatment
Enough is Enough
Living it Up
Pooh Unplugged
A Different Kind of Intimacy

Aroused

A Collection of Erotic Writing

edited by

Karen Finley

THUNDER'S MOUTH PRESS • NEW YORK

Aroused: A Collection of Erotic Writing

Compilation copyright © 2001 by Karen Finley
Introduction © 2001 by Richard Hell

Published by
Thunder's Mouth Press
An Imprint of Avalon Publishing Group Incorporated
161 William Street, 16th Floor
New York, NY 10038

Book design: Paul Paddock

Library of Congress Cataloging-in-Publication Data is available.

ISBN 0-7394-2460-2

Printed in the United States of America

Distributed by Publishers Group West

For
the
love
of
Estelle

KAREN FINLEY was born in Chicago. She received her MFA from The San Francisco Art Institute. She performs and exhibits her work internationally. She lives in New York.

Contents

Photography

Aroused

by
Karen Finley

Silk moist panties
Fan on my wet spot
and blow the taste
of semen, sweet grass and gone bad love
everything smells like fucking
oh, sweet sweet fucking

Get me in that subway
heat, flesh
Bodies so close like orgy

Get me in that elevator
alone, stranger
See I'm not wearing panties

Get me on the veranda
so I can get a closer look at you
pulling on what makes you a man

With windows wide open
I hear your moans
and play with myself
till we come at the same time

Sometimes there isn't a name
Sometimes it goes on for years
Sometimes it never happens
but the desire is in that someday it will.

Sometimes it is paid for
There are so many ways to
get it up
wooed to
yelled at
stroked
tender
kiss me

In the backseat
In your parents bed
Over the phone
On the kitchen table office desk shower mind fuck
garden delight imagination
fuck me bite me lick me close the door wait on the roof
seeing the moon

the tension
the ultimatums
till I make you jealous and ignore you and hate you and
want you back and
fuck you over
fuck over and over again

After all night drinking
and then once sober
looked over at in the morning
please be someone else
loved til death do us part
comfortable
routine and ritual
the other woman
frenzied
come for me
you always do

Sometimes it is all so complicated
the best friend, the triangle, affair,
downstairs upstairs

boss teacher neighbor
the intimacy of it all
the power
the guilt
the shame
the cheating
somehow makes it all
so more arousing
let me
take me
want me
I'm wearing perfume for you

I never want to see you again
I wake up thinking of you

Sometimes I love you
but I don't want you in me
and I don't know why
Sometimes I don't love you
and that is why
I want you in me

I could tell you about last Sunday
where he gave me a rainbow neck
to let all others know
he owned me
marking his territory

I could tell you about the time
on the rocks
in cold icy chicago
and the steam of dick crazy and pussy heaven

I am so wearied with the politics of it all
and satisfied in the chaos
of our differences the desire
for climax

I am dropping the preaching

for now
dropping the should of
dropping the look of your mommy
Put it in me daddy
Let's get this relationship over with before it even starts
Can't you get married so we can have an affair like
other decent people?

I don't want to untangle my
anxiety too much
for I am afraid of
loosing my passion for you

Oh, Lord
Here I go again
Wanting
Nervous
Out of breath
Can't eat
Faint

It's that delicious feeling
of sickness
like taking heroin

We all know from a glance
from here comes booty
from eyes up and down
touch me
I want you
I wanted you from the moment I saw you-

Ah, the arousal of it all
Please accept this sensual pleaure
Please receive this sensation
This gift
From us to you
Please be
Aroused

Writing Sex

by

Richard Hell

It's hard to write about sex. It's like writing about your mother. (I mean your mother, not mine, and me saying things about her.) Sex is charged. Some artists who treat sex behave as if people should respond to the sex in their work neutrally, as if it were any subject at all, but that's naive or disingenuous.

One place the Bible makes sense is in Genesis where loss of paradise is signified by sudden shame at nakedness (nakedness being genitals, being sex, of course). There's no going back. What removes us from the unselfconscious Eden of the other animals is that we have these oversized brains that aren't innocent. The goddamned "human condition" is that we're physical creatures ceaselessly batted around by biological needs and impulses inherited from our instinct-driven ancestors while at the same time we've evolved these super-complex brains capable of imagining and desiring (and demanding) other, ideal behaviors. It's embarrassing and infuriating, this discrepancy between what in some moods and states seems self-evidently desirable, even necessary, while in others seems depraved—or impossibly idealistic. (The very same activity can seem problematic because it's evil and because it's impossibly good, like, say, mate swapping, or having sex with your mother—that's your mother. . . .)

But beyond a doubt: people have a visceral, involuntary response to the presentation of sex. So how can one write it well when people react to it irrationally? I don't know, but I think a way to judge one's success at it is by whether the writing makes enough readers interested in having sex with the writer. Really. Ultimately, art for most artists is an elaborate sexual display, and, so, specifically sexual literature would have to stand or fall according to its seductive powers.

Of course there are many readers who are turned off by explicit sex writing, and the way to reach them lies elsewhere. But what an artist is doing is showing what he or she is made of so that the right people will be attracted. I do not think this is ignoble and I'm not trying to be a wise guy cutting down the pretensions of artists. I'm as pretentious as the next guy and I care more about books and writing and beauty than just about anything, but no more than I do about people wanting to have sex with me. Yes, art is also about making sense of the world (or excitingly reflecting its nonsense), and heightening the attender's own sense of being (inspiring him or her), and creating sensual and mental pleasure (beauty), etc., etc., but what are these but definitions of the seductive?

(In parallel, the act of writing itself is a kind of sex. That's not news either. Corny writers are always calling their books their children. But the need to write can also be a desire for immortality similar to what sex provides: reproduction. Sex is so pleasurable because our strongest drive is the preservation into further generations of our genetic material: a kind of physical immortality. Writing can be the means of doing this for a mind, a consciousness. A book survives because its author's consciousness as embodied in the writing is that interesting and affecting to readers. "Good" writing survives because readers like the company of the writer. Which brings us back to sexual display. . . . So suppose I'm writing about sex; then I'm having sex about sex in order to solicit sex! It's all sex!)

Probably the main objection to sexual writing is that it is vulgar, it violates refined discretion. Again, it's the reason we're not supposed to fart in public or to eat with our mouths open: embarrassment at out instinctual, involuntary, non-intellectual nature. I respect that—I try my best not to fart in public myself (though I enjoy it in private), while I regret losing the readers who can't abide sex-writing because it offends them. I don't claim that writing sex is right or good or necessary, and I'm not putting down readers who reject it. I just insist that it's legitimate. There is no subject that is beyond the bounds of good writing, just as there is no unworthy or indecent form or medium. I myself have a hard time reading very *long* works. So no matter how much I like Nabokov and Joyce, I've never read *Ada* or *Ulysses* all the way through. Though I read all the time, I haven't read *In Search of Lost Time* or *Don Quixote*. I have never finished reading an epic poem. This is a handicap of mine, an unfortunate disadvantage. It doesn't mean that epics are inferior. By the same token I resent being sneered at or dismissed for writing sex. I believe it's the reader's loss to be unable to enjoy sex in art, however understandable his or her reflexive reaction may be.

In a way I think that writing sex is especially interesting because of its difficulty. The gender and sexual preference of the writer immediately render some kinds of writing more or less problematic. (Not to mention cultural background—writing about sex in France is different from writing about it in America, or Iran.) Say for instance I'm speaking of male heterosexual writing, then the writer must contend with: male readers tending not to like other men's sexual display, and women possibly being made to feel objectified and not liking that. . . . The general difficulties have to do with penetrating (ahem) the readers' skepticism and resistance by winning their confidence with one's candor and depth of insight and (as above) one's personality, one's character, one's being itself as represented by the writing. (And again, finally, what other real standard for writing is there but that you like the company of the writer? You trust him or her, you like the shape of his or her mind and view of things, you appreciate the values inherent in the work. . . .) It's hard! I myself have had writers I liked suddenly and fatally tainted because of what they revealed about themselves in their writing about sex. Just as readers do, of course, writers have awful blind spots and handicaps in their psychology where sex is concerned, because it's such a complicated subject in which people have so much of themselves invested.

I think maybe gay men have the best chance of writing sex well. In fact when I think of good sex writing, the first names that come to my mind are Dennis Cooper and Allen Ginsberg and William Burroughs—Verlaine and Rimbaud were good too—not, say, Henry Miller and D. H. Lawrence and—who?—Philip Roth?—Erica Jong?—Kathy Acker? There's Nabokov, but he's really discreet. Apollinaire did some good pornography, but it was more purely pornography than those more "ambitious" kinds of writings I'm thinking of. (I believe pornography—writing done with the overriding purpose of arousing—is necessary and good, but that's a slightly different subject. The distinction is vague though—there's a lot of overlap. I've masturbated to Botticelli and dug the formal beauty of photos in *Sister Spank* magazine.) The reason gay men writers have a better chance I expect is that gay male sex is more accepted as being largely about arousal and the path to its consummation (pure lust, in other words, rather than, however indirectly, the path to creating a family), so there's less room for confusion and ambivalence and fewer grounds for outrage and resentment in the reader. (Incidentally illustrating the difficulties I'm describing, I have to disqualify myself regarding lesbian sex writing because it makes me too jealous to assess it fairly. When I read it, if I like the writer, I want to be the person she's desiring. I haven't found a way into heterosexual women's sex writing either. There isn't a whole lot of it by interesting writers. Lee Ann Brown is cool.) Allen Ginsberg's writing hasn't meant that much to me, but I think his sex writing is good for its unusual matter-of-factness, which I think largely follows from his queerness. Dennis Cooper and William Burroughs are two of the best American writers of the past 50 years and they both do a lot of sex and it's very good, conspicuously better than those heterosexuals, and I think this is made possible in part by this same advantage.

For some reason, I am interested in and compelled to try to know and describe dirty secrets of the sort that are obvious even though they're "secrets." Supreme examples being the biologically decreed pre-eminence of sex in our lives (and the sexes' separate interests there), and the inevitability of flat, final, death (and the implications of that). (Of course these are interestingly intertwined, being that sex provides the most effective way or two of detouring death.) But the list of such hypocrisies, illusions, and self-deceptions is endless (and the writers who've dwelt on them many—for instance, Voltaire, Swift, Flaubert, Nathanael West, Burroughs, Lenny Bruce—or maybe it's the only story there is—as Jim Thompson said, there's just one plot: things are not as they seem . . .). When I get uncomfortable with my own sex writing as I sometimes do (most often when I'm faced with reading it aloud in public, or when I think of relatives or "wholesome" people I admire reading it), or I'm subject to rejection or disapproval because of it, my justification for myself is always that I'm only being true to life. Maybe it is a poverty of material, but god knows it is half the material of our existence. (Or maybe I'm embarrassed because one doesn't like to be overheard shamelessly flirting. I think of writing as directed at one person, the reader. It's weird to have one's private offering, one's personal letter, heard by a crowd or discovered by one's family.) Then again, it's also embarrassing to have described my own contributions to this book as solicitations for your favors, but if you're who I care for you to be, the small embarrassment is worth the reward.

Little Trophy

by

Jerry Stahl

I was third in line the first time I ever actually "did it." This was 1970. I was fifteen. The girl involved was a plump, freckled nursing student named Sharon Schmidlap, a ponytailed barber's daughter who lived with her parents three blocks from the small-town boarding school to which I'd been shipped and who had, apparently, been of special service to a select few of my schoolmates for a season or two before my own arrival in eleventh grade.

"Who's the nervous Nellie?" young Sharon giggled, gaping up at me through gapped teeth while Number Two in line, a carbuncled southern boy named Tennie Toad—on account of his Tennessee roots and his bumpy epidermis—humped away and turned his sizable head to wink repeatedly in my direction.

Number One was a boy named Farwell whose father'd been ambassador to Turkey until his mother found him hanging from a chandelier in the embassy banquet room. Rumor had it Daddy Farwell checked out in stockings and heels, and his mother'd slapped the body in a tux before the guards came. His son hadn't said one way or another.

When Tennie was done, or when I thought he was done, he hopped onto his knees, reached under Sharon's ample hips and kind of flipped her onto her stomach on the wall-to-wall shag that covered the rec room floor. (A shade of purple, incidentally, that matched the nubby aureoles around her nipples, and the much-chewed-upon fruity gloss of her lips.) "This is what she *laks*," he giggled, in that half-screechy, half-cackling way he had, like Alfalfa from the Little Rascals, but grown up and nasty. "My gal laks a l'il bit o' spankin', donchu honeybutt?"

Before I knew what to make of that, Sharon gave a little coo. She adjusted her pillow-sized nether-globes upward for maximum impact, and Tennie let rip with a meaty thwack on her left buttock. I was amazed, horrified, nervous, and sort of in love. Sharon kept whipping her head from side to side. Her chocolate-brown eyes rolled back, so that the whites showed down to the bottom, reminding me of pictures I'd seen of horses in barn fires. She looked scared. She looked like *she liked it*. I thought my brain would look out of my ears.

By the time Tennie rolled off of Sharon and into the shag, her whole body had sprung a sheen, a glistening coat of sweat that made me think of supermarket chickens. Skinless and boneless.

I'd become so transfixed, when it was my turn I all but forgot I had to mount the girl myself.

Sharon wrapped a strand of mousy hair around her finger and ran it between her incisors, teasing, "Whatsa matter, Hercules, your pants glued on?"

I never even liked undressing in gym, and now I had to de-pants in front of two older guys and a girl who looked like she could eat me on toast. But I had to do it. *I had to!*

Without letting myself think about it, I took a deep breath. I fixed my eyes on the rec room TV, a Motorola with tinfoil balls wadded on each rabbit ear and a one-armed brass bowling trophy plunked beside it. That trophy began to speak to me.

I knew the thing was just broken. I knew that Sharon's barber dad had probably gotten drunk after a tournament and dropped it stumbling out of his Pontiac. But *still.* . . . It may have been the marijuana and spot remover—we'd huffed a busload on the way over—but that trophy wouldn't let go. *Look at this bowler*, I thought to myself, *he's got one arm, but he's not afraid! He's not ashamed! He probably gets heckled every time he steps up to the lane. They probably laugh at him, but HE'S not going back to his room and sitting under a blanket. HE'S got a goddamn trophy. So what do I care if it shrinks up and people call me "Nugget" the rest of my life? I'm a brave guy—I CAN TAKE IT!*

By the time I finished my crippled-bowler meditation, I was loaded for bear. I was finally hard and large, though not so much from the sight of Sharon's spread pudenda as my own visions of handicapped ten-pin glory. The noble feelings it instilled. I must, however, have looked like I was dawdling, because Tennessee Toad stepped up and shoved me hard between the shoulder blades, right into Sharon's saddle.

Amazing, the softness of her, the slightly tangly, slightly vinegary taste of her skin. But when I tried to kiss her, she moved her head so I got just a lick, a slurpy smush from just below her chin up under her ear.

"Oh, a *romantic,*" she sneered, and I pulled back just enough to see her roll her eyes. "Cory Grant wants to *smooch.*"

Still making a face, she reached between my legs with her left hand and grabbed me. Then she snapped her fingers with her right and Tennie tossed her a Trojan. She snagged it in midair, as if she'd been practicing for years. Sharon Schmidlap, Queen of the Condom Toss! I had a sudden vision of her naked on *The Ed Sullivan Show,* wowing them between Herman's Hermits and a troupe of plate-spinning, festive Romanians. Sunday nights have always made me nervous.

I wasn't too sure what was happening, but Sharon made short work of it. She kept up the patter as she unwrapped the rubber. "One size, fits all, lucky for you!" Right then, I remember thinking, *But I thought she was a Methodist. . . .* There was no time to muse, though—she was already wrapping me. "Okay, big boy, let's get dressed for church!"

At the same time Sharon was covering my hood ornament, Tennie was uncovering my behind. He grabbed me by the ankles and pulled my pants off over my shoes, then followed up with my undies.

"Voila!" he sang, and I found myself staring into the milky whites of my partner's eyes, wondering what to do with my arms, whether to actually *lay* on top of her or keep a respectful distance, as if we were strangers on a crowded bus.

Farwell chose that moment to put on a record—Mr. Schmidlap favored Perry Como—and Sharon plugged me in at the exact instant Perry asked the musical question, "How Much Is That Doggie In the Window?" I actually *liked* that song. My father used to whistle it. That's how I knew when he was happy. I imagined Dad looking down from the sky, summoned from death by that cheery tune, watching his son fumble his way to Shameville atop the spongy Sharon.

Toad got me out of my reverie. "Newsflash for Bobby," he chided me. "You're supposed to move. Don't just stick it in and take a nap."

"I *know,*" I cried back at him, adding inanely, *"I'm just warming up."*

More than what was happening in front, it was the action behind that had me squirming. I became, the second Tennie spoke, uncomfortably aware of him staring at my behind. I had never, to the best of my knowledge, showed my hindquarters to anyone before. Not, at any rate, for extended viewing. Self-consciousness burned my cheeks. I felt, with almost crippling intensity, split between two planes of reality. On one, I was timidly lunging into Sharon, poking her, or so it felt, like the fork my mother used to check if her cupcakes were done. On the other, the plane I couldn't see but the rest of the world could, my rear end was popping up, then popping down, popping up, then popping down again for Tennie Toad and Farwell to gawk at and mock.

I was so sure they were making fun of me I actually tried to crane my head all the way around, like an owl. Before I could get there, Sharon grabbed my face and held it.

"You pay attention, you little turd! Pay *attention*!"

My apathy, or whatever she thought it was, had the odd effect of making Sharon more passionate. And as much to my horror as my excitement, she began to mumble like someone possessed.

"You don't give a hoot about me. . . . Oh now, you're not like my boyfriend, you're not like *Charlie*, with his *roses*, with his chocolate-covered cherries. . . . Ho no, you don't care. . . . You just want my *hole*. You just want to . . . Oh! You just want to . . . Oh! Oh! You just want to . . . You little bastard, you little creep, you just want to fuh, wanna fuh . . . you just wanna *FUCK ME*, you wanna *FUCK MY GIRL-HOLE*, my *VA-GEE-NA*"—that's how she pronounced it, va-*GEE*-na, like Pasadena, where they hold the Rose Bowl. "Oh yeah, that's what you want. . . . Oh God, oh goody God, that's what you want! *THAT'S WHAT YOU WANT* . . . !"

She went on like that, until I actually got scared. *Confused*. I kept feeling those eyes on the back of my skull. Finally I did turn around to find that Tennie wore a new look on his pitted face. An expression, I realized, of respect. I had just gotten the hang of it, the in-and-out, the shoulder-holding, the whole idea of nipple-squeezing, hair-pulling, pawing—in a mild way—when Sharon went after my tongue. But no sooner did she start to kiss than she stopped. She pushed me off, called me a Communist, and repositioned her face on the woolly carpet.

"Now what?" I heard myself whimper. Toad made a swishing

motion with his hand, as though signaling a runner home from third, then Farwell chimed in with a single clap. This was as animated as I'd seen him since the embassy thing.

"Well?" Sharon angled her face sideways, so that I could see her tongue wiggle out of her lips. "Daddy don't wanna go fishin', Daddy shouldn't bait the hook."

"What?" I said.

"What do you mean *'what?'* Tennie leaped off the couch. He grabbed a book off the end table—a *Reader's Digest* condensed including *Treasure Island, Gigi,* and *The Man in the Gray Flannel Suit*—and swung it off the back of my head.

"Ouch," I hollered. "What are you doing?"

"What are *you* doing?" he hissed back at me. "You silly fuck! Give it to her!"

At which point Sharon herself chimed in. "What do I gotta do, paint a bull's-eye?"

Her voice had gone all low and throaty. Tennie dropped the book. He backhanded me across my left ear, but not as hard this time. Then he leaned in so his breath tickled the back of my neck. I could smell the cheesesteak he'd eaten earlier that afternoon, what seemed like a century ago, when I was still a virgin, as opposed to a half-virgin, or a near non-virgin, or whatever I was now.

"I've been *bad*," Sharon cackled, with a low little laugh. "I've been so dirty-bad, you don't even know."

"Huh?"

"Jesus, you're a *feeb*!" Tennie whispered. Still leaning in, he reached over my shoulder and clapped one of Sharon's ample haunches, leaving a handprint the size of a pie-plate. "Didn't you *see* me before?" he asked. "Did you think that was *my* idea?" He was so close his lips grazed my earlobe. I wondered if I'd catch something. Lumps and rashes of one kind or another had plagued Toad as long as I'd known him. "It was *hers*, you retard. She *laks* that stuff."

As if I were, indeed, too feeble to act on my own, he drew my arm out to one side and swung it so my hand flapped off Sharon's buttock. "Git it," he snapped at me. "You git it, stud-boy, or does Tennessee gotta slam the Spam in for you, too?"

"Okay," I protested. *"Okay!"*

But it wasn't okay. Not even close. I wasn't inside her now. I was just . . . *in the air.* Worse, so much time had passed, my organ had begun to sag. Panic grabbed me by the throat. What if the rubber slipped off? What if I just shrunk? What if I went back to acorn status? If I had to unpeel the Trojan and slink back to the dorm with Tennie and Farwell calling me Droopy, or Homoloid, or worse.

"Daddy, *spank*!" Sharon whispered, breaking my reverie. Perry was now singing "When You Wish Upon A Star." No matter how I squinted, my dead father's face peered out from the blank TV screen. He was shadowy, but he was *there*, and he wasn't happy about it. Sharon reached around and slapped herself. She did it again, then slipped a finger under me, tickling beneath my testicles. The sensation was so strange I juked sideways and swatted her hand away.

"Cut it out!" I repeated, my voice still Jiminy Cricket-like, and cracked her across her goose-bumped caboose. I slapped her again before I could think about it. To my surprise, I was re-erect. More surprising, each time I spanked her Sharon gave a tiny cry—a pouting little "Meanie!"—and wiggled her behind asking for more.

"Now you git it," Tennie hooted. "Now the cowboy's gittin' up to a gallop. That's what you're *s'posed* to do," he said, speaking very succinctly, as if teaching a Mongoloid to wait at the curb for the light to change. "That's what a girl wants, that's what a boy gives her. It's just po-lite-ness, son. It's just *na*ture."

The Mewling (abridged)

by
Kathe Izzo

Girl, my mewling girl, let me tell you one more thing about last night, and then we won't talk about it anymore, I promise. You probably know all this already, you've been fucking girls so much longer than me. You know I've cried after I've been fucked like I was raped and beaten and it was just a long slow fuck of love. I've been so many places on a fuck, like a voyage, like the dream, and then you suddenly see, like the choke of reality and technicolor and the blast of light, like the movie big but tiny, like the movie like blood cells, pumping central and filling endlessly but now you have enlightened me. When you are the one being fucked you have a lot of time to think about things, like the color of the air and the flavor and whatever could be possibly on your mind, what ever could possibly be bothering you, there's so much interference, like your last lover or your mother or your dog, whatever the fuck you could possibly have on your mind. Now I know what it's like. Who would have ever known. Like time against the wall, like bang, like last night, against the girl. You got the girl and you got to make her happy, like ripped empty. You got the girl and you don't know what the hell is going on. Like a small perfect place that you don't fit, bust it open. Crack of darkness, like so much light. You gotta fit and you will. You hate it. You know you do. You want it so bad. Like I can't believe it.

It's almost suburban, really, Lemon and me, lying in bed in the morning, watching cartoons. I watch her. I watch her play with the cats, curled up in the sun on the floor in her yellow pajamas. How can so many people screw this up? Lemon = mewling and I know I am so lucky. Got a mewling every night. Got a mewling every day. In her yellow pajamas, in her dirty coveralls, hair all messy like little chick fluff. Mewling = pink lips, you can't miss them, even though she thinks she's so tough, tiny veins in her wrists. Can't stay away from them, the small places, tiny wrists and tiny little paws, dirty tiny neck fits right in the cradle of my hand, thumb perfect, forefinger behind her ear. I never know when it's going to happen. You can't plan these things. I mean, I could be confused in the afternoon, wanting something but I don't know what. I could be the baby doll sitting in her lap but now you know she's tired, her head falls forward, her hair falls over her eyes, her eyes are closed, she's smiling a little bit, my hands are in her mouth, words fall out but I don't care. Now she's leaning on me a little more than I'm leaning on her and I am so very awake and she is out, gone, limp, a change of plans, tough baby girl, got my fingers in your kitten mouth, got to suck now, I know mewling wants to bite but you're tired, so very tired. Your clothes are all twisted. I pull you up somehow, curl you up without moving a muscle, without disturbing you, my sweet somnambulist, pull you up my handful of damp sweet Old Spice. It's just the way it happens sometimes, your head against mine, got your belly in my hands and you are one thing, one ownable thing, mine, my hand can take you, your whole body at one time. It takes nothing to slide my hand between your thighs, so slight they barely meet each other, to turn you over and lick the nub beginning of a tail.

It's been two long weeks since the kids have spent a weekend with their dad and I find the Mewling pacing in the kitchen. She's sharp, nasty with me. I can tell she wants to scratch but I whip back with a quick pout and a few tears. You are hurting my feelings. I walk away. I am a girl, after all who likes to get her own way and who knows how to do just that. I don't get it. I hold my own as the curvy girl, run a tight ship, but later when the kids go, I get all messed up. Suddenly it looks like it's her tonight, looks like the shower scene, against my designs, has turned into the blond girl smashed against the tile with my knee in her ass and I become large, uncontrollable and imperfect and she is so pink so beautiful so tight. Still pink, still pink, later curled up on the couch with just her Harley shirt on playing with the remote like she doesn't know I'm there and I'm beyond restless irritation beyond rumbling bang bang and I feel helpless like I'm going to fuck it up, like I'm going to crush her or rip something bad. Got to slow down, got to slow down, how did she get so perfect, how did my hands get so big. I touch the Mewling with one finger and split her open. I am ten times her size and she can't be saved.

She had her hands on me the other day, she was making me do something I didn't want to do. She had to. I didn't want to do anything. I was way down the road. I hadn't looked up for days. I was working, feeding the kids, taking a shower, talking on the phone like I was everybody's friend, but my skin was just a map hovering over my body like a micronetwork of fragile antennae all crisscrossed. It wasn't as high-tech as it sounds, it played more like the early space travel of my youth, no pictures just astronauts, disembodied voices. Everything is twitching and blinking, each antenna tiny and confused, trying to find the light, tied by strings just barely, a minute density of thread tied to a worn peculiar parchment deep underneath the skin in a territory I can only imagine, a tug felt somewhere inside when the twitch of tiny alarm gets one step past agitation and something moves inside. The Mewling has my hands tied behind my head and now she tells me to fight. She sits on my chest and sticks her cock in my mouth. All I can do is bite and she slaps me, tells me to stop being such a weenie, such a doll, got a body use it. I have no hands, no fingers, I can't kick, she's leaning on my legs, and like I said she's getting bigger. How'd she get so big, that little suckling girl. Got to watch out more. All I can do is push with my whole body, push up into her, my ribs spreading her legs even further apart; try to buck her off.

Now the Mewling is smiling quietly with a slight snarl to her mongrel kitten lips. She's got her hands around my throat and she presses down with her body until I start to go for her. Five, 10, 15 miles down the road without looking and she's waiting for my collision. I can't stop moving through her, but it looks like she's got something to say about who's moving through who, got my legs spread, rips my pants off, got her paw wrapped inside my underwear, got her fist up inside my solar plexus, feels like a baby being born and she's laughing and I'm crying like it's so beautiful, like I'm at a wedding, like I'm rain at the top of where it begins, and we're together and now my skin is soft and on and we're open right there for business to the public and we're traveling together on a small path with lights in the dark and I am happy.

The Boy is Peeling

by

Alistair

McCartney

This is how I want it to be. The door is open. The door is red. I wanna draw a picture of you fucking me in red crayon on white paper. I want a man who's skinny as a wand. The picture will be simultaneously romantic and graphic. Anatomically correct. It will be realized on butcher's paper. Be a dear and go to the butcher's and get me some of that nice butcher's paper. The butcher's is next to the draper's. Don't get lost or raped on the way. The draper's is dark and musty and dusty, like the hole of a boy, but the butcher's is bright and clean. The butcher's is gay and antiseptic. It cheers you up on a gray day. The meat smells sweet. The butcher is a nice man. He has hairy hands. Huge knuckles. He wears an apron that is blue with thick white stripes. The stripes are neither neat nor precise: they are shaky. Like whoever was responsible for the stripes had the D.T.'s. He has a lovely assistant, much younger, smooth. Tiny knuckles. Skinnier stripes on his apron, it's a hierarchical thing. Why do we desire power? A question a dead bald French philosopher posed before he died. He thought it was quite understandable to die from desire. The butcher fucks his assistant every day at five, after they close. He makes the assistant strip, but then he has the assistant put the apron back on. It's a turn-on, like a naked busty boy in stilettos with long painted nails and big hair that rapidly accumulates dust. The butcher's assistant is whimpering. The butcher places a piece of red raw meat in his little pursed mouth. He makes him wear a red meat dress. He takes him out in his red meat dress. In a red flashy sports car. Red fuck. Paint me a red fuck. He takes him to expensive restaurants, ones with small servings and dancing. He twirls his loyal assistant around in his red meat dress. Until the poor thing gets quite giddy. Sometimes he even takes his lovely assistant in his red meat dress to red meat balls, the kind that are intent on raising money for charity. The door is red and raw as the butcher's assistant. Once the sex is over and done with, the butcher is surprisingly tender to the boy. Tenderness is a surprise. He is tender almost as an afterthought. We fuck so we don't have to think. The butcher gives his mistress-assistant gifts of raw meat. Little treats. Giblets and such. He washes the boy in the antiseptic usually reserved for the meat. Until the boy is clean, so clean, there's no such thing as dirt. The door is red raw, open as a boy in pleasure, and the paint is peeling. Pleasure is to do with peeling. Beneath the red you can see the door used to be green. Sex makes me see. Sex is concerned with layers. Beneath the red is green; like just beneath me you can see my nerves. Like coral waits for us patiently beneath the sea. Longs to scrape us. My nerves are just like my glasses: gold wire. And twisted. Oh, by the way, did I mention to you that I wear glasses? Do you mind that I wear glasses? Or would you rather me take them off? I'd prefer not to see you anyway. I wear glasses, you see, because I work in a library. I'll steal books for you. Hardcovers. I'll teach you the Dewey Decimal System. The door could do with a lick of paint. Maybe you should lick the door. And I'll watch. I'll make sure no one comes. The door is almost off its hinges. Unhinge me. I never lock my door. There's no point. Men are always breaking their way in. Fill a Grecian urn with your cum; write an ode to me. Fly me to Germany. Men in ski masks, just like terrorists. They come to see me for political reasons. I used to have a key it was gold but I lost it. On purpose. Threw it in the gutter. My ass is a silver gutter. My asshole is a keyhole: gold. Your fingers are skeleton keys: gold. A fuck is a gold grip. Hold me in your gold grip. You can look through my hole. The world is much much smaller. You can't get entirely in. Our bodies won't fit into the world. The door is open; look close and it's been clawed. I'm as open as the door. Clearly. Animals have been clawing their way in to see me. Can you place the animal to the claw? Sex relieves us from language. The door is wide open, red and peeling. When I cum it's like getting caught in a red downpour. When you're inside me I am I am I am. You push open the door even more with the metal tip of your shoe. It's going further than before. It creaks like me when you splay me open. Don't worry baby: I'm not a haunted house. You use your shoe because you don't want to leave any fingerprints. Any traces. You find me restrained. With rope. "A cowboy does everything with his rope except eat with it." It's necessary to show restraint. I've recently been raped by cowboys. I don't hold it against them: all boys are lonely, but cowboys are the loneliest boys. Although I've been raped I'm surprisingly calm. The ropes aren't tied tight, they're tied loose, it's theatrical, for effect, the rape was fake, the cowboys who raped me weren't even real cowboys, they got their costumes at a costume store. They got them for Halloween but decided to keep them. I could get out of the ropes if I wanted to, but I don't want to. I beg you to help me. Like a blind beggar. In rags. In a fairy-tale. Like a deaf old man begging a young boy to let him blow him in the forest. He wants to make his life into a fairy-tale. Sex takes us back to childhood. But instead of untying me you grab the paddle conveniently placed beside me and beat me into bruises, colors we have names for: red, purple, yellow, green, then these bruises come up like divers in colors we've never seen before, colors no one can name. We have to get beyond surfaces. If you come up too quickly from sex, you can get the bends and die. Little bubbles in your bones. And then you rape me also, just like my fake cowboys. Just like my Halloween boys. My hollow boys. My halogen boys. My hollow spaces. We'll make sure that every day is Halloween. Then you pull up your pants and leave me exactly the way you found me.

First Love

by
Hubert
Selby, Jr.

Y ou comfortable?

I guess so.

Would you like to start?

I suppose.

I realize this must be difficult for you, so anytime you would like to stop just say so.

Yeah. . . . But I don't think you know how I feel.

I assume I do not know exactly how you feel, but I would think that you feel self-conscious talking about the events—

No, no. That's not it. It's her, not me. I'm concerned about what you'll think about her.

I see.

No, you don't . . . not really. You see, I love her. With all of me I love her. She opened up a world I never knew existed.

Yes . . . love can do that.

Yes, and beyond.

Would you like to start?

Yes.

How did it all begin?

It began with her mouth. She had a way of moving her mouth that stimulated every muscle and bone in my body . . . and my mind. At first I was just amazed at the feelings—

Do you remember what you were thinking?

I don't think I was thinking. I was totally overwhelmed by the feelings. But I do remember having trouble breathing for a few minutes. It was that overwhelming.

What did you do then?

I don't really remember doing it, but suddenly . . . my ah . . . my thing was in her mouth and I almost passed out.

The sensation was stimulating . . . erotically?

Erotically? I don't know. I had never been with a woman before. It was my first time. I only know part of what happened—

Only part?

—the feelings seem to surround me . . . sort of wrap themselves around me and I don't remember where I was or where I went but the feelings more and more kind of swallowed me and I remember I could hardly breathe and I couldn't really see—

You lost your vision?

No, no, it's not like that, it's just that I couldn't focus on anything, it's like the air was spinning and I wanted to yell and scream and cry and I was spinning around and the feelings sort of ate me up and I sort of disappeared into the feelings and that's all there was . . . was this . . . this feeling . . . I was just one big feeling . . . yeah, it ate me up.

I see. How long did this . . . experience last?

Don't know.

Well, what time did it start?

I don't know.

Let me try it this way . . . what was the last time of the day you remember?

It was daylight.

Daylight. What time in the daylight . . . morning, afternoon, what?!

I don't know . . . daylight—

Come now, there must be something you can remember that will give us a point of reference with respect to the time of day. Really!

Well . . . I did eat lunch . . . yeah, I'm pretty sure I ate lunch . . . I think. Hmmm . . . yeah, peanut butter and jelly sandwich. Yeah. On Graham crackers. Not really a sandwich I guess, but—

Yes. Well, that does give us a point of reference. So it was afternoon. I assume you do eat lunch in the afternoon.

Oh yeah. One o'clock. Lunchtime, you know.

Yes . . . lunchtime. What time did you regain your memory?

It was dark. I mean sort of.

Of course. "Sort of." That narrows it.

You know, it was dark and it looked like the sun had just gone down.

Well, apparently you were in ecstasy for at least four hours.

Ecstasy?

Never mind. What happened when you awoke?

Well, I just sort of lay there. . . . I mean it took a while to realize where I was—

In what way?

Well, it's sort of confusing. I didn't recognize things at first. It took a little while for me to realize it was home. But when I tried to move I was weak, very weak. My body felt wobbly.

You felt drained?

I guess. I tried to move and I realized my arms were still around her and my thing was still in her mouth and she was looking at me with her big pretty eyes and—

Your, "thing" was still in her mouth?

Yeah. And she looked at me . . . you know, sort of sideways. And when I tried to move she started sucking on it again.

I see. And you had another . . . memory lapse?

Well, sort of.

Sort of. You either did or didn't.

Yeah . . . but see, I remember it was dark and I went to my house . . . leastways that's where I woke up.

I don't suppose you know what time that was?

Sunrise. I remember lying in bed and watching the sun and she seemed to sort of wiggle out of the sun . . . sort of.

Wiggle out of the sun?

I mean it really wasn't her, but you know how you can see the sun when it first comes up and she seemed to wiggle out of it and her breasts were like two suns and beams of light came right out of the nipples into the room and started going up and down on my body and my thing got all big and hard like concrete and it hurt . . . an itchy sort of hurt and she came right through the window and at first I had to close my eyes the light was so bright, but it got dimmer and I could feel her sucking and licking my thing and her tongue was warm and wet and her lips were so soft and she just kept doing it and my thing was so big but she put it all in her mouth and I kept trying to move but I was so weak and her tongue was licking me all over—

All over?

Yeah.

What do you mean by, all over?

You know . . . everywhere. Ah . . . *those* places.

Be specific. You ashamed to tell me exactly what she did?

Yeah, sort of. I'm afraid you'll think bad things about her.

I wouldn't think bad things about her. Tell me everything . . . in detail.

Well. . . . She would bend over me and rub her lips all around the top of my thing and look at me with those eyes . . . her eyes were so soft and sweet and—

Yes, yes, but what did she do?

Well . . . she would put her lips around the top of my thing and rub it and twirl her tongue around it all the same time, then put it deeper and deeper into her mouth looking at me so sweet and twirling her tongue and I could feel my thing hitting the back of her throat, all the way in, and she sang a song or hummed and something kept rubbing the tip of my thing and her tongue kept licking and then she would slowly oh so slowly raise her head—

Still using her tongue?

Yes. Her tongue. And she slowly raised her head until it was just the tip in her mouth, then she would slowly put it all in her mouth again, over and over and I felt like my heart would stop and she took it out of her mouth for a moment and smiled then started running her tongue up and down and around it and then she . . . she kept going.

Kept going? What do you mean?

Well, she kept moving her tongue all the way down my thing and then started licking my things an—

Things? What in the hell do you mean?

My things . . . my . . . sacks.

Ohhhh. Go on. Continue.

Well. . . . You won't think bad things about her?

No, no. What did she do next?

She kept licking and kissing the inside of my thighs then down to my . . . you know, my. . . .

She stuck her tongue in your asshole? She rimmed you?

Rimmed????

Never mind, never mind. Keep going.

Well, I can't hardly be sure.

You what?

I kept forgetting sort of . . . like I was out of my body but lost in it or something. I never felt anything like this. She kept doing these things to my thing and then my tummy, then back to my thing and sacs and bottom and everywhere and I was going in circles and all the time those big eyes were smiling at me and then it would seem like everything, every part of my body, all the feeling would go into my thing and it felt like it was swelling up and huge and was going to burst and she would always put it back in her mouth and rub it up and down with her beautiful lips and I would explode and she would keep going and—

She swallowed it.

It?

Forget about it, go on, go on.

Well I just seemed to float away and I think I screamed or something and I just seemed to collapse but then I would hear her sort of humming and feel her mouth around my thing and then her finger was rubbing my bottom hole—

Ahhh. . . .

—then she put her finger in and out as she kept rubbing up and down on my thing with her mouth as she sucked and licked all the stuff from my thing and then I would explode again—

How many times?

Huh?

How many times did you cum?

Huh?

Explode for gods sake?

I don't know. It just kept happening, over and over, all day.

All day?

Yeah. Then she just held me for a while and kissed me and let the gooey stuff from my thing drip into my mouth then put her breast in my mouth and told me to bite her nipples and she squirmed and moaned and I kept biting and squeezing and something came over me and I started kissing her everywhere and biting her and she put my hand in her thing

Your whole hand?

Yeah, she just—

You fisted her.

Fist—

Go on.

And she moved around and up and down on my hand and it slowly went up her thing and all my fingers went in, and then my knuckles disappeared and she kept moaning and squirming and pushing down on my hand and I was in past my wrist and she kept squirming and pushing and moaning and saying yes, yes, harder, fuck me, fuck me and I was feeling squirmier and squirmier and rolled around and my thing was all big and hard and felt itchy sort of and she pulled my hand out of her and I didn't want her to and shoved it in further and further and chewed on her breasts and she rolled around and around and finally slid off my hand and sat on my thing and I lay there watching it going in and out of her thing and it was all wet and dripping and I wished I could lick both our things while she was doing it but she shoved me down and bent over me and stuck her breasts in my face and told me to chew on her tits and I did and I kept biting harder and harder and I could taste blood in my mouth and she sat up and moved around on my thing and pulled the lips of hers apart and pointed to some little thing in there and told me to rub it and I did and it sort of flapped back and forth and she started moaning again and saying yes, yes, o fuck, fuck, yes, yes and I pinched it and rubbed it harder and harder and it seemed to get bigger and soon I was getting all jelly again and she kept bouncing up and down harder and harder and I felt so weak but I felt like I wanted to tear her thing out and pinched harder and harder until I exploded again and I couldn't rub it any more but she kept moving, but slowed down and soon she just sat there and every few seconds she would sit up and I could see all the gooey stuff on my thing and dripping from hers and then she finally got off and rubbed her thing up and down on my tummy and then licked my thing and sucked it until all the goo was gone and then she kissed me and I could taste it and I sucked it out of her mouth and my thing started getting itchy and then she rubbed her thing on my chest then knelt over me and put her thing on my mouth and told me to open my mouth and I put her thing in my mouth and she peed in my mouth, real slow and it was warm and made my thing itch and get hard and swollen and then she moved her thing slowly down my body and peed all over me and put my thing in hers and kept peeing and told me to pee and I did and I stopped when she said to and she got off and closed her thing then knelt over my face and let the pee drip all over me then told me to pee in her mouth and I peed too fast and she grabbed my thing and squeezed it so hard I couldn't pee and she . . .

Why do you stop?

I don't want you to not like her.

Believe me, I like her. What else did you do?

I don't know . . . lots of things.

How long were you doing this?

Don't know. Seems like the sun came up and went down many times.

How many times did you . . . explode?

Didn't count. Lots I guess. Over and over and over.

What else did you do?

All kinds a things. Can't remember everything. Ropes and things. . . .

Did she look like the women in those magazines you have?

Sort of I guess. Not really sure what she looks like. Think shes prettier.

How long have you been collecting those magazines?

Couple of years. Since mother died.

And you have been living alone since then . . . since she died?

Yeah.

You can't remember everything you did?

No. . . . But I think there was a lot of biting. Seems like I remember her saying over and over to bite her nipples. . . .

Biting her nipples. . . . Did you also kiss them and lick them?

Oh yeah, lots of licking . . . yeah.

And you fondled them and stroked her pu—vagina?

Vaa . . .

Her thing.

Uh huh. Lots.

And it got wet and. . . .

Oh yeah. It got wet and slippery like and it dripped all over—

And you licked it and kissed it?

Uh huh. She pushed me down on my back and kneeled over me and told me to stick my tongue out and she'd spread her thing open and slid it up and down on my tongue then just sit on my face and tell me to bite her thing and sometimes she'd pee and rub her thing all over my face and tell me to keep licking and biting . . . yeah, over and over.

And you nibbled her clit during a golden shower. . . .

Huh? I just bit where she said.

And she turned over and you licked her ass.

Oh yeah. She kneeled over me and spread it open and told me to put my tongue in there too and everything made my thing get big and she'd put my thing in her mouth while she moved around on my tongue and wiggled and I started biting her even when she didn't say to and it made me dizzy and my body would jerk around and everything was yelling, even my toes, then I'd explode and I'd feel like my body was going to snap like a twig, then I would feel like jelly, all wishy-washy like jelly.

And she kept your thing in her mouth.

Yeah . . . oh yeah, and kept doing things and I got all hard and swollen and—

And you kept biting her tits and nipples and ass.

Uh huh. She kept saying like you, bite my ass, bite my nipples. Yeah.

And you kept biting and it felt good to sink your teeth into her ass and nibble on her pussy.

I kept biting even when she was bleeding. I think I bit one of her nipples off . . . or almost. Maybe.

Oh Jesus, you bit it off, just bit the fucking thing off her tit?

Don't know. Maybe. . . . Why you taking your thing out?

Show me how she kept your thing so hard.

Oh, you got that gooey stuff dripping out. . . . Hmmm, my thing was bigger and harder.

Put it in your mouth and do what she did . . . oh . . . oh. . . .

How did you feel after you killed her?

I'm not sure. I woke up holding her and I thought maybe it had been a nightmare, but there was blood and she was dead.

Why did you kill her?

I don't know. Couldn't think of anything else to do I guess.

What did you do then?

I ate her.

You ate her.

Well, I didn't just eat her like she was. I wouldn't do that. It wouldn't be right. I baked her first.

Baked her.

Yeah. Sorta slowly. Then I ate her. It took a long time, days I guess . . . many days it seems like.

What did you do next?

I don't exactly know. Seems like I slept a lot.

Then what?

I think I called the police.

Why did you do that?

Seemed like the right thing to do.

Do you know where you are?

Police station—some sort of jail I guess.

You're in a hospital.

Hospital?

Yes. And I am a doctor. Specifically, a psychiatrist.

Why would I be in a hospital? I didn't get hurt.

The police checked your story and theres no evidence of a crime.

What do you mean?

There was no womans body or . . . remains.

But I ate her.

Yes, that is what you said. But all they found were the bones and hide of a lamb.

What are you talking about . . . this is crazy . . . what do you think I did with her.

There was no woman. It was all a hallucination.

Hallucination?

You made it all up in your head.

She was real. I just think about her and my thing gets all hard.

I know you believe it.

It was real. . . .

Now, tell me again how you put your thing in her mouth and tickled her tonsils, then bit her nipple off. . . .

Night on Twelfth Street

by
Marilyn
Jaye Lewis

In the half-light before dawn, the double bed jostles me from sleep; shaking with a distinct rhythm, like riding the double L train from First Avenue into Canarsie. It's Manny jerking off again, I realize. Lately he seems to need this furtive sexual stimulation before dashing off to work at the last minute—strictly solitary sex is what he's after. Sex that doesn't involve me, that lands his jism in a tee shirt. The tee shirt winding up in the tangle of sheets for me to discover later when I'm alone. And I'm the one who he says is possessed by demons. Nympho demons, the kind of demons his aunt, the Mother Superior, warned him about when he was a teenaged Catholic boy in Buffalo. He's only 20 now. Six years younger than me.

Manny came into my life almost as an afterthought, like an unwanted conception late in life, and I can't figure out how to get him to leave. Whenever I suggest it might be time for him to move from my little hellhole on East Twelfth Street and find a home of his own he punches me repeatedly and starts smashing dishes that are irreplaceable heirlooms from my favorite dead grandmother.

The one nice thing about this Catholic boy, though, is that he's so hung up on his Catholic upbringing he's psychologically incapable of coming in a girl's mouth. I can suck him until the proverbial cows come home and never have to swallow so much as a drop of his spunk. The sin of wasting his seed in this specific way weighs heavily on his conscience. But all the other sins have found a home in him. His soul is blacker than tar, mostly because his mind is so fucked up. Let's face it, he's too inquisitive to be Catholic, but he was raised by a father who beat him regularly, who alternated between using a leather belt on his ass and bare fists on his face, and a mother who was a sister to the top nun. It's left a seemingly permanent schism in his psyche. Four months ago, he was a straight-A student at the university, studying to be an architect. Now he works as a ticket-seller in a gay porno movie house over by the West Side Highway. It's run by the mob and it's the only gay porno house left with a back room for sex in these days of AIDS.

There are a lot of things about Manny that don't make sense if you weren't raised Catholic, which I wasn't. Still I've heard him babble on enough these last couple months to put the pieces together. He started out a trusting little boy with a good heart, but dogma has doomed him to a destiny of sociopathic perversion. I try to tell him to get over it already, that this isn't Buffalo anymore, it's New York City. He can be whoever he wants to be. Sometimes he listens to me intently and makes love to me in the dark like he's starving for a sanctity he believes he can find in a woman's body. Other times the black cloud rolls over his face and the fist flies out, connecting with my cheekbone.

It was never my intention to save Manny from himself, just to lead him to the vast waters of the variety of human experience and let him drink. But the variety proved to be too much for his conscience. Sometimes without my knowing it, the things I'd want to do to him in bed would push him over the edge and instead of succumbing to orgasm I'd end up dodging his fists. Lately I don't have the strength to wave so much as a white flag. I'm reduced to trying to read his mind and staying the hell out of his way.

I like it when Manny's at work. I like the fact that the movie house is open around the clock and that his shift in the little ticket-taker's booth is 12 hours long. It doesn't matter a bit to me that he's back to doing blow, either. Even though it makes me spit each time I discover he's stolen my hard-earned money from my wallet, I'd rather he spent all night in the horseshoe bar on East Seventh Street without me. Then he's more likely to skulk around the Lower East Side looking for more blow at four o'clock in the morning, increasing the risk of landing himself in the Tombs again. He hates the violence of the Tombs. He's come out of there sobbing. But having him locked in that mad monkey house is preferable to having his unpredictable rage lying next to me in bed.

I wish I could get him to give me back my key. I wish I could afford a locksmith to change the lock on my door. I'm going to find a way to get him out of here. I'm going to do it soon. Ruby's band is back from their tour of northern Africa and Marseilles. She's trying to quit junk again, which means she's wanting to have sex with me. It's her pattern and I've come to count on it. I love her so much it's scary.

I can't explain why I love Ruby. We have next to nothing in common. We don't seek the same highs. We don't like the same music. When we're lying together in bed we run out of things to say. I don't hang out in dyke bars like she does. I don't wear black leather. Even our tricks are from different worlds. I don't venture into the park after midnight to support a heroin habit. A cheap handjob in the shadows is not for me. My tricks are uptown men who shoot their spunk in broad daylight. Restaurateurs, or entrepreneurs, wealthy men whose emptiness is too complex for what can be gotten in 10 minutes at 20 bucks a pop behind some bushes. Ruby wouldn't fare well in those uptown luxury apartments. She's not okay with being handcuffed. She doesn't own a pair of high heels. Holding on to a man's dick in the dark is the limit of what she can stomach. Pussy is where her heart is.

The first time I made out with Ruby, in a toilet stall in CBGB's, I didn't know she was on junk. I only knew she was a good kisser, which was why I'd followed her into the stall. We didn't do anything wild in there; we just kissed. We didn't unzip our jeans or pull up our T-shirts—nothing. But kissing Ruby was enough to make me fall in love. Her face up close to mine like that, her brown eyes closing when we kissed; her dark hair brushing lightly against my face. Then the soft groans in her throat, as our bodies rubbed against each other in that suggestive rhythm. I understand now why she seemed to be in slow motion. It wasn't some trance of Eros; it was the gold rushing through her veins.

I couldn't compete with the junk. It wasn't good enough for me. I wanted the whole girl. When I told Ruby that, we didn't kiss again for a year. I blew my money that year on the gypsies on Avenue C. Mostly on the youngest girl, the 14-year-old with the stray eye. I paid her to hold my hand in her lap, palm up, and tell me a pack of lies. I was too in love to leave anything to chance. I wanted my destiny spelled out for me. I wanted Ruby to come to her senses. She did, after three men in the park raped her one night. She called me collect from the pay phone in the emergency room at Beth Israel. She was ready to try it another way.

She moved back in with her mother in Queens. Six weeks later, she showed up on East Twelfth Street, doubtful seeming, but her veins were clean.

If Ruby could find a way to keep off smack for good, there wouldn't be cracks in my world, where vermin like Manny can wriggle in when I'm blind on bourbon and crying for myself. It's not that I kick Ruby out when she's shooting up, it's that she stops coming around. So I plug up the holes with whomever I can find. Now I have this dilemma. I want Ruby back in my bed. Nothing compares to her.

The first night Ruby and I made love it was the height of summer. Salsa music blaring from some Puerto Rican's boom box clashed with the tin calliope sounds of an ice cream truck parked under my open window. But in my double bed at the back of the flat, the intrusions of the neighborhood faded. It was finally just Ruby and me. Both of us sober. When I saw her naked for the first time I felt elation, like how an exulting mother must feel as her eyes take in the body of her newborn for the first time, that unshakable faith in the existence of God. That's what it felt like to see Ruby without her clothes on. How else can a mind account for something so perfect, so entrancing, so long desired? Her firm, upturned breasts with tiny eager nipples. Her narrow waist, slim hips; the dot of her navel and the swirl of black hair that hinted at the mystery hiding under it all—at first, it made touching her a little daunting. But she lay down next to me and fervently wanted to kiss. The force of passion coming from her slender body made the rest of it easy. I didn't worry about how to please her then. I knew intuitively what her body wanted. I could smell it coming off of her. Her nipple stiffening in my mouth needed more pressure. I twisted it lightly with my fingers instead. Tugging it, rolling it, pulling it insistently, while my mouth returned to her kisses. She moaned and her long legs parted. That's how simple it was.

I knew she would be wet between her legs. My fingers slid into her snug vagina and her whole body responded. An invisible wave of arousal rolling over her that I could feel in the pressure of her kiss. The muscular walls of her slick hole clamped around my two probing fingers, hugging them tightly, making it too plain that the thick intrusive pricks of the pigs who'd raped her could only have succeeded in finding a way into her through sheer masculine determination. I knew how she had suffered. Struggling, succumbing, three times successively. It was hard to believe her body had with-stood the repeated violation. I shoved the pictures from my head. I centered my thoughts instead on the rhythm of her mound, how it urged my fingers to push in deeper. They did. Feeling my way, my fingers found the spot inside her that opened her completely, causing her thighs to spread wider, then she held herself spread; bearing down on my fingers as her slippery hole swelled around them.

I kissed my way down her ribs, down the flat expanse of her belly. Following the wispy trail of hairs that led to the world between her legs. I wanted my mouth all over her down there. It was what I had dreamed of, ached for. At last, she was offering it to me; wide open and engorged.

Sometimes I think about how easy it was to make her come. Two fingers up her hole and my tongue on her clit, then the river of shooting sparks gushed through her. And because I loved her it made me happy to make her come, even though, afterward, we lay together entwined with nothing left to talk about. Ruby and I are always silent when we're finished making love.

With those wealthy tricks uptown, it's more complicated. They need to discuss each detail. They practically draw you a map: the tit clamps here, the enema bag now, the length of rope like this, the gag last. The timing must be meticulous and the monologue rehearsed.

And with an uptight, paranoid guy like Manny it's even worse. There is no plan, no map—no discernible guideposts. Each gesture, every word is a toss of the dice: will it lead to a kiss or a bruised lip? I try not to lose sleep over it. If worse comes to worst, when Ruby arrives we'll shove the heavy bureau in front of the locked door. We'll go to my bed in the back of the flat, strip out of our clothes and make love. Then I'll call the cops on Manny at last, when he's shouting obscenities out in the hall and slamming uselessly against the barricade.

The Youth Hostel

by

Wallace

Shawn

from *A Thought In Three Parts* (1975)

T wo sparsely furnished rooms, not connected, dimly lit with no windows. Room 1 on the left, Room 2 on the right. Room 1, Dick sitting on the bed, thinking. Room 2, empty. Sounds of birds outside. Long silence before Dick speaks.)

DICK

Well—seem to be alone here. Nobody else in. Birds singin' outside. Nothin' much to do—just sit around I guess.
 (Pause. Room 2, Judy enters. She turns down the bed, neatens the room, as the scene in Room 1 progresses.)
Fun to play with toys, but don't got none.
 (Enter Helen.)
What!? Oh hi, Helen!

HELEN

Hi Dick.

DICK

Aren't you out with the others?

HELEN

Nope. Guess not. (Pause.) I guess I'm just different—like you, Dick.

DICK

Yeah, I guess so, Helen. (Pause.)

HELEN

Mind if I sit down? I'm feelin' a bit ill.

DICK

Why not. Go ahead.

(She sits down.)

HELEN

Yeah. My stomach's been gettin' to me. Makin' me sick. I hate bein' sick—y'know?

DICK

Yeah.

(Long pause.)

HELEN

Can you guess what I was doing just before I came in here, Dick?

DICK

No. What?

HELEN

I was doing fuckin' nothing.

DICK

Yeah. That's too bad. *(Pause.)* I hope you're in a good mood now, though, Helen.

HELEN

Well I hope you are, Dick.

DICK

Well, I might be.

HELEN

You stupid asshole.

DICK

Yeah.

HELEN

You stupid asshole.

(Room 2. A knock at the door.)

JUDY

Yes—who is it?

BOB *(outside)*

Well—It's me—Bob—

JUDY

Oh—*(Pause.)*—Hi Bob!

BOB (outside)

May I come in?

JUDY

Oh—(Pause.)—sure!

(Bob enters.)

Gee Bob—you look all upset. (Pause.) What's wrong?

BOB

I don't know, Judy. I guess I can't sleep.

JUDY

Can't sleep? Gosh—Why, Bob? Are you—too upset?

BOB

No—not exactly. I can't quite explain.

JUDY

You can't?

(Pause.)

BOB

You see—I'm too nervous to sleep. I'm just too disturbed—

JUDY

Gosh, Bob—

BOB

Can I sit down at least?

JUDY

Of course—I didn't mean—

(He sits down.)

BOB

You see, I've never had a girlfriend, Judy, and—

(Pause.)

JUDY

I see—you're afraid you just don't know how to talk to girls.

BOB

Yes.

JUDY

Well—(Pause.) I think you're doing just fine right now . . .

BOB

Gee—thanks, Judy. You're the kind of girl a fella might really like to talk to. Really.

JUDY

Well, thank you, Bob.

BOB

No—I mean it.

JUDY

That's nice, Bob. I really appreciate it.

(Very long silence.)

BOB

Judy—Judy—you know how bad I'd like to touch you.

JUDY

Oh now Bob—don't frighten me like that.

BOB

No. I don't mean to frighten you. But I want so bad just only to look at you—

JUDY

Only to look, Bob?

BOB

I want to see your breasts, Judy.

JUDY

What—you mean naked, Bob?

BOB

Yes, Judy. I need to. Really. I won't touch you. I promise. I promise. But I just can't sleep. I can't leave this room. I won't look hard, Judy. But just to look.

JUDY

Bob—I don't know you—

BOB

You have to, Judy. I just can't leave.

(She sits silently for a long while on her bed. Then she takes off her shirt.)

Thank you, Judy.

JUDY

Now will you go, Bob?

BOB

No—I need more, Judy. Your pants too.

JUDY

Oh Bob—please—

BOB

No—I really need it, Judy. I have to see it.

(She slowly takes off her pants. Nude, she sits on the bed so that he can see her genitals. She looks sad. He looks at her carefully from his chair.)

Thank you, Judy. Should I touch it?

JUDY

No, Bob.

(He stands. Stripping, he approaches her. Then he slowly penetrates her and makes love to her until he comes.)

BOB

It's not enough, Judy. *(He leaves her.)*

JUDY

No.

(Bob goes back to his chair.)

BOB

I expected more.

JUDY

I know.

BOB

Why do you hate me?

JUDY

I don't hate you, Bob.

BOB

I want more.

JUDY

No. There's just nothing, Bob.

BOB

Let's get married, Judy.

                    JUDY

No, Bob. Put on your pants. You'll catch cold.

                    BOB

Thanks, Judy. *(He picks up his pants, but doesn't put them on.)* I appreciate it. I hate you. But I love you, Judy.

                    JUDY

I know, Bob. I'm very cold. I'm going to get dressed. *(She puts on her shirt.)*

                    BOB

Thank you, Judy.

                    JUDY

Let's try to stop now.

                    BOB

I know, Judy.

                    JUDY

I'd rather go to bed now. I'd like to sleep.

                    BOB

I know, Judy.

                    JUDY

Don't you want to leave now, Bob?

                    BOB

No, not really—I'll just stay here. I think we'll fall asleep soon.

                    JUDY

I know, Bob—but don't you think you should leave? I'd like to masturbate.

                    BOB

I'll watch you, Judy.

                    JUDY

No, Bob, I could never do it then.

                    BOB

Get onto the side of the bed, and I'll get on this side, and we'll both do it, and we won't see each other.

                    JUDY

All right, Bob. We'll see who comes first.

BOB

I'm sure you will, Judy.

(They go to opposite sides of the bed and both masturbate.
She comes first.)

JUDY

That was wonderful. Are you coming, Bob?

BOB

Not yet—now shut up.

JUDY

All right, Bob. I feel terrific—really exhilarated. Gee whiz. Oh come on, Bob—you sure are slow.

BOB

Oh—oh—that helped me! *(He comes.)* Get me some tissues, Judy. I feel like a fool.

JUDY

All right, Bob. Here. Ugh—What a mess.

BOB

Gee thanks, Judy. Give me a kiss. Here—right here.

(He points to his cheek. She kisses it.)

Thanks, Judy. I guess I'd better go. I hate myself—but I'd like to sleep somewhere else.

JUDY

Good going, Bob. I'm going to jerk off some more. So get your ass out.

BOB

Don't be vulgar, Judy.

JUDY

I'm not, Bob. I just love to jerk off.

(Bob leaves. She lies on the bed and masturbates.)

I really love this. It turns me on. There! *(She moans.)* Ah! Ah! Ah! Oh God—I can just drink that in. Good feelings. Feel goodings. Goo goo. Goo. Goo. Goo. Goo. Jerk jerk jerk.

(Long silence. She lies in bed, but doesn't sleep. Room 1. Helen is
wandering around the room. Dick is sitting in a chair.)

HELEN *(playing with flowers)*

I like flowers.

DICK

Yeah.

HELEN

They're really attractive.

DICK

Are they?

HELEN

Yeah. I sometimes feel they're really great.

DICK

Yeah.

HELEN

Why don't we get a few more? Really decorate the place.

DICK

Yeah. Why not?

(Pause.)

HELEN

I feel so lonely, Dick. Could you hug me a few times?

DICK

Well I really don't want to, Helen.

HELEN

No?

DICK

Fuckin' sorry, but I'm feelin' sort of sick.

HELEN

Yeah. I'll fuckin' hug myself. *(She climbs onto the bed, gets under the covers, and throws her pants out onto the floor. She touches herself under the covers.)*

DICK

You really make me sick, Helen. You really do. I really hate you.

HELEN

Really, Dick?

DICK

You're not the kind of person I like now, Helen.

HELEN

Oh, aren't I, Dick?

No. You really aren't.

Well what sort of person do you like now then, Dickie? Why don't you tell me? I'm really interested.

DICK

Well, people more like Joan, Helen—or people like Alice.

HELEN

Alice? Really? Is she the one you like, Dick? I'll bet she is.

DICK

Well—I do like her, Helen.

HELEN

Yeah—she's really your type. She's really your type, Dick.

DICK

You dripping cunt—will you leave me alone?

HELEN

She's really your type, Dick. Just the type you wet your pants for. Should I tell you all about her, Dickie?

DICK

No.

HELEN

I'll just tell you a few things. I think you'll be interested.

DICK

Go eat yourself, Helen.

HELEN

To start with, sweetheart, her asshole is covered with shit. She's never used toilet paper in her fuckin' life. She's got dirt on her arms up to her elbows. And she's a fuckin' liar, and she stole my razor blades twice in a row, and then she fuckin' hid them—Do you want to hear more of this?

DICK

Go on—why not? What the hell do I care?

HELEN

She eats shit in her room. Wendy watched her. It's not even secret. She'll never do it for me because she knows I hate her, but she does it in front of everybody, all the time. She hasn't shaved her body once since the time she was born, so she looks like a big hairy tree, with big black roots running into the ground. I once tripped her up and stripped off her shirt just to look at her. She looked like a dirty, filthy pig. I pulled down her underwear to look at her crotch, and I was almost sick. It was like a stinking forest growing in all directions. I wanted to look, but she tried to stop me. She stuck her fist in my eye. She almost blinded me. She could have killed me. I tried to smash her head on the ground, but she hit me in the nose, and I was bleeding all over.

DICK

That's great, Helen.

HELEN

Why do you like her so much? Why? Why? Why don't you tell me?

DICK

I don't know. I think she's a decent person. She seems like a good person, like a good person. She's a person, a decent—A person, a person, a decent—I like her. I don't see why you don't like her.

HELEN

Have you ever eaten a meal with her?

DICK

A thousand times. I've always liked it. She's a pleasant companion.

HELEN

Did you watch her eat?

DICK

What do you mean did I watch her eat?

HELEN

I mean, did you watch her eat?

DICK

But what do you mean did I watch her eat? What do you mean did I watch her eat?

HELEN

I mean, did you watch her eat?

DICK

I don't know what you mean.

HELEN

I mean, did you watch her eat, Dick? Did you watch her eat?

DICK

I don't know what you want me to say. I don't know what you want. I don't know what you want. You want me to say things, Helen. What do you want? I don't get it. I don't get it.

HELEN

I said, did you ever watch her when she eats? She doesn't eat the way I think you mean I think I think, Dick. *Now* stop me.

DICK

I'll stop you, Helen, and I really mean it, so you better listen. Now, Alice is my friend. A fine person. I want to know her. I do *not* want to discuss these things, to fight, to argue. We're talking here about my friend Alice, and if you don't like her you can go and drown yourself in shit for all I care, but I don't want to hear these insults and lies. I want the truth.

HELEN

Oh do you, Dickie? You want the truth?

DICK

Yes.

HELEN

You want the truth? Well here it is—your great friend Alice is hated by everyone, including me, and she knows it. Consequently she's taking revenge by making herself disgusting to everybody, and she's leading you off to be a friend of hers so she can make you just like her. She'll catch you off your guard and you'll be eating shit too, Dickie—just like Alice.

DICK

Well well.

HELEN

Yes—that's the truth, baby Dickie. So like it, honey. I hope you like it.

(Pause.)

DICK

You really get to me, Helen. You really do.

(Long pause. In Room 2, Judy gets out of bed, puts on a skirt, and sits in a chair.)

HELEN

I wish I were dead.

DICK

Is that right? Why is that, Helen?

HELEN

Go fuck yourself, Dick.

DICK

Gee thanks, Helen.

HELEN

"Gee thanks, Helen." You really are an asshole, Dickie.

DICK

Yeah, thanks. Thanks a lot, sweetheart. Why don't you leave me alone?

HELEN

Well why the hell should I?

DICK

Because I want you to. I'm sick of you.

HELEN

Really? Really? *(She lifts up the bed covers.)* Are you sick of this?

DICK

Oh come on, Helen.

HELEN

Come on, Dick. Just finger me, Dickie.

DICK

Why the hell should I?

HELEN

Well why don't you, Dick? Please? Please?

DICK

You're just sitting there, Helen! *(He goes to the bed and fingers her.)* I'll feel your asshole too.

HELEN

Oh God.

DICK

Is that okay?

HELEN

Okay! Okay! Oh! *(She comes. Pause.)*

DICK

Yeah—Well—Look what you've done to my fingers. God!

HELEN

Well—so what?

DICK

Yeah—so what for you. *(wiping his fingers)* You've fuckin' wrecked my whole day, Goddamn fuckin' shit—

HELEN

Yeah—Well—Thanks, Dick.

DICK

Yeah—thanks for nothing. Get the fuck out of here.

HELEN

Yeah. Okay, Dickie. See you around.

DICK

Yeah. So long, Helen.

HELEN

So long, Dick. *(Exits.)*

DICK

Yeah. Well. I'm sick to death of these pushy people. What's the point? Do I need that? I'm going to lie right down here and jerk myself off, and if anybody tries to stop me it's their tough luck. That's my fuckin' point of view.

(He lies down and begins to masturbate. Judy leaves Room 2 and enters Room 1.)

JUDY

Oh, hi Dick! Are you jerking off?

DICK

Well—I *was*. I'm gonna go nuts!

JUDY

But what's the matter? Don't you feel like talking? I thought you'd be lonely.

DICK

Oh Judy—I've been trying to be by myself for hours. Helen's been in here giving me a hard time.

JUDY

Oh—really? Here—let me do it. *(She starts to jerk him off.)*

DICK

No—really—Judy—you really don't need to.

JUDY

I want to—honestly, Dickie.

DICK

I know, Judy, but—

JUDY

You don't want me to? Do you want to have me?

DICK

No—I only—

JUDY

(pulling up her skirt)

Look—here—here—let me get right on you. Oh—oh—you see?—wowee—

(She sits on him, and they make love.)

Oh, boy—this is really enjoyable! Yes! Yes!

(She comes, then he immediately comes.)

Oh, gee—

DICK

Yeah—I have to admit that felt awfully good, Judy. I'm glad you did it to me.

JUDY

Thanks, Dick.

DICK

You've really got a good, sticky hole. It's really a good one.

JUDY

I like you too, Dick.

DICK

But why aren't you out with the others, though, Judy?

JUDY

'Cause I'm in here fuckin' you, Dick. Now, you know that.

DICK

No, but I mean—

JUDY

No but *I* mean I came here on purpose to fuck you.

DICK

You did? But why, Judy? Do you like me that much?

JUDY

Well—do you really want to know how much?

DICK

Well—how much, Judy?

JUDY

I love you, Dickie!

DICK

What? You do? But what do you mean?

JUDY

From the first time I saw you. You looked really special to me. Different! Really!

DICK

Why Judy! I'm amazed!—Of course I always liked you too, Judy— in those cute little shorts—you could almost see your vagina—and those downy hairs on your thighs—

JUDY

I knew you loved those shorts, Dick. I only wore them 'cause I knew you loved them.

DICK

God—and to think I didn't know—never even thought you felt anything about me. And here we are! Gosh—isn't it great?

JUDY

Yeah—it really is. Oh God—let's do it some more.
(*They make love again and both come. They lie quietly. Long silence.*)

DICK

Judy?

JUDY

Yes?

DICK

You have a beautiful body. I've never seen tits like that—they're so small and petite.

JUDY

I know, Dick.

DICK

I just love everything about you. *(Pause.)* It's dark in here.

JUDY

Yeah.

DICK

There used to be a bear that lived over there. You see?—that spot was some of his urine.

JUDY

Gee, Dick—

DICK

You see, he lived in a kind of forest, with yellow leaves . . . do you see that big red house there?

JUDY

Gosh, Dick—

DICK

But you'd better go away now, Judy, though, really. *(Pause.)* I'm beginning to get that sickie feeling again, you know.

JUDY

What, Dick? What sickie feeling?

DICK

I'm beginning to wonder what I like about you, Judy. I'm beginning to feel a bit strange—and I don't think I want you here any more— I'm beginning to wonder if you're too thin for me, Judy.

JUDY

Dick—I don't understand—

DICK

No—I really mean it, Judy. You're too thin—your ass—Please, Judy, please go before I get you now! I'd have to get you, Judy—so get out now! You'd better get out!

JUDY

All right! All right! But you're an odd person, Dick! Why are you so odd?

DICK

I don't know! Just hurry up and get out of here! Get out! Get out! Now! Now!

(Judy exits, leaving her skirt behind.)

I'm mortified. I kicked her out just like a dog. But what could I do? I hated her! She's too thin! She's just not healthy! When I saw that ass, like a pushed-in face—No! No! I really could have killed her! My God! My God! And she was so good-looking—that wonderful vagina, those breasts—so tiny! I loved them so much! But I felt too angry. It's all so hard—It's so *difficult* . . . *(Pause.)* Oh God,—God,—tired's not the word. I need such a rest. A rest, quiet. Lots of swimming. *(He masturbates, making sounds. He comes, with more sounds.)* Ah—That was great. Good orgasm! God—I really needed it. *(Pause.)* Wow. Now I'll close my eyes. Boy oh boy. Sleep. Sleep. Coming. Soon. Good. Here. Goo.

(He sleeps. Judy enters, looking for her skirt.)

JUDY

I'm sorry, I left my—Hey, he's asleep! *(Pause.)* God, he doesn't look so frightening now! Hi, sleepyhead—where'd you put my skirt?

(Helen enters in a skirt and top.)

HELEN

Oh—hello there, Judy.

JUDY

Well—well well well! Hi, Helen!

HELEN

Hi, Judy.

JUDY

Have you come to see Dick? He seems a bit grumpy.

HELEN

I think he's sleeping, Judy.

JUDY

Yeah—Well—You know what I mean. *(Pause.)*

HELEN

Yes, I've been feeling a bit bored, you know, lately, Judy—

JUDY

Uh-huh—

HELEN

And I thought I might visit a little penis he has, you know?

JUDY

Oh—Really? Why not visit mine, Helen?

HELEN

That's very funny, Judy. *(She lifts Dick's blanket and puts her head under it.)* Let's see who's here. Hello? Hello? Does he have one in here, somewhere, d'you think? I can't seem to find it.
(Judy lifts up Helen's skirt and puts her head under it. Helen shrieks.)
Oh God, that tickles!
(She pulls away, laughing. Judy follows her, laughing wildly. Helen climbs onto the bed to escape. Judy climbs on also. Both are laughing wildly. Dick wakes with a start.)

DICK

Hey! What!? What!? What the—

JUDY

Hi there, Dick! Just grabbing a little bite here—
(She rips Helen's skirt off and starts to kiss her genitals. At first Helen fights her, laughing wildly, but then she relents. Dick watches them.)

DICK

Hey—how's she doing there, Helen?

HELEN

Well I'm not too sure. *(Pause.)* She's really a pig. Ow—come on now, Judy!

DICK

Is she really that bad?

HELEN

Oh really, Judy! Really! Really!
(Judy looks up.)

JUDY

What's wrong, you shit?

DICK

You cunts. How disgusting.

HELEN

You made him grow a penis there, Judy. See?

JUDY

Hey, I think I like that. *(She starts to suck Dick's penis.)*

DICK

Hey! *(He starts to laugh loudly.)*

HELEN

You like that, huh, Dick.

DICK

She's not bad at this, Helen!

(Dick is laughing wildly. Helen is looking for something.)

HELEN

Where is that fuckin' thing?

(Helen finds a dildo and begins to masturbate with it on the bed, while Dick continues to laugh. Finally he comes. Helen continues masturbating.)

DICK

Not bad, Judy.

JUDY

Hey, look what she's doing.

DICK

Hm . . . Rather appealing.

JUDY

Thinks she's pretty clever, I can certainly see that.

(Helen comes.)

Can I borrow it, Helen?

HELEN

Go eat your titties, Judy.

JUDY

Why not?

(Helen begins to masturbate again with the dildo.)

Oh come on, Helen. Why not?

(Helen ignores her.)

Why not?

HELEN

It's really something—

(Judy rushes at Helen, as if to grab the dildo, but Dick pushes her away.)

DICK

Get out of here, Judy. Come on, get out.

(Judy yells at them.)

JUDY

You disgusting pieces of urine!!

(She goes out, slamming the door. Helen masturbates more and more vigorously. Dick gets out of bed, goes to a big box, takes some food out of it, and eats it. Bob enters.)

DICK

Hey—hi there, Bob.

BOB

Hi, Dick—My God—what she's doing!—

DICK

You like that, Bob?

BOB

You're naked, Helen—I can see your—

(Pause.)

DICK

Do you like that, Bob old man?

BOB

Oh God, gee—I can hardly stand this, Dick. I can really see in there. Every part of her vagina. What she's doing—what she's doing—

(Helen comes, lies exhausted for a moment, puts down the dildo.)

HELEN

Oh. God. Well hi there, Bob.

BOB

Hi, Helen.

HELEN

Hi. Hi hi.

DICK

Well go ahead, Bob. You want to jerk off, you just go ahead. We won't stop you. *(He returns to the bed)*

HELEN

He wants to jerk off?

DICK

Well, don't you, Bob?

HELEN *(to Bob)*

Yeah, we can't stop you.
(Pause)

BOB

Really? Really? You mean you want to see it?

DICK

If you want to show it.
(Bob takes out his penis.)

BOB

See? Look.

DICK

It seems all right.

HELEN

Yeah. It looks like a penis.
   *(Bob is sitting on the bed with Helen and Dick. He masturbates.
                 Helen and Dick watch.)*
          BOB *(masturbating faster and faster)*

I'm coming soon!

DICK

Oh boy.—

HELEN

Oh—God—

BOB

Oh! *(He comes, shooting sperm toward Helen and Dick.)*

DICK

Whoops—catch!—Yuck.

(Helen is laughing hysterically.)
HELEN *(to Bob, laughing)*

You're such an asshole!

BOB

Oh wow—that was good—

HELEN

Yuck! Yuck! What an asshole.

BOB

Well—why not? Can you equal me, Dick?

DICK

Can I what? What?

BOB

Well—can you?

HELEN

Yeah, Dick. Let's have a little contest. Let's see how you do. *(Pointing to either side of her.)* Now you sit there, and you sit there. And now here's my pretty little belly, and on the next step up are my nice little tits, and all the way up is my cute little neck. Now aim this way, and let's see who gets higher.

DICK

Oh come on, Helen.

BOB

Yeah, let's see it, Dick.

DICK

Are you really serious?

HELEN

Come on, Dick! Stop wasting our time.

DICK

Well come on, Helen! I don't think I'm in the mood.

HELEN

I hate him! I hate him! All right, I'll start you. *(She kisses him until he starts to laugh.)*

DICK

Okay! Okay!

HELEN

I really hate you, Dick.

(Bob and Dick both start to masturbate.)

All right then, come on boys. Let's see a little speed. Let's go. Let's go!

BOB

I'm closer—oh God—

(Bob comes. Then Dick comes. Silence. Then Helen speaks.)

HELEN

Boy, I'm feeling pretty wet up there, Bob. I'm really soaked.

DICK

Well I thought mine was higher.

HELEN

Oh come off it, Dick.

DICK

Well—wasn't it, Bob?

BOB

Well you did pretty well there, Dick, but I thought mine was up to her face.

DICK

You what?

BOB

Think I'll try it again.

HELEN

Could you aim for my mouth?

BOB

Well there's no harm trying. *(He starts to masturbate.)*

HELEN

Well come on then, Dick.

DICK

Go suck yourself, Helen.

HELEN

Well come on, Dickie! Don't wreck everything! Come on! Come on!

(She touches his penis.)

BOB

No fair! Dammit!

HELEN *(to Bob)*

You shut up and keep working. *(after a while, to Dick)* You're getting no place, Dick. You're just pathetic. *(She removes her hand.)*

DICK

You're a shithead, Helen.

(Helen starts to masturbate with the dildo. Dick watches her for a long while. Then he speaks.)

I said you're a shithead.

(He grabs the dildo and throws it across the room. She tries to run to get it and he grabs her and wrestles her down to the floor and starts hitting her. Grunts and cries. Judy enters. Bob keeps masturbating.)

JUDY

Hi there, Bob.

BOB

Hi, Judy. I'm just doing this.

JUDY

I can see that, Bob. *(She looks at Helen and Dick.)* Those disgusting farts. *(to Helen)* I'm taking your little thing, you disgusting vomits. *(She picks up the dildo and licks it. Dick and Helen stop fighting for a moment to look at her, and Helen rushes at her, pulling her to the floor by her hair and hitting her. Dick tries to pull Helen off, and all fight violently. Judy is screaming. She still holds the dildo. Then Bob comes, dripping sperm over them, and they stop fighting and separate. Silence for a moment.)*

HELEN

Oh, wow—

DICK

God, thanks for the sperm there, Bob.

(Judy is sitting at some distance on the floor from the others. She begins to masturbate with the dildo, more and more vigorously.)

BOB

Gosh, what a wonderful feeling. I love the way it feels right here, just right at the edge. *(Pointing to the head of his penis.)*

HELEN

Hey, my hand is bleeding.

(Judy finally comes and drops the dildo on the floor.)

BOB

God, it's freezing in here. I hope we don't catch cold!

(Judy exits. Suddenlly all feel cold. Bob sneezes loudly, takes a blanket and wraps himself up. Judy enters Room 2 and lies down on the bed. She masturbates with difficulty, manually and with her pillow. Bob leans against a wall of Room 1 and shuts his eyes. Dick washes himself with some water in a corner of the room and finally lies down on the bed. Helen wraps herself in a blanket and gets some food from the big box. She eats it, huddled to the wall. All are shivering. Judy continues to masturbate.)

JUDY

It's so unfair. Just so unfair.

(Judy comes, and then sleeps. Long silence. In Room 1, Bob and Dick fall asleep. A long, long silence. Then Tom enters Room 2. He switches on a rather bright light and kisses Judy.)

TOM

Hi, darling.

JUDY

Hi, Tom *(waking up).*

TOM

How's my sweet little wifc?

JUDY

Am I your wife, darling?

TOM

Of course, my angel. You remember that.

JUDY

I know, Tom.

TOM

I've brought some breakfast. I sure could eat it.

JUDY

So could I, Tom. I'd really love to.

TOM

Here. Fix it yourself. However you like it.

JUDY

Thanks, Tom. That would really be great.

(Judy fixes the breakfast and they sit at a table and eat it.)

TOM

Smells like sperm in here, Judy. Did you have visitors?

JUDY

Only Bob, darling. He made me do it.

TOM

Bob? He's crazy! I think he's odd—I really do.

JUDY

He is odd, darling. A peculiar person.

TOM

Does he love you, darling?

JUDY

I don't know, Tom. Sometimes I think so. I wish *I* were odder.

TOM

I know, darling—I guess it's difficult.

JUDY

Do you think Bob loves me?

TOM

I'm not sure, sweetheart. He certainly seems to.

JUDY

I'm glad. I like him. I think he's nice.

TOM

Don't you like me, Judy?

JUDY

Yes, but he's nice too.

TOM

I know, darling. I was only teasing.

JUDY

All right, Tom. I knew you were. *(Pause.)* Have some more food.

TOM

Thanks, Judy. *(Silence.)* I ran into Baby Naylor last night. He's playing trumpet with Leiku Kanefian.

JUDY

Really, darling?

TOM

Yes—that's what he said.

JUDY

That's great. How nice. What a good position! *(Pause.)* Gosh, Tom, I wish *you* had a job. Why *don't* you get one? You know you're qualified.

TOM

I know, Judy. But I just can't concentrate.

JUDY

Does your mother support you, sweetheart?

TOM

You know she does, Judy

JUDY

I guess I thought perhaps she'd stopped it, Tom.

TOM

But why would she stop it, Judy? That's silly. You know she cares about me.

JUDY

I know that, Tom. I certainly know that, my darling. I know that, baby. I know. I know. I do know that, darling. I know, darling. I know, darling. I know, darling. I know, darling.

TOM

I know you know, Judy. I know that, dear.

(Silence.)

JUDY

Bill—

TOM

I'm Tom, darling.

JUDY

I know you're Tom, sweetheart. I was just talking to you.

TOM

I know that, darling.

JUDY

Tom—don't you think we should clear out some of our odds and ends, darling? Our possessions have accumulated so. There are so many things we don't even need.

TOM

Or want. That's true. Really. Let's chuck them all out.

JUDY

But Tom—don't you like our things?

TOM

Well—I don't know, darling. Not really too many of them. They're mostly junk, after all.

JUDY

Well I guess so, darling. I picked them carefully.

TOM

Well—all the same. I think they're junk.

JUDY

I guess you're right, Tom, and we'd better chuck them out.

TOM

Okay, Judy—if you want to.

JUDY

If I want to?

TOM

Well—it was your idea.

JUDY

Well—I suppose it was, darling, but it was really your idea.

TOM

Well, I suppose it was, darling, but it was really your idea.

JUDY

Well, it was really your idea, darling. But let's throw them all out. *(Silence.)* Tom?

TOM

What?

JUDY

You're in a bad mood, sweetheart. What's the matter?

TOM

Nothing's the matter.

JUDY

No, really, darling.

TOM

I'm sick of my job. The goddamned boss—he gets into my hair. Crosses me every chance he gets. Damned son of a bitch.

JUDY

Don't make jokes about jobs, Tom. I wish you had one.

TOM

Well so do I, dammit. So why are you stopping me, then?

JUDY

I'm not stopping you, Tom.

TOM

You liar—don't you say you're not stopping me.

JUDY

Don't say it, Tom?

TOM

I said, don't say it. *(He slaps her.)*

JUDY

Okay, Tom. You win. You win.

TOM

You bet I win, baby. That's what winning's all about.
(Long silence. Then he hits her again. They fight violently on the bed. Long silence. In Room 1, Helen shifts her position against the wall, still cold and shivering. Long silence. Tom is almost asleep. Then Judy gets up, touches her face.)

JUDY

Very interesting. Tom, you know you've wounded me. You've really harmed me.

                    TOM
What?
                    JUDY
I say, you've really harmed me.
                    TOM
I have?
                    JUDY
But not too interested?
                    TOM
I thought I was sleeping.
                    JUDY
I think you're an asshole, Tom.
                    TOM
I thought I was sleeping.

                    JUDY
Are these dreams, Tom? I really feel bruised. These welts really hurt.
You've finally hurt me, Tom.
                    TOM
"You've finally hurt me, Tom."
                    JUDY
Do you like me, Tommy? Do you really like me?
                    TOM
Your mouth is open, Judy.
                    JUDY
Do you really like me? Do you really like me? *(Pause.)* "Here we
finally are, Judy." "I think I understand you, Judy."
        (They sit for a long time. Both feel cold. Judy shudders.
                    Silence.)
                    (Blackout.)

12 Assholes and a Dirty Foot

by

John Waters

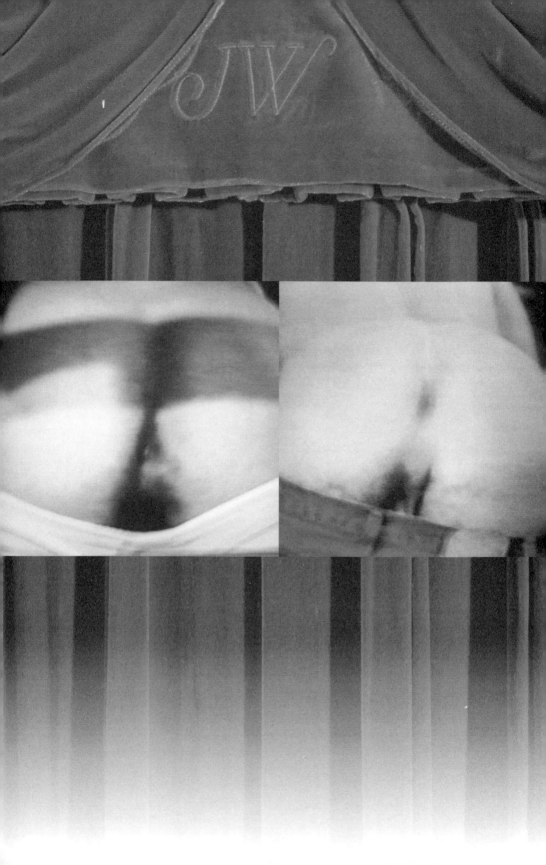

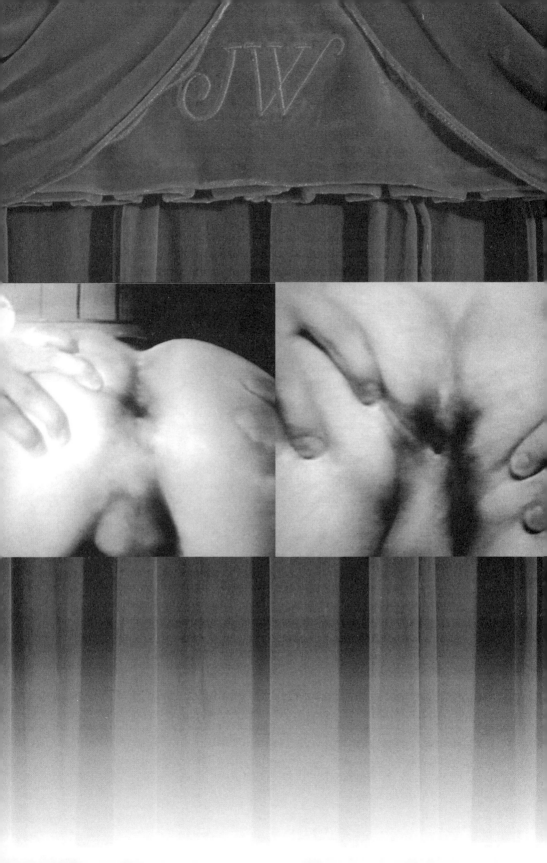

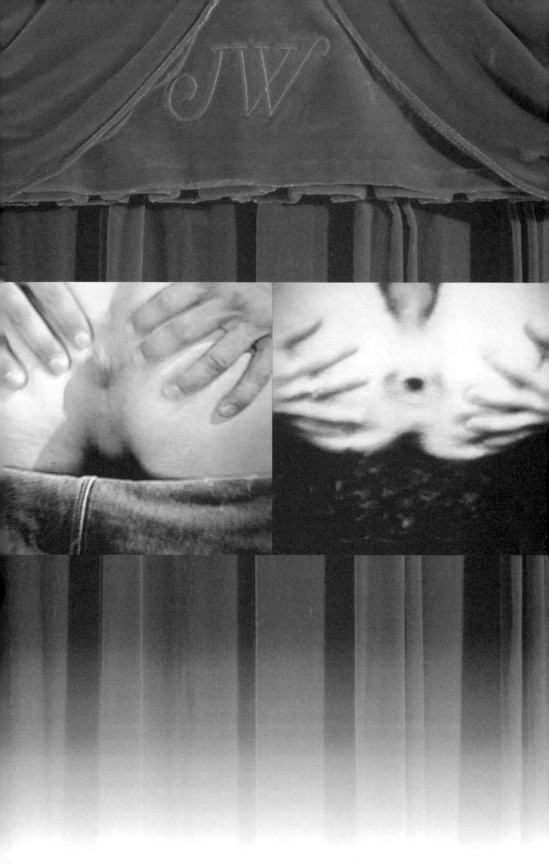

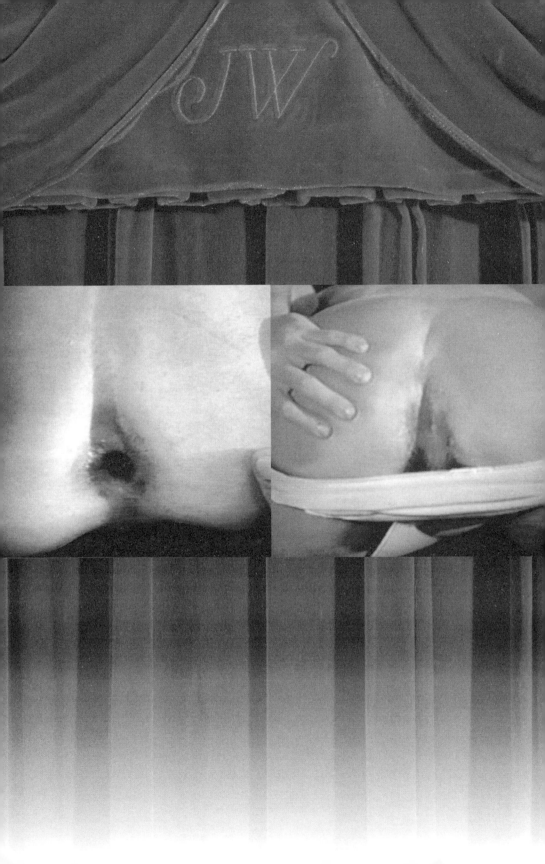

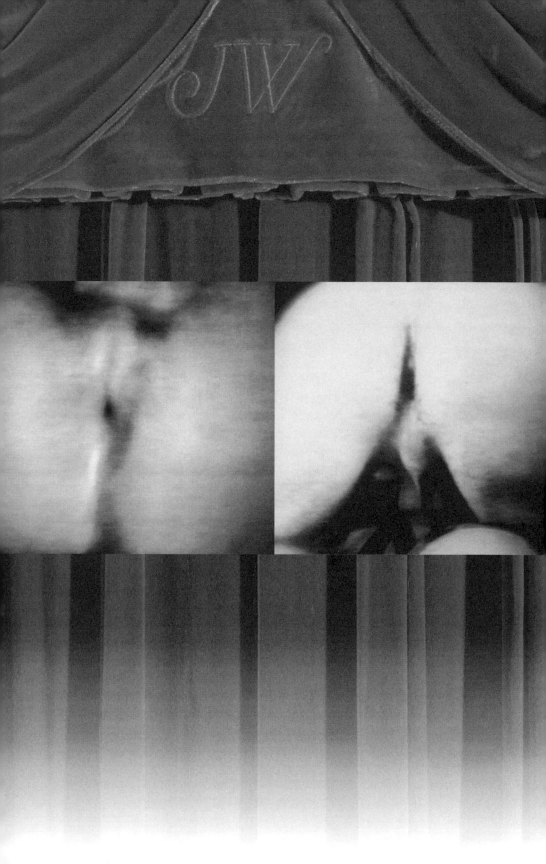

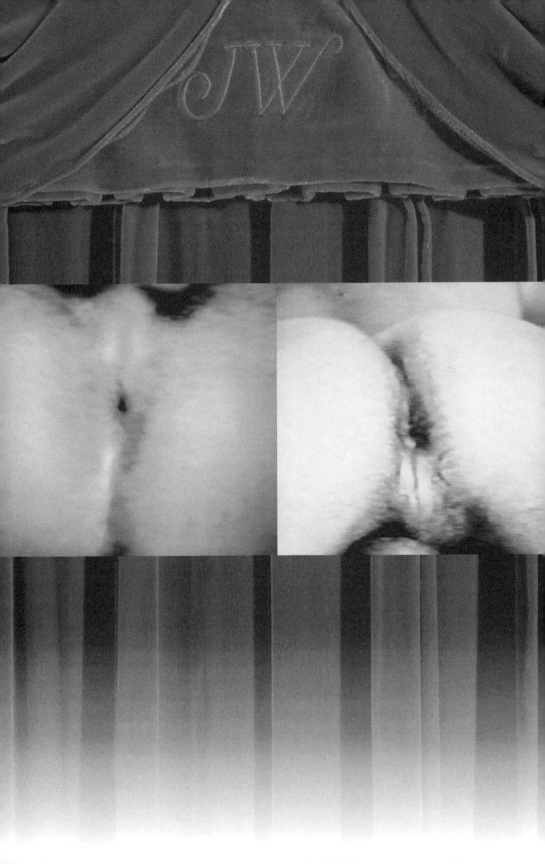

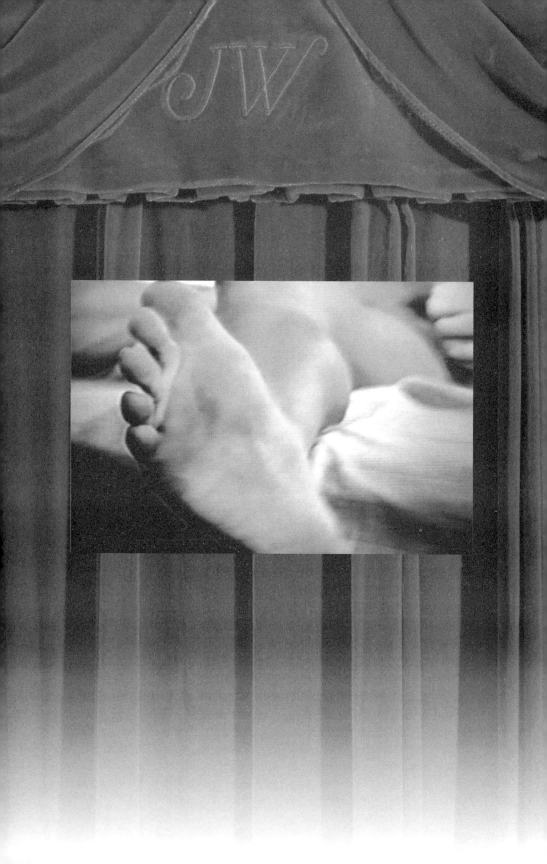

Folksong 1999

by

Mary

Gaitskill

On the same page of the city paper one day:

A confessed murderer awaiting trial for the torture and murder of a woman and her young daughter is a guest on a talk show via satellite. His appearance is facilitated by the mother's parents who wanted him to tell them exactly what the murder of their daughter and grandchild was like. "It was horrible," said the talk show hostess. "He will go down in history as the lowest of the low." There was a photograph of the killer, smiling as if he'd won a prize.

A woman in San Francisco announced her intention to have intercourse with 1,000 men in a row, breaking the record of a woman in New Mexico who had performed the same feat with a mere 750. "I want to show what women can do," she said. "I am not doing this as a feminist, but as a human being."

Two giant turtles belonging to an endangered species were stolen from the Bronx Zoo. "This may've been an inside job," said the zoo president. "This person knew what he was doing, and he was very smart. We just hope he keeps them together—they're very attached." The turtles are valued at $300 each.

It was in the middle of the paper, a page that you were meant to scan before turning, loading your brain with subliminal messages of fascination as you did. How loathsome to turn a sadistic murder into entertainment—and yet how hard not to read about it. What dark comedy to realize that you are scanning for descriptions of torture even as you disapprove. Which of course only makes it more entertaining. "But naturally I was hoping they'd report something grisly," you say to your friends, who chuckle at your acknowledgment of hypocrisy.

And they did report something grisly: the grandparents of the murdered girl who wanted to know what only the murderer could tell them. You picture the grandmother's gentle wrinkled chest, a thick strip of flesh pulled away to reveal an unexpected passage to Hell in her heart.

Then you have the marathon woman right underneath, smiling like an evangelist, her organs open for a thousand. An especially grotty sort of pie-eating contest, placed right beneath the killer, an open body juxtaposed against the pure force of destruction. Why would a woman do that? What do her inane words really mean? Will she select the thousand, is there at least a screening process? Or is it just anyone who shows up? If he had not been arrested, could the killer himself have mounted her along with everybody else? If she had discovered who he was, would that have been okay with her? Would she have just swallowed him without a burp?

You picture her at the start of her ordeal, parting a curtain to appear before the crowd, muscular, oiled, coifed, dressed in a lamé bathing suit with holes cut in the titties and crotch. She would turn and bend to show the suit had been cut there, too. She would "ring-walk" before the bed, not like a stripper, more like a pro wrestler, striking stylized sex poses, flexing the muscles of her belly and thighs, gesticulating with mock anger, making terrible penis-busting faces.

Might the killer enjoy this spectacle if he could watch it on TV? He may be a destroyer of women, but his victims were regular, human-style women: a concerned mother trying to connect with her daughter on a road trip in nature—the trip that delivered them into the hands of the killer. You picture her reading "Reviving Ophelia" the night before they left, frowning slightly as she thinks of the teenage boy years ago who fucked her bottom and then took her to dinner at Pizza Hut, thinks also of her daughter's coed sleep-over last week. Getting out of bed to use the bathroom with only the hall light on, peeing in gentle darkness, remembering: grown-up pee used to smell so bad to her, and now the smell is just another welcome personal issue of her hard-working body, tough and fleshy in middle-age, safe under her old flowered gown. The daughter is awake too, and reading *Wuthering Heights*. She is 13, and she is irritated that the author has such sympathy for Heathcliff, who abuses his wife and child. What does it mean that he is capable of such passionate love? Is this realistic, or were people just dumber and more romantic back then? She doesn't think that the mean people she knows are the most passionate; they just want to laugh at everything. But then she remembers that she laughed when a boy in class played a joke on an ugly girl and made her cry. Sighing, she puts the book down and lies on her back, her arm thrown luxuriantly over her head. On the ceiling, there are the beautiful shadows of slim branches and leaves. She does not really want to take this trip with her mother. Her mother tries so hard to help her and to protect her, and she finds this embarrassing. It makes her want to protect her mother, and that feeling is uncomfortable too. She rolls on her side and picks up the book again.

Thought and feeling, flesh and electricity, ordinary yet complex personalities, the like of which the killer had found impossible to maintain inside himself from the moment of his birth—and yet which he could erase with the strange, compulsive pleasure of an autistic child banging its head on the wall. You picture him as a little boy alone in an empty room, head subtly inclined as if he is listening intently for a special sound. In the top drawer of his dresser, there are rows of embalmed mice stacked neatly atop one another. At age 12, he has killed many animals besides mice, but he only embalms the mice because uniformity satisfies him. He likes embalming because it is clean, methodical, and permanent. He likes his mind to be uniform and inflexible as a grid. Below the grid is like the life of animals, sensate and unbearably deep.

There are people who believe that serial killers are a "fundamental force of nature," a belief which would be very appealing to the killer. Yes, he would say to himself, that is me. I am fundamental!

But the marathon woman on TV would be fundamental too. She would not show her personality, and even if she did, nobody would see it; they would be too distracted by the thought of a mechanical cunt, endlessly absorbing discharge. However, with her lamé bathing suit and her camp ring walk, appealing to everyone's sense of fun, she would be the fundamental female as comedy: the killer could sit comfortably in the audience and laugh, enjoying this appearance of his feminine colleague. Maybe he would feel such comfort that he would stand and come forward, unbuckling his pants with the flushed air of a modest person finally coming up to give testimony. Safe in her sweating, loose, and very wet embrace, surrounded by the dense energy of many men, his penis could tell her the secret story of murder right in front of everyone. Her worn vagina would hold the killer just as it had held the husband and the lover and the sharpie and the father and the nitwit and every other man, his terrible story a tiny, burning star in the rightful firmament of her female vastness.

Hell, yes, she would "show what women can do!"

In the context of this terrible humanity you think: the poor turtles! They do not deserve to be on the same page with these people! You think of them making their stoic way across a pebbled beach, their craning necks wrinkled and diligent, their bodies a secret even they cannot lick or scratch. The murdered woman, in moments of great tenderness for her husband, would put her hands on his thighs and kiss him on his balls and say to him "secret Paul." She didn't mean that his balls were a secret. She meant that she was kissing the part of him that no one knew except her, and that the vulnerability of his balls made her feel this part acutely. That is the kind of secret the turtles are, even to themselves.

But now all natural secrets have been exposed, and it is likely the turtles have been sold to laboratory scientists who want to remove their shells so that they can wire electrodes to the turtles' skin in order to monitor their increasing terror at the loss of their shells. You think this idea is absurd and grotesque. But rats have been tortured with electroshock each time they press a lever to get a food pellet. Rabbits have been injected with cancer and then divided into control groups, one of which was petted and the other not, in order to investigate the role of affection in healing. Scientists do these experiments because they want to help. They want to alleviate physical suffering; they want to eradicate depression. To achieve their goal, they will take everything apart and put it back together a different way. They want heaven and they will go to hell to get there.

But still, there is grace. Before the mother met the murderer, her vagina had been gently parted and kissed many times. Her daughter had exposed her own vagina before her flowered cardboard mirror (bought at Target and push-pinned to the wall), regarding her organs with pleased wonder, thinking, "This is what I have."

And maybe the turtles were not kidnapped but rescued: There

are actually preserves for turtles, special parks where people can take turtles they have found or grown tired of, or rescued from the polluted, fetid fishtanks of uncaring neighbors. Or maybe they were simply set free near the water, wading forward together as the zoo spokesman had hoped, eyes bright in scaly heads, each with the unerring sense of the other's heartbeat, a signal they never knew to question.

And maybe she didn't start the marathon in a gold lamé suit. Maybe she appeared in a simple white gown with a slip and a bra and stockings and beautiful panties that the first man (hand-selected for his sensitivity) had to help her to take off to the sound of "The First Time Ever I Saw Your Face." Maybe they even took time to make out, acknowledging romantic love and the ancient truth of marriage. It would be the stiff and brassy acknowledgment of showbiz, but deep in the brass case would be a sad and tender feeling—sad because they could only stay a moment in this adolescent sweetness, they could not develop it into the full flower of adult intimacy and parenthood. But this flower comes in the form of a human; it must soon succumb to disease, atrophy, ruined skin, broken teeth, the unbearable frailty of mortality.

The marathon woman is not interested in mortality or human love. Right now, the marathon woman has infinity on her mind. Roberta Flack's crooning fades. The first man mournfully withdraws. Then: the majestic pounding of kettle drums and brisk, surging brass! It's *2001: A Space Odyssey*! The lights go up! The silhouettes of naked men are revealed on the screen behind her bed above which spins a giant mirror ball! Men step from behind the screen and array themselves about the bed, splendid in their nakedness, even the ugly ones, like gladiators poised to wade in! This one now, number two, is very short and muscular, covered with hair. His face is handsome, his body exudes physical swagger shadowed by physical grief. The woman cannot know that, at 18, he was a gunnery mate on a PT boat in Vietnam, or that *Time* once ran a photograph of him posed with his machine gun, the brim of his helmet low across his eyes, a cigarette sticking up at a jaunty angle from between his clenched, smiling lips. She can't know it but she can feel it: the stunned cockiness of an ignorant boy cradling Death in one arm, cockiness now held fast in the deep heart of a middle-aged man. Just before he enters her, she pictures his heart bristling with tough little hairs. Then she feels his dick and forgets his heart. He pulls her on top of him and she feels another man ready to climb up her butt while number four bossily plants himself in her mouth, one hand holding his penis, the other on his fleshy hip. The referee, a balding fellow in a smart striped shirt, weaves deftly in and out of the melee, ensuring that real penetration is taking place each time. The music segues into hammering dance music, the kind favored by porn movies, only better. The music is like a mob breaking down a flimsy door and spilling endlessly over the threshold. It celebrates dissolution but it has a rigid form and it hits the same button again and again. It makes you think of Haitian religious dances where the dancers empty their personalities to receive the raw flux of spirit—except this music does not allow for spirit. This is the music of personality and obsession, and it is like a high-speed purgatory where the body is disintegrated and reanimated over and over until the soul is a dislocated blur. It is fun! People dance to this music every night in great glittering venues all over the world, and now the woman and the men fuck to it. They are really doing it and it is chaos! The referee furrows his brow as he darts about, occasionally giving the "roll-over" signal with his forearms, or a "TKO" hand-sign barring a man who's trying to sneak in a second time.

And because it is chaos, there are moments when the woman's mind slips through the bullying order of the music and the assault of the men. There are many trapdoors in personality and obsession, and she blunders down some of them—even though she doesn't realize that she has done so. Like the killer, she is now only able to occupy her surface because extraordinary physical demands are being made on her surface. By turning herself into a fucking machine, she has created a kind of temporary grid. But underneath, in the place of dream and feeling, she is going places that she, on the surface, would not understand.

What no one would guess about this woman who is having intercourse with a thousand men: She is afraid of men. Her father was weak and ineffectual; his own weakness enraged him, and so his daughter grew up surrounded by his silent, humiliated rage. Her mother smothered her own strength in order to make her father look strong; that didn't work, so the girl grew up with her mother's rage too. She had no way to put male and female together inside herself without rage. This is the core of her fear. Her fear is so great that she cannot afford to recognize it. It is so great that it has taken on a thrilling sexual charge. Because the woman is courageous by nature, she has always gone directly toward what she most fears. When she began to have sex with boys, it was as if she was picking up a doll marked GIRL and a doll marked BOY and banging them together, hoping to unite herself. As she grew older, the woman inside her became more insatiable and the man became more angry. He became angry enough to kill.

Because this woman is decent, she will not kill. But in deep sleep, she dreams of terrible men. In the worst of these dreams, a killer with magic power came to her childhood home. He bewitched her mother so that she let him in. He turned her father into a dog chained to a post. He carved his name on the girl's face. He butchered her mother like a cow.

This dream was so terrible that the girl forgot it before she woke. It is still inside the woman. He is part of her, the male who would kill. The female he wants to kill is part of her too. Deep inside, she is still trying to bring them together. And for one moment, down a special trapdoor, she has found a way. If the corporeal murderer who guested on the talk show had been fucking the marathon woman at this moment, he might've had a feeling of subconscious unease: For she has entered the deep place of sex and it is not a place the killer wants to be. This is a place without form or time. There can be no grid here. Even the shape of his heart will no longer hold; it will be forced to open. Sorrow, terror, hate, love, pity, joy: all human feeling will come in and he will be unable to bear it. He will dissolve. His killing nature will be stripped to abstract movement, a bursting surge overtaking the weaker prey, the principle of pouncing and eating. In this place, all pouncing and eating is contained, because this place contains everything. This place is her ovaries and her eggs, bejeweled with moisture, the coarse, tough flowers sprouting in her abdomen, the royal, fleshy padding of her cunt. Some people say that nature is like a machine. But this is not a machine. This is something else: a million dark wombs giving birth to millions of creatures, wet and rank, eyes sealed blind with darkness, humans and animals, all forms derived from every formless entity swarming in boundless black nothingness.

When male turtles fuck, they thrust deep inside their mates, they stretch out their necks, they throw back their heads and they scream. They don't have to drop through trapdoors or travel down layers. They are already there. Animals want to live because they are supposed to. But they know death better than a human killer. Life and death are in them all the time.

The marathon woman is more than halfway through, and she is tired. You are tired too, just from thinking about it. The theme from *Chariots of Fire* is on the sound system, but you are hearing a very old song from the Industrial Age called "John Henry." It is about a steel driver of great strength who outperformed the machine invented to replace him. He won, but in doing so, he died. The song ends "He lay down his hammer and he died." This song is not about sex or about women. The marathon woman is not going to die, nor is she going to win. She has no hammer to lay down. But she is like John Henry anyway because she is making herself into a machine. But she is not a machine. She is something else.

Analgesic

by

Lydia Lunch

T his," he said, pointing to his crotch, "has never happened to me before . . . " He sat shoulders slumped, knees spread wide apart, in the center of the couch. Pulling, squeezing, strangling, the offensive object between his legs. Talking to it as if it were almost human instead of merely an appendage. An appendage which no longer functioned. Or at least was not at this moment functioning.

He was 22, 36, 54. Blonde, bald, salt and pepper. I picked him up in a bowling alley's moldy bar, the faded lobby of a downtown movie theater specializing in badly dubbed Hong Kong martial arts flicks, or possibly in the underground car park of an ex-lover's duplex. He was beautiful enough to be arrogant. Clever enough to play it off.

I threw out some cheap line about how intoxicating the nostalgic aroma of sweaty leather booths were, Jet Li versus Bruce Lee, or the possibility of structural damage during a geological shift in the San Andreas faultlines. Whether or not he feared, as I pretended to, the potential collapse of an apartment complex whenever he was forced to descend the three stories below in order to retrieve his car I have no idea.

We went for a nightcap, dim sum, to a book store which special-ized in old world maps. Strolled the periphery of a reservoir, scoured skid row, passing out fried wontons and fortune cookies, or drove out to the beach, a lagoon, the lake. We discussed solar flare ups and their effects on the earth's atmosphere, female infanticide and get rich quick scams on late night TV. I invited myself back to his place after concocting a fabulous lie about accidentally locking my keys in the trunk of my car.

Where and how they lived revealed only as much as a Tarot

reading, the throwing of the I-ching, a daily horoscope, or the numerological breakdown of the letters in their name. How they reacted to what was about to happen, exposed the true core of who and what they were, and what they were, or weren't capable of expressing.

I excused myself to the bathroom. Tousled my hair, checked my lipstick, and removed the tube of Chinese analgesic from my purse. Smeared it between my fingers, on my hands, wrists, forearms, even the bottom of my feet. You never know. . . . Dabbed a little on my lips. Rubbed feverishly against my breasts. Smudged a little against my mound. Was so thorough, I even massaged a little into the crack of my ass. As masquerade, I dabbed a slutty dose of perfumed oil into my hair. Slunk out of the bathroom. Ready to play.

"Mmm . . . Tuberose? Gardenia? Myrrh?" he questioned, kissing the nape of my neck, nestling deep into the delicate web of flesh connecting the earlobe.

"Mogra," I whispered. Not that it mattered, he wouldn't have a clue to the origins of this mysterious Indian intoxicant. I knew, however, its musky undertones would completely remove the arnica, capsicum, burdock, and chaparral which combined in the proper dosage allowed the analgesic to do its work. To prevent swelling.

I grabbed his face, sweetly pulling it up toward my lips. Slipped my tongue in his mouth, allowing my swollen little nugget to prance around inside, teasing his anxious tip. Sucked on it. Ran my fingers lightly over his closed eyes, careful that the capsicum cream made no contact with the moisture forming at his temples. My desire was not to blind, just to incapacitate.

I played the aggressor. Told him to just sit back, enjoy, allow me to do the work. Tugged at his hair, if he had any. Pulling his head back enough to nuzzle under his chin, into collarbones, shoulder blades, nipping like a baby piranha. After the first audible gasp, as the initial shudder subsided, I unbuttoned his shirt, just enough to expose his nipples. Grabbed one between thumb and forefinger, twisting. Bent my head to suckle. Took it between my teeth. Chewed on it a little. Could feel the heat radiating from between his legs. Spread them a little wider with my right knee. Enough to smell his heat. Cooing in his ear to just drink it in . . . sup on it. Surrender.

I nibbled my way down his belly, unbuckling his belt. Exposing the greedy beast whose visible throbbing ebbed and flowed with each intake of breath. Full, rich, deadly, thick. Purred on it. Circled it with my mouth. Took it in, swallowed the meaty fiend. Slurping loudly. Making a show of it, knowing how soon the curtain was to fall. All I had to do was place my hands upon it. Stroke it a few times. Pull on it. Twist. And it would recede. And so I stroked. And his erection faded.

The analgesic was working. It never failed. He went soft. Mushy. Limp. Quickly. It was beautiful. The hurt look of complete amazement, priceless. The stammering and fraudulent explanations. He must be tired. He had too much to drink. He's under too much stress. I was just too beautiful. I was intimidating. "This has never happened to me before . . . " and on and on. An endless litany.

Of course they always offered to get me off. To satisfy me. Whatever it took. To lick, finger, tickle, massage. But it wasn't their sex that I was interested in. Or the sex they could supply me with. I wanted something else. Something bigger. I wanted their humility. To watch their confidence erode, crumble, collapse. So I could slowly build it back up again. It allowed me to play saint, martyr, mother. I could whisper to them how I understood, it was no big deal. It didn't really matter. It happened to everybody at one time or another. It was nothing to worry about. They should just relax. Enjoy my breath against their cheeks as I held their face to my breast. Not place so much importance on the act itself. Recognize and relish how intimate the moment was. How beautiful. How erotic. That we could be so close to each other, and not feel pressured to perform. I'd suggest they take a hot shower. It would help them to unwind. I'd make myself comfortable. We could have a nightcap when they came out. Smoke a cigarette. Watch some old black and white movie. Just relax. Enjoy.

I'd listen for the water heater to kick in. When enough steam had filled the bathroom to deaden the sound, I'd call a cab. Tell them to meet me at the nearest intersection. I'd leave a note on the couch. Telling them what a wonderful evening it had been. How sweet they were. How well I understood. Not that they ever would. How could anyone? The most exciting thing to me, the biggest turn on, was an extremely beautiful man who was unable to get hard. Who had almost been reduced to tears over just how incredibly useless it actually was. A cock. Such an overrated little tool. So sad. So ultimately foolish.

Cumming to the Conclusion

An Erotic Trilogy from Hell

by

Richard Lewis

An Act of Goddess

So I just had what I thought was a very productive, mature and sober day in New York. After hours of press for my nightclub gig, and a great session with my New York therapist I was happily walking back to my hotel after the sound check at the club, when as if dropped from heaven, I passed one of the most beautiful, if not *the most* incredible-looking woman I have ever seen. She smiled in a way that to a fool would immediately suggest that she would, without much encouragement, want to spend the rest of her life with me.

Before you cynics have a field day with my one-sided fantasy, let me be perfectly clear that not only did I know that she recognized me, but was glowing to boot, at the one-in-a-million chance of spotting me. She was unquestionably an actress or a model as she was carrying a huge black portfolio, so even if she ultimately faked caring about me (and could, I'm certain, have thought of ways to use me), I nonetheless gave her unknown character the benefit of the doubt. She had the kind of expression that screamed that she was not only very available, but dying for me to stop her and make some charming quip that could not only lead to paradise but also (and this is the downside), undo every bit of monogamous drudgery I had been feverishly working at for years now. Namely, the act of restraining myself from acting out on my girlfriend, and allowing myself the opportunity to really have a mature, loving, dynamic relationship with one woman.

Somehow I managed to keep walking in the opposite direction, all the while knowing that I was doing the right thing, but also feeling like a dead man. After a block of "hellos" and "you're greats" from passing fans, which now meant nothing to me with this goddess image in my head, I had the insatiable urge to turn around and run as fast as I could and catch up with her, not caring at all what kind of emotional hangover I might have eventually; assuming I was lucky enough to find her and have some sort of intimate liaison.

At this stage in my sobriety, approaching her was as dangerous to my existence as approaching a drink with my name on it. I somberly walked back to my hotel in excruciating pain, lamenting what might have been. But rather than feeling proud of my alleged maturation and faithfulness, I instead felt pitifully foolish in having chosen abstinence. This was more than just a drink. This was a new, never-before-tasted liquid, packaged in a glass of flesh and blood and raw sexuality. I told myself I wouldn't even lose a day of sobriety if I had this affair. I could whisk this strange woman away, have the greatest sex I've ever experienced and then quietly excuse myself, and make it back to my room, still sober as a motherfucker. What would be so wrong with that? Sadly, at this stage in my life, *everything*.

Suddenly every fiber of my being felt empty. All of my creative drive and unbridled enthusiasm to get back to the hotel and work into the night (poring over the hours of new material for opening night), instantly drained from me and became a task, instead of the joy it usually was. In fact, more than just a task, it felt like a self-imposed prison sentence. Time that was once time spent gloriously filling my life with authenticity was now a moment-to-moment hell, a constant obsessing over just what it might have been like sucking her breasts, or licking her vagina or making her laugh. I'd seen yet another beautiful siren and let her go, to be gobbled up by some other guy while I crashed into the rocks of unsettling monogamy and self-pity.

The rap I gave my New York shrink just hours before about how indebted I was feeling to have stayed in love for almost two years already, and how grateful I knew I *should* feel to be loved by a real soulmate, now sounded like a bunch of pure bullshit. Just hours before this female vision of heavenly delights could have become a part of my life, I had thought I should feel appreciative; but somehow I didn't and even took it for granted.

Then in an almost overpowering realization, I saw that my *ingrained reluctance* to accept true love from my true love (or any woman I really got to know and adore), was the innate, toxic ingredient in my open-ended horniness and endless dissatisfaction at not feeling content in a relationship. What a nightmare! When will this end? When will I allow myself to feel at peace, at ease with one woman, rather than feel the relationship is more like a quiet cross I must bear and schlep with me everywhere my whole life, and will probably cling to until the very last second as I am lowered into my grave?

And yet, I am *writing* now instead of *fucking*. I'm writing now, instead of fucking my girlfriend over. I'm writing now instead of being affectionate to someone I'm not available for. Even crazier, I am not with someone I know nothing about except what she *could be* beneath her heart-stopping looks. Stranger than that, I have no desire to even leave my room; satisfied with daydreaming over a loss I'll never have, and living off of room service and fantasies until I open in a few days. Strange because I can't imagine ever again seeing a woman as astonishing as the one I'd just walked away from. And even if I had played it out, and took a chance on sabotaging my real love affair, in my heart of hearts I knew I'd still be conflicted, conflicted that my cock was perhaps being treated too gloriously by a veritable stranger, a stranger who would ultimately leave me feeling drained and guilt-ridden. So what's the point of torturing myself again? Unless, of course, I just want to cave in to my addictive personality, my distrust of being loved by someone with not only substance, but a track record of caring, and while my earthly time runs out, simply spend it having no conscience or regard for my responsibility to any woman—*ever*.

I wonder where that missing goddess is now? I wonder if she is telling her friends that she passed Richard Lewis and that neither one of us had the courage to try and pick each other up? I wonder whether she is screwing her boyfriend or maybe her girlfriend and fantasizing that it's really me? I wonder whether she is even thinking about me at all.

I mean, I did stare at her for almost a block after she passed me, and she never looked back. That's generally not a good sign. Maybe she remembered something I once said and was merely smiling about that without a real appreciation for my total body of work, and without having anything close to remorse over not meeting me. Even if it was a rare, once-in-a-lifetime, golden opportunity. Perhaps she just regarded me as some well-known, aging comedian, and was just chuckling and marveling over the fact that I still had a great head of hair. Or even worse (ego-wise), what if her brief smile was only in extraordinary anticipation she felt about racing home to tell her parents (who would be much closer to my age than she is) that she'd passed *their* favorite comedian, the one she thinks is cute but too obscure for her taste, and who on top of that makes her nervous to watch.

There are so many scenarios that are better written by the goddess herself. She knows far better than I do.

At least for tonight I avoided some drama, remained devoted to my chick and put a little character in the bank. Oddly enough, even with this progress made in character building, I have both an off-putting sense of emptiness and worthlessness, and a surprising feeling of sanity at the same time.

It's hard being an adult and a baby simultaneously.

Maturity, for me tonight, equals masturbation plus time. Time without the goddess.

I pray to God she isn't in the front row opening night. My penis is *very* anxious to run away from home.

The Next Night

Well, I didn't fuck around. I spent the day writing and coming to the aid of other alcoholics while getting ready for my show. Even before I spoke to some pretty spiritual cats over the phone, who like myself are there 24/7, I managed to feel better about myself. I called my girlfriend, my real goddess, and let her know how hard it had been staying sober while being under so much pressure, and about the guilt I felt at not being able to enjoy or appreciate having a great woman like her in my life.

Of course I didn't feel it was necessary to needlessly relate my recent feelings of despair over the prospect of not only never meeting that dream girl again, but also the loneliness of the prospect of never even chasing that kind of rush again. My girlfriend, although not addicted to the hunt like me, is making my struggle even harder because (and I know this sounds stupid) she herself had lived a lifestyle with men she knew down deep were wrong for her, and that made it difficult for her to give herself totally to anyone out of a fear, similar to my own, that they would ultimately turn out to be phonies and abandon her. I actually love a woman who not only understands me but also understands my dilemma. When I told her of my fears she not only tried to comfort me but also said she had similar defense mechanisms against getting too close herself. And furthermore, then added that for the first time she was able, with *yours truly,* to really be herself in a relationship. This wasn't supposed to ever happen to me. She seemed perfect. And that's the rub.

To desperately try and ruin a good thing that I don't feel capable or deserving of having, I had almost hoped sometimes that my honesty about my problems with my wandering eye would one day push her to the limit, making her really upset, so I could then crazily interpret it as her being possessive, or pushing me away. A tried-and-true self-fulfilling prophecy I have down perfectly. To make doubly sure that I could escape from this healthy relationship without a sense of remorse, I can easily put a spin on her acceptance, and see it as a halfhearted love of me which would then throw me into *rejection mode,* where I'd feel a sort of irrational, justified hurt or rejection and then allow myself the luxury of acting out with other women in some comic game to get even. It's obviously impossible to be loved if I continue to feel, at my core, worthless and inadequate.

I immediately called a couple of guys like myself, who although in recovery, are having the same difficulty in staying away from affairs. I told one similarly tortured man that after I'd stopped drinking and now was not cheating on my woman, I felt that I needed some sort of symbolic, ticker-tape parade to validate how hard I've been working on becoming a better person. He told me that it really wasn't about her giving me the kudos as much as me doing it for myself. He was so right. It was identical to the process of stopping my drinking. It wouldn't have mattered if God himself pleaded with me to quit; it would have failed unless *I wanted to.* So to show me how much progress he felt I was making, as a favor to me he said that in his own head he would throw me a parade. We giggled (like adolescent girls at a sleepover party) and his compassionate make-believe confetti made me feel like a million bucks.

The topper was what my other friend told me. He too felt good for me, but very simply and properly put my addict's temperament in proper perspective, by stating matter-of-factly that, *"Being two places at one time is being no place at all."* That phrase sounded so familiar, mainly because it was so right on. He was so on the money. And as hard as it was being with myself, it was at least someplace tangible and identifiable. And even though being human is my biggest problem, it sure felt good feeling like a somebody not in free fall.

Instead I jerked off before I went to sleep and felt better, in the process, better than I would have jerking myself *and* two unsus-pecting women around.

Tomorrow I open, and I'll feel pretty good about who I am standing on that stage whether they laugh a lot or not; because at least for one day I can look in the mirror and recognize someone who more resembles who I think I am.

Thank goddess.

Of course, on stage, getting a few laughs wouldn't hurt. Like I've said, I'm only human. Damnit!

It's a Tough Act to Swallow

"Shit! This can't be happening to me."

That was the feeling I had while lying naked with a potential Mrs. Right as she suddenly stopped performing oral sex on me and matter-of-factly said (trying to retain some semblance of passion), "I've never *swallowed* before."

I went into shock and so did my penis. I was both erectionless and speechless at the prospect of spending the rest of my days (perhaps) with this genuinely wonderful woman, who would always make me feel uncomfortable now, because I knew that she felt uncomfortable swallowing my orgasmic *honey*.

Time stood still as I tried to come up with some sort of sympathetic white lie to cover my colossal disappointment. To make matters worse, I started to immediately escape from this reality by remembering days past when many (mostly much younger women who were all wrong to plan a life around) treated (and God bless them) the act of swallowing semen like it was some kind of deeply religious duty. And a pleasure. What a sickening irony that such an intimate act can so often be cherished by the wrong person and eschewed by the right one.

As I continued my reverie into the past, the honey memory was painfully vivid, and seemed to validate my current lover's dilemma. It was a reference used once (I swear) by a hot young bee farmer I was sleeping with back at college in the late Sixties (when everyone seemed to be doing something involving sperm every hour or so). This is a hazy recollection because I was stoned and she was drunk. Attempting to blow me while keeping herself from falling off the bed she somehow straightened up enough to shout, "Did *you* ever taste this shit?!"

Of course not . . . except, well (here's another deep, dark secret I won't be taking to the grave with me) once in college, completely ripped and alone in my room, I tentatively tasted a tiny drop after jerking off. Instantly panic-stricken, I called 911, whereupon I was immediately scolded before being given the more appropriate number (that somehow I was supposed to know, even in a state of duress) to call when accidentally swallowing foreign substances, poison, or any type of crazy shit.

I called the other hotline and was greeted by what sounded like the world's most insensitive bitch! Not only did this woman seem dispassionate (although I had yet to tell her *what* I'd swallowed; only that I *thought* I might drop dead) but she also seemed tragically undertrained for such a serious position. This was reinforced by her tortuously slow questioning, as if she were reciting from some dumb protocol, and by a curious tendency to simultaneously hum Steppenwolf's "Magic Carpet Ride."

Though a pretty good singer, she kept distracting me every few seconds by asking me things like, "Do you feel like you're close to death?" "Does anyone have a gun to your head?" "Do you think we should get out of 'Nam?" "Is Hendrix better than Clapton?" Well, I wasn't in a party mood after my forbidden act, so, finally, desperately afraid of the Grim Reaper in my grass-induced and paranoid state, I told her to shut up. Then I spit out the bitter truth.

"Listen, babe, cool it for a second and let me know if you think it's fatal if I ingested some pepperoni pizza, marijuana, and my own semen." Then I began to sob uncontrollably.

Her long pause gave me a chance to reflect on what the consequences of my dumb swallowing act might be. The thought of dying and the ensuing autopsy that would come out, suggesting that at the time of death not only was I on drugs but *giving head,* filled me with panic. And though I'm not homophobic, it was just too much to handle because my dad had a bad heart condition and clearly this sort of news would've done him in.

Undaunted, the operator started to sing again. Then, as if in an attempt to quickly relieve me of my unfounded fear and enigmatically try and help fill me with some gratitude (this struck me as sort of romantic), she commenced upon some long-winded, stony and yet rather entertaining tale, about the emotional background of the legendary Yankees ballplayer who foolishly sat out *one* game, only to be substituted by Lou Gehrig; and how this poor guy had to watch his pathetic misfortune grow, one day at a time.

This yarn oddly enough cheered me to the point that it extricated me from my self-imposed death watch. One thing led to another over the phone, and we soon realized that *my* grass dealer was *her* brother. Instant pals, she came over when she got off work. We shared a few joints, and I blew her mind; turning her on for the first time to potato pancakes and Procol Harum. And in return, she gladly blew me (and swallowed, I might add).

But that was a long time ago, and this latest episode took place, with my potency running out and my heart running in, with its two cents. I was convinced that I may have soberly stumbled upon *the love of my life.* She felt the same way about me. The down side to all this good news is that from day one, I've always felt truly fucked-up (even sober) when I've tried to convince myself that true love could really be legitimate. And, even more fucked up now, as I tried to believe this woman isn't lying.

Not totally out of touch, I realized that this had to be close to "the real thing," because historically I automatically go into my mode of "looking for flaws" if frightened by something more than just physical attraction.

That brings us back to the blow job. I knew down deep (in order to quickly put distance between my devotion and my new sweetheart) that I was just adolescently case building, because of her initial reluctance to swallow. I mean, who was to say that she couldn't in time develop abilities to give the greatest blow job ever? And as for me, I might just grow up. But if she hadn't openly admitted to being a tad squeamish swallowing my hearty broth of "liquid children," I still would have, lightning quick, found some other blemish of hers to turn me off and prevent me from moving ahead with someone who, all in all, seemed to be the greatest.

But that said, given my bad luck with women and my childish and selfish approach to love, why should I have had much confidence that she *was the one,* in the first place? Relationships have always ultimately *sucked anyway* (pardon the expression). At least from my damaged perspective.

Unfortunately, no matter how I twisted my logic, this woman seemed so right for me on paper. But what was driving me crazy was this sense of impending maturity. I seemed to once again be fighting off growth (which for me makes compromise with another person almost toxic).

Was I looking for an easy way out? You bet! But what for? And to go into what? Like I didn't already know! Once again I'd (sooner or later) waltz into yet another endless string of would-be "dynamic" relationships, with women not yet born when the Beatles broke up. These would ultimately prove to be just wasted notches on my sex belt (and blown time) added to my ever-growing list of Mother Goose–endorsed relationships.

Allow me to share. . . . At my lowest point of immaturity I once found accord with some screwball acquaintance of mine, Jake. *He* felt that since he could never find the right chick (certain that his hearty appetite for vodka and cocaine every day had nothing to do with his perception), maybe he should, although he was 35 at the time, actually ask a 15-year-old he yearned for to move in with him. Granted, he admitted it was a little embarrassing having to ask the waiter at a high-profile eatery in Beverly Hills to get a phone book for his new love to sit on so she could reach her plate without standing on her chair. Yet like myself, being full of fear about intimacy and also an addict (though he never tried to lick his disease), he insanely concluded that due to her youth she not only would have very little "baggage" but she would be able to comprehend very little about his own past wreckage, and that could only serve to make his future with her look brighter. And I agreed. Heavy, huh?

Well, fortunately for the "tot," she came to her senses and left him for a high school quarterback and had a storybook wedding.

Jake didn't fare that well. Apparently, after doing too much blow in a vain attempt to ward off his depression after "Poopie" left (he called her that, much to her chagrin), he once again pursued a much younger girl and dropped dead of a heart attack while showing off on a see-saw.

I think I finally see light at the end of my penis. I really hope so this time.

I've been a tough act to swallow.

Beyond Masturbation

Cutting to the chase, if a guy can blow himself and does, is he gay? Likewise, if a woman can go down on herself, and does, is she a lesbian? Of course, if they are gay or lesbian this is all academic and they are very lucky campers. Not to mention very flexible. (And in one case, at least, probably pretty well-endowed.) But if they are straight, doesn't it present sort of a nightmare if these heterosexuals are as neurotic as me?

Believe it or not, I was suddenly struck with this notion almost 30 years ago while spending a summer traveling throughout Europe. I was pretty broke, except for the few hundred bucks my dad gave me as a college graduation gift, when the nightmare happened.

One heavenly, carefree afternoon in Copenhagen, I was sitting a few rows back from the smelly sawdust at what was billed as a magical, one-ring, circus extravaganza. Much to my shock and amazement, about midway through the show, one of the top acts *(The Two Rubber Men)* came out. One black and one white, tall with muscular bodies, they proceeded to contort themselves in such a way that both were able to fit inside a see-through container the size of a shoe box.

Immediately, and seemingly without any rhyme or reason, I began to cry and puke my guts out. And I have never been the same since.

Before I humiliate myself further and give any more reasons for my former therapists to feel like failures (should they read this fear-based story), I must mention a few things that were going on outside this tiny menagerie, on the world's stage . . . Viet Nam . . . First men on the moon (as far as the U.S. was concerned) . . . The Manson Trial. A college sweetheart, waiting impatiently for me back in the States, and then, of course, the dreaded fear of having only one more semester before being thrown into that bizarre world outside the cushy pressure of midterms and scoring hash.

Yet, even with about 10 countries left on my amazing journey, alone, for the first time ever, feeling as if I was living in a dream with nothing pressuring me, except my insatiable desire to see as many museums as possible, and to touch—obsessively and mischievously—with my own hands, the very pictures I had seen in art history books, there I was, a budding psycho, obsessing about the lifestyle of these flexible circus guys.

And not just on how they ever decided to learn to fold themselves up like dry cleaning, but whether or not they gave oral sex to themselves. And if so, whether or not they felt they were doing anything more than masturbating.

Of course, it wasn't about them, but me. Don't get me wrong, getting to the moon first was sort of cool, but the prospect of living in a small box if times were hard fueled my paranoia about ever making a living. And mostly, the fantasy of giving myself head endlessly (and never wanting to do anything else, all the while still feeling like a ladies' man) seemed too good to be true. And I was at once struck with such a disturbing degree of jealousy, I almost felt like killing myself. Well, not really, but darting out of the tent back to my "bed and breakfast" to see whether I could suck myself off and then having to figure out what kind of letter I would write my parents about how I fell in love with Denmark and could never leave, without admitting that I'd probably never stray from my room again and would die a happy man but never graduate college is something I could not do. I mean what would be the point? It would be like telling a great collegiate basketball player not to leave school before graduating and miss participating in the NBA Draft with a potential for a $90 million contract, but rather, to stay one more year and risk injury; and for me it would mean perhaps being in a plane crash on my way back to the States, and the sacrifice of a lifelong dream (even then), of satisfying myself without fear of abandoning anyone.

Maybe a blow to my parents' ego but what a trip for me. Hey, man, one small step for Armstrong but one giant blow job for Lewis. Seems like a no-brainer, doesn't it?

It's not like I'd ever had a pressing need to have children. In fact, I never had a pressing need to have much of a life, outside of my career. So if I could have satisfied myself, without the need for counseling, I think it might have been a good move.

Sadly, the big obstacle has always been my bad knees, which not only fucked me up for Yoga but posed the risk of getting me into some serious surgery if I even tried to get into the "Blow-tus Position."

Hence, it still remains unanswered, whether I could ever feel as easygoing "getting off," by blowing myself, as I have felt (millions of times) jerking off. Moreover, what about phone sex? An act I clearly enjoy could be severely hampered if I really started to fall in love with myself. Seriously, I don't even think the world's greatest ventriloquist could pull that off.

So in the final analysis, after several heated debates with famed orthopedic surgeons, I decided to put my knees first, and never blew myself. And although stranger things have happened, I probably never will.

Yeah, it's kind of a drag. But all things considered, perhaps it's best it worked out this way (as it will probably help keep my dating options open), while I continue to confound my self-loathing by considering myself one hell of an eligible bachelor.

Miss Anne

by
Lori E. Seid

When I came bounding out of the sunny day, into the bar, she was sitting on the steps clutching her belongings. Even though my eyes were unadjusted to the dark I could see her beauty was painted on. But the look in her eyes stopped me in my tracks. I knew she wasn't who I was looking for but I asked anyway.

"Excuse me, are you Robin?"

"No I'm not." She held out her hand and said, "I'm Anne Smythe, I am here to audition for the go-go position."

She held out her hand so femininely I wasn't sure if I should shake it or kiss it. Shaking it, I introduced myself as one of the people in charge of the audition and we sat down on those cold dark steps together still holding each other's hands, just chatting.

When the auditions began I knew that onstage Anne would possess exactly what we wanted: the illusion that she could be yours. She took the stage, her eyes looking right through me, her body moving so slow and so teasingly that even the other dancers onstage had to stop to watch. But she quite obviously wanted my attention. This was not a problem. She got it. She also got the job.

Anne started work the next evening and came early to find me to say hello. She would do this every night. My job at this club was temporary; I was making a living traveling throughout the world offering salons in a theater festival environment. I worked at the club every day and 10 dancers rotated in the available shifts.

Every set Anne danced she made sure I knew she was doing certain moves to me. No matter where I was she'd find me and catch my eye. This was my business but still she made me blush with shyness and desire.

After each shift she would again look for me and offer to buy me a drink. I always politely declined. This woman intrigued me in the way a character in a book does. Miss Anne, the name I'd taken to calling her, treated me gently and carefully, almost stereotypically the way a woman treats a man who has something she wants. What I could give her was a mystery to me. I mean she already had the job.

It stunned me when another dancer pulled me aside.

"Listen if I tell you something privately will you promise not to embarrass the person it's about. . . ."

"Of course," I replied.

He paused, and then said, "Anne thinks you're a guy. . . ."

"Excuse me?"

"Anne, you know, the dancer, thinks you're a man." She said 'I don't know what to do, I'm falling in love with *him* . . . *He* is the sweetest and most gentle man I've ever met."

"Maybe she meant Steve," I said. "There is no way—"

"She means you. I checked, she means you."

I stood there stunned. If I was in a cartoon, swirling lines would be coming out of my head as my eyes rolled around in separate directions. Gender confusion was not completely unknown to me. Sometimes people called me "Sir" in quick exchange situations but they realized their mistake before too long. But Anne and I had been working together for three weeks now. What had she been looking at?

"Did you tell her I was a woman?" I asked.

"Yes, of course I did."

"What did she say. I mean is she freaked out or. . . . "

"No," he said. " . . . She seemed stunned and embarrassed at first, then she seemed downright turned on by the idea."

"Okay, enough. You've told me enough, thank you." I cut him short.

"Have fun," he teased, running off to the dressing room.

After her shift she looked for me as always and asked me if she could buy me a drink. This night she seemed just a little more everything. A little more dressed, a little more made up, a little more perfumed and a little more eager. Maybe it was me who was a little more turned on.

For the first time I accepted her offer of a shared drink, but only if she went out with me. After our doors shut I usually had a nightcap at this place called the Art Bar. This bar was guest list only and her type of dancer was never invited there. Part of the idea behind our events was to change how people looked at strippers and how they looked at themselves. It would do me proud to take her there. We walked over to the bar and she was clearly getting anxious about what lay ahead.

"Look," I said as we waited for a light to change, "you're with me and that makes me very happy. If you're uncomfortable going to this bar and really don't want to, fine, we'll go somewhere else, but if you're nervous because you feel you won't fit in there we should talk about it right now."

Her response was not what I expected; she tightly grabbed hold of my right arm, held back tears with a smile and said "I'll go anywhere you take me." I knew she meant more than crossing the street.

When we got there the place was packed but not so much so that we weren't immediately noticed. The room stopped.

"Fuck 'em," I thought. "A dyke and a stripper. Deal with it."

We walked straight to the bar and I ordered a bottle of expensive champagne. That was her drink but she was accustomed to buying it by the glass. She just kept staring in my eyes like this was a fairy-tale come true but I didn't mind. By now I was believing in it also.

We went out to the tables on the back terrace. The moon was full and low and a bit overwhelming.

I poured two glasses and we played with each other's fingers while the bubbles settled, silhouetted by the moonlight. We held our glasses up, quietly touching them to each other, leaned forward and gently kissed.

"So, Miss Anne, why do you think that whole room was watching us?"

She sweetly smiled and glanced nervously and looked down at her glass. "In some ways this is a very small town, you're new here, everybody likes you, respects you. I have been around a long time, everybody knows me too well."

"Jesus, what could they know? That you are a go-go dancer, a stripper?!"

"Even in my simple life it's more complicated than that. Let me have tonight—okay?"

I sat and watched the stars twitch in the pitch-black part of the sky.

I wondered if this woman really knew what she was getting into. We sat, not speaking, just listening to the world around us.

The bottle was empty. It was time to leave. We walked back through the party inside, nodding our good-byes without stopping. We continued in silence all the way to the taxi stand. "Come on, I'll drop you off," I said.

Getting in, I asked her address and her pause in answering made me say, "Do you want to stay with me tonight?"

As I said it I saw the driver's eyes dart into the rearview mirror making sure memory served him and we were two women. She nodded. The driver grimaced as I leaned forward and gave my hotel address. The car pulled out quickly and I fell back on top of Miss Anne. She moved over just enough so my shoulder was still over-lapping hers. She took hold of my hand and we sat still listening to the pounding of our own hearts.

The awkward silence continued, as we walked through the lobby, the hallways, and the stairway of my hotel. It was made painfully apparent by the steady clicking of her six-inch high heels. Finally my door opened and closed behind us.

Still not speaking, we went right to the bedroom. We both knew why we were there. We got near the bed and started a frenzied kiss. Before that first kiss was finished we were on the bed with me on top, our legs entwined.

I soon found out everything on her was fake. Her tan rubbed off on my white T-shirt, her makeup on the white crisp hotel linen. Her body hair was waxed off to mannequin perfection, her breasts were filled with silicone. It made me want her more, to tear it all off and climb inside her.

My hands were all over her, touching, stroking, and pulling at her clothes. It wasn't long before they were gone. She pulled away abruptly and looked away from me in shame.

"I haven't been with anyone in three years," she whispered covering her breasts with her arms. "I hate these, but I had to, I'm old now, I have to keep my job, I'm sorry please don't look at them." She did suddenly age, all her makeup wiped off, her eyes vulnerable and pleading.

I had never been with a woman with fake breasts. It seemed so weird to see them never move with the rest of her body, to stay full, perfectly round and erect. I wanted to touch them.

I moved her arms gently away as I again straddled her under me. I tenderly kissed her nipples wondering if they had any feeling because they didn't seem alive. Tears quietly slipped from her eyes down the sides of her temples and I gently licked up her breasts, up her neck, up the path of her tears, to the corner of her eyes. I whispered, "You are here now, with me, and I think you are beautiful. I thought that the moment I saw you and I especially think it now. Hold on to me and I'll take you past your pain. . . ."

She put her arms around me and tightened the grip of her legs around my waist. Her nails, lightly tickling at first, scratched deeper into the flesh of my back as she bit on my ear and groaned, "Fuck me."

I did. For a very long time. She took me so deeply, so strongly, so fully, I felt as if we'd pierced through each other and would never part. There was sunlight bursting through the edges of the curtained windows. Finally we lay quiet, listening to a new day begin.

"No one's ever made me feel like this. I mean I have never been with a woman before, but no man has ever. . . . " She paused a long time, distracted. She pulled away, panicked, then resisted the urge and settled herself back in my arms.

". . . my last boyfriend," she slowly continued, "is the man that runs all the biggest strip clubs in this city. I used to work at his club. I was the biggest draw. I was famous, people from all around knew me. But I did more than just strip, I was his creative side. All the most popular shows I designed, they were all my ideas. Everybody knew it. But then things started going wrong. He started beating me and beating me and beating me. He wouldn't stop and nobody would help me. He is a very powerful man. One day, I couldn't take it anymore. I told him if he beat me one more time I would leave. He did and so did I. I hid at a girlfriend's house but he found me and beat me worse than ever. But for me the most painful thing was that everyone just looked on. Like it was my fault for challenging him. I spent two weeks in the hospital. Besides other things, he broke my jaw. As soon as I could, I left town, but I had nowhere to go. My mother is dead and my only family, my father and my sister, they want nothing to do with me because of how I earn my living. I don't do anything wrong. I'm not bad, this is what I do. Finally, a year ago I moved back to town. What could he do to me, I thought, I am already dead. When I got back to town people were happy to see me but he warned all the best clubs not to hire me. That's why I only can work at the lunch place. It doesn't compete with his nightclubs. And you, you are only temporary. . . ."

She looked at me for the first time since she started speaking. She had snapped us back to the present, and the reality that I was only in town for a few more days. I felt so much for this woman in the pit of my stomach. I wanted to keep making love to her just because I had no words that could ever express my emotion for her. All my mouth could do was kiss her. Deeper and deeper. We started fucking again, and my whole hand slipped inside her, as she sat on me grinding all her weight into me. More and more of my forearm disappeared inside her like she wanted me to bust through her, to break her, and I wanted to as much as she did. We were something impossible, a desire that could not be stopped, like the painting on the ceiling of the Sistine Chapel.

My thirst for her only seemed more intense and the need to keep going only bigger. I rolled her on her back and started down her body with my mouth. I spent more time in her armpit and underarm area than her breasts. I still wasn't sure what they could feel and didn't want her to get sad again. Besides, they still felt strange to me; the skin felt like plastic and I didn't want to get too lost in my own thoughts on the whole subject. I lightly licked under her breasts, tickling her ribs with my tongue. When I got to her hips I nibbled what little bit of flesh I could get my teeth on. She started to squirm and I felt this roughness stir up in me. I put my left knee over both her thighs and wrapped my left hand tightly around her neck. I bit down hard on the flesh over her cunt.

She let out a gasp and whispered, "Oh Daddy, I have been so bad, Daddy, if you spank me I'll be a good little girl, Daddy. . . . I'll do anything you want. . . . Daddy hit me, Daddy."

I lifted the weight off her thighs so she could turn over. I kept my hand firmly around her throat, feeling the tightness each time she swallowed. Her ass rubbed and rotated and pushed into my pussy. I could feel the power she was working in me. I held her arms over her head with one hand as my right hand softly rubbed the skin on the cheeks of her ass. I slipped my finger around the wetness of cunt and slowly eased my thumb into her asshole while the rest of my hand firmly clenched her pussy. Her whimpering only made me rougher and sterner.

"Oh Daddy. . . . I have been bad, but I will be good, so good, you'll see I can make Daddy so happy. . . ."

Every now and then I'd lift my hand from her ass with a

quickness that made her hold her breath wondering how hard I could be.

I finally started slapping her ass. Her moans were so deep and so grateful she just kept raising up for more. The more I slapped her, the harder it became and we both were in a semi-trance from the sound, movement, and feeling. As her ass raised higher and higher I could smell the wetness coming out of her cunt. There was no way to stop now, we were both in a frenzy.

My hand slipped off her red cheek and two fingers grabbed her clit. It was hot, swollen and throbbing. I slid my knee under her so her ass had to stay in the air. Four fingers went into her as my thumb pushed back into her asshole. She cried but not in pain. Every time I could feel her muscles tighten, close to orgasm, I slowed down. *Not yet*, I thought, *not fuckin' yet*. When I thought she could wait no more, I pulled my hand out some and turned her over on her back again. Before she realized what was happening my face was hungrily spreading her legs wide apart and my tongue and teeth went for her clit, as my whole right hand pounded inside her. Within seconds she came with the most powerful push and I just kept drinking her in as my hand pushed in and out with her cumming. Our pace slowed but it was a long time before we finally stopped.

We lay still in the same position for a very long time. I felt parts of her body twitch uncontrollably and I slowly and gently took my hand out of her cunt. She never opened her eyes and as I lay on her we both fell into a very happy, deep sleep.

At dusk we woke up and I ordered coffee from room service. We watched the colors in the sky change the shape of the clouds and we both got privately sad, knowing that soon we would have to go on and be the same people we were before. The coffee came and we drank it. We smiled unspoken conversations at each other.

Miss Anne reapplied all her stuff and transformed into her public self again. I watched her, like a child watches its mother, amazed by the ritual of it all. Finally complete, she softly kissed me, getting lipstick, foundation, tanner, and stinky sharp perfume all over me again. She threw me another kiss as she quietly shut the door behind her. I thought of the sounds of her lone heels retracing the steps we had taken together. In its stillness I looked around the room. The smell of sex still hung thick in the air. I smoked a cigarette sitting on the edge of the bed and I thought about the illusions and the reality of desire.

I took a long hot shower and got ready for work.

A Wedding Day

by
Tim Miller

At the age of eighteen, I gave up men after only a few months as a homosexual because I decided that men were pigs. Then, early in 1977, I met a nice woman at the improvisational modern dance jam I frequented every Friday in Santa Monica called "Get High on Dance." Her name was Danielle, and she lived a few miles south on Santa Monica Bay in Redondo Beach. She knew I was a big fag, but decided what the hell.

We danced up a storm to Pink Floyd and we began to make out on the dance floor there on Santa Monica Boulevard. It strikes me as not among the lesser ironies of my life that the only time I have made out on Santa Monica Boulevard, holy of holies of homodom in LA, it was with a woman! We charmed, seduced, and delighted one another with our artsy undulations on the dance floor that night. She and I proceeded to have bad sex with each other a couple of times a week over the next two months.

On my brother's wedding day a few weeks later, I rushed to the reception in Marina Del Rey, figuring to put in a brief appearance. Danielle and I were going to meet later at her house in Redondo. I endured the photo shoot of groom and attendants in front of the yacht club. My brothers and I did a high-kicking impromptu for the camera that landed me on my butt. Brushing the grass off my bell bottoms, I told my Mom I was off to see my friend Danielle. She hurried me on my way, waving me off with the overeager hopefulness of a mother thinking her queer son has seen the light at last. I drove down Pacific Coast Highway in my '65 VW bug, feeling the tasty whiff of heterosexual privilege fluff my wide powder-blue lapels. It was like a powerful drug, this forbidden world suddenly made available to me. I could participate in my brother's wedding and then go to my girlfriend's house in Redondo.

The dreary litany of KFC, Taco Bell, and Pizza Man (their motto was "Had a piece lately?") assaulted my sensibilities as I drove down PCH in my erstwhile trusty VW. Unfortunately, I was not wise in the way of cars and hadn't noticed the oil light that had been blinking on my dashboard for the last two weeks. When the burning smoke began to pour out of the VW's rear engine, I was perplexed but not delayed. As the oil-less engine burnt to a crisp like a heavyset bagel trapped in the toaster, I merely discarded my car by the side of the road as casually as I would toss a crumpled Butterfinger wrapper in the garbage can. I knew I could hop on the bus and still make my date with Danielle! I sat on the bus bench in Hermosa Beach with my tuxedo and vest and shirt opened all the way down to my thin, hairless torso and indulged a Travolta-esque Kodak moment.

I hopped off the bus two doors from Danielle's house on F Street, rapped smartly on the door, and was whisked inside. Danielle's roommate Anna and a friend of hers from Chicago named Steve were also there. Great!!! Party on! I had danced and undulated with them all the week before at "Get High on Dance." Quickly we laid out Indian print sheets and old pieces of foam mattress on the living room floor so we could give each other massages with sweetly scented oils bought at the health food store in Santa Monica. Taking off all our clothes, we flopped down and the massage oil began to flow. Stroking each other, pulling the taffy of one another's tension, Danielle and I began to kiss while we massaged the knots of tension from our necks.

During this period I had always seen myself as the ultimate bad date for women. I could lure them in with my sensual and sassy post-modern dancing, but when push came to shove it was hard for me to get it up and get it in. I did my best. Danielle knew how to work with me and always found a way to get me to rise to the occasion. Anticipating early 90s queer sex, I think she liked getting the faggot to fuck her! As we kissed, I felt the room begin to levitate. All the possibilities! Anna and Steve were making out too. I put my dick in Danielle (from behind) and began to fuck her. Anna lay down next to her and Steve got on top of her.

This was *my* wedding! Only two hours before, our dull Congregational minister had been leading my brother and his soon-to-be-wife through their wedding vows and now here I was where I belonged in my own chaotic life. I saw these two women lying side by side as Steve and I fucked them. Danielle and Anna began to kiss, then Steve and I began to kiss. His tongue filled my mouth as my cock slid in and out of Danielle.

I felt the scratchy upper lip of Steve scraping over my nose and lips as we kissed. Finding myself in the position of fucking my new girlfriend Danielle while I kissed a man gave me a front-row-seat opportunity to examine my position that "men are pigs." His probing tongue in my mouth and the feel of his rough beard made the three cherries line up and ring on my psycho-sexual slot machine!

I was now at a new kind of wedding—a wedding between the different potential parts of myself. The wedding between two men and two women. The wedding between the four people in the room and our parents and the best man and the bridesmaid. Steve and I came in Anna and Danielle as we kissed. Was I more in the kiss or the fuck?

The room floods back, the reality of that special moment. I feel my tongue in Steve's mouth and my softening cock inside Danielle. I know that there is no question, on this wedding day, that I am fated to walk down the aisle with Steve rather than Danielle.

The next morning my Dad thought he was coming to rescue me from yet another automotive mishap, but instead he would make his way to the west side of Los Angeles for another kind of wedding—his youngest son collapsed on a tattered, sex-drenched mattress with two women and another man. My father regarded the refuse of the wedding night's orgy. He stared at the candles sputtering their last breath in their pie plates, the spilled massage oil slick on the hardwood floors crosshatched by Danielle's dog's sharp paws, and a thermonuclear ghost cloud of dope smoke blessing the chaos of limbs and hearts and heads.

My father saw the sleeping forms of the two women lying next to each other against the wall. I saw my stock prices as a son begin to rise, but then he noticed Steve collapsed on the couch in the corner, the Star Wars sheet barely covering his butt and my personal Dow Jones crashed.

"Let's go."

On this day-after-the-wedding I saw the anger behind my father's eyes that I had burned up a perfectly good VW engine as well as my bridges to these two women. I would never give him the marriage that he wanted me to have. We went home.

He Delivers!
A Straight Woman
Looks at Gay Male Porn

by

Karen Finley

Have you ever seen a man topped?" asked the gay male executive editor of an online magazine.

"Have *you* ever seen a nine-pound, 21-inch baby come out of a bleeding raw pussy?"

I bit my lip and didn't say it, as I was working on my competitiveness and would take it to therapy. So I thought to myself, "He's gay, but he is still a guy," taking a whiff of him over the phone. He needed to change his socks. *Men.* I shook my head and acted bored for a moment until he said that he wanted me. *He* wanted me. This gay executive editor wanted me to write about a straight woman's reaction to gay porn.

"Well, I've seen gay porn. Really, really I have." Once I was editing a video in a primo porn production company and behind me on many screens were hundreds of handsomes being sucked, pulled, inserted, and duplicated.

The editor, whom I'll call Edward, gave my deposition a second thought and added, "Well, I'm sure you have imagined."

I tried to remember my fantasies of man being topped, and I recalled fantasizing about Jesse Helms pulling his teeth out and gumming the chocolate off my twat as he is topped by Rush Limbaugh. "Yeah," I said to Edward. "I have thought about it."

"I'll call my video house and get you some tapes of bears, boys, . . . will you watch S&M?" He said it with his voice lowering an octave. He sounded paternalistic, and I have always had a daddy thing. "I'll watch S&M, Edward," I whispered.

I fell in love with *him* right then and there, as he was selecting the gay porn *for me!!!* Edward is such a guy! He does the ordering and picks up the check. I could hear him say, "Take off your clothes *now, bitch*." And I would. I love it when my Edward gives orders. Edward selecting the tapes for me. That he couldn't think of any other straight woman but me to write the piece. It was all so vary romantic.

Trying to got the tapes in my hands heightened my passion. In the following two weeks I would run over to *his* office, calling on my cell phone to *his* voice mail. It was all so exciting and he is such a guy, a dick, never available. Keeping me waiting.

Finally he e-mailed me: "I hope the quivering male flesh will be worth the wait." I wanted to blush but breathed in at the next line: "Beast, I mean Best."

And then on second thought he wrote, "PS: rather I should say beast."

Beast?

Beast!!!

My beast. I wanted to watch *Beastie.* Boy male beasts with tails and gills and claws. Beastie boy male manes satisfying their Beastie bodies thick hair extra limbs limp then hard their erections like volcano waves triple beast cocks balls by the dozens taking damsels in distress or dukes or ducks or dicks. *Who cares*—it's my beast, my *beast* baby, beast.

A triangle had to happen. And it did when Edward assigned his intern to deliver the tapes to me. *Big guy executive editor too busy too busy work man dick dad stud work money business power dick.*

There was a knock at my dressing-room door. "Ms. Finley? Someone is here with a package that must be *personally* delivered, *hand delivered.*"

"Why, let him in, by all means." My voice became Blanche Dubois—and she did fancy Stanley, that beast!

The intern was delivering my trousseau, the copies of gay porn. I instantly imagined the exchange as a metaphor for the gay male editor who had assigned the piece standing over me, holding his golden genitalia and saying, "I insist on hand delivery." And I respond with fire in my eyes, "Let him in, by all means," as I open myself and wrap my long legs over the beast shoulders and he mounts me and I become his animal.

I looked through the tapes for some titillating titles. I noticed that the labels had been worn off by the wear and tear of sweaty palms, overuse, cummy hands—and I felt disgusted. But then I felt a thrill. Each label had its own libidinal quality, its own labia feel. The tape, the image going in and out in and out by male hands larger than mine holding their cocks, boylike or bruisers, and than I felt all the men either alone or watching with another as a way to connect or just get off, to get off, to cum.

I desired their sex with self, their moment of jerking either to get the day started or to end the day or to feel for a moment their hot cum through their fingers, washed off like a baby, a baby alone. Not too intimate, this is close enough. I see you selecting the tape, I see you putting it in, I feel you getting comfortable, holding yourself holding yourself, I wish I could hold you for you, carry your load. . . .

I wanted to hoard the labels from all the video porns and have their need their need carried in my purse like a tampon, like a phone number of a long lost lover.

Edward had asked me this: He wanted to know where a woman puts herself in gay porn.

A woman who is capable of endless orgasms attained in one sitting, orgasms that the man has to hunt for a month to have. It may look like the male is so sexual in his cruising and his endless search for more and more hole—or to be a hole—but the female, when put into cruise control, is much more sexually economic. With her need for one sperm for one egg she will sit back and go into orgasm over and over and over without having to take a rest.

The female, with her capacity to be a mother, is capable of crossing emotional and physical boundaries, of experiencing others—and otherness—as her own. So, besides the obviousness of bodies, cocks, thrusting pure *sex*, there is for me the ability to get off in my maternal feeling when seeing any creature get aroused. That makes me happy and satisfies me. When a mother is nursing and hears another child, any child, cry she immediately has a letdown. A letdown means that her breast starts to release milk. Even after nursing is over, when I hear a cry my breast still pangs for other children. This physical reaction happens with other sensations as well, such as sex and violence. All those physical stimuli enter into the sexual stimulus—and I am just explaining why a woman does not have to identify in order to respond to gay porn, but can, from an empathetic place, experience a symbiotic sexualness.

The young female is thrown into a world where sex with men has its dangerous and life-changing components. Every time I have sex I look at my partner and know that this man could be the father of my child; that I could get pregnant—and it has happened. Having multiple partners makes it all the more confusing if you do get pregnant. Having one man at a time is a protective device that nature put in place before DNA testing. Also, the fact that women are less physically strong than men makes us less willing to take a risk with an anonymous sexual partner, as a gay man might. That is why for me, when watching the gang-bang video that was choreographed from the opening act of *A Chorus Line,* my intuition gets in the way because the gang-bang rape is not a fantasy but a possibility, and there is an image I won't go back to: the time when the gun is at my head and his dick is in my hand. . . .

Being with gay men can be very relaxing for me, for I feel that I am not going to be hunted. I enjoy the sensual element of no potential danger, and the gay male–straight female relationship is erotic by its denial.

But let's go to the videotapes.

The first one, featuring a hockey team and an Eastern European look, turned me off in the credits. The title, *Souvenir,* made me think of some refrigerator magnet. The story line was simple: locker room, most of the players depart, then two guys wimpily go at it, then the boyfriend of one of them shows up. As I recall, there is the usual kiss body chest suck fuck—except that the jealous boyfriend looks at a picture of them as a couple. I didn't get aroused but I will tell you how I would.

Instead of an inside rink have it outside. The men cold but sweating and the sensation of the cold breath the hot flesh pushed against the frigid air. The bodies moving graceful fast slow, so the figures become human cocks on skates. We see the teams, the players, the winning, the losing, the focus to get that damn puck fuck in the net with sticks—the puck me puck me puck him in the net, the iciness and the zipper cold against the skin that I just want to undo and slip your cock out. He is against the snow, fallen, and his opponent has a palm gripped on his muscled thigh, pushing down and grabbing his inner thigh. We see his face gripped in tension but in pleasure, knowing he is being touched and wanted. We see the cold breath and the lips meet and their hot membranes melt, tongues swirl; we see eyes on fire as the lips icicles fudg-esticles collide. We know there is that moment of who is going to satisfy, of who is making the move, and our friend in the snow still has his opponent's hand on his thigh, and then a new lover's lips are lowered onto his cock. It is so cold and quick and needed. There is no need for anything else—he just wants to eat him in the snow eat him in the snow.

The transsexual tape bordered on an amateur-hour swingers party tape made by admirers of *Star Trek*. It starts out with commercials for 800 numbers with transsexuals being sucked, fucked, dildoed, clamped—it looked like a psychic hot line and about as inauthentic. The dingy quality exasperated me, and I felt that the transscxuals should have been treated better. Given better clothes.

The tape starts out with an overstuffed white chair-bed. The fabric looks like it must have smelled: grassy. We see the transsexual and a man sit on the chair together. They are asked questions by an interviewer: Had the man ever been with a transsexual before? Then they take their clothes off clumsily, revealing that the transsexual has fake breasts and a real dick. So? So who cares. I have been with overweight men who have titties. I like sucking on a man's nipple, but this didn't excite me. I felt like this was a tape for some straight guy in Idaho saying, "Oh, this is *so* extreme!"

I would get the transsexual off the couch and strutting her hybrid self into Bloomingdale's. We see our trannie in the underwear department trying on lacy bustiers and then unloading her big gland out of its turquoise thong and having the lady salesclerk on her knees in the dressing room going down on the cock. Other customers wait in line. Women are waiting to be fucked by her majesty in her throne room-dressing room.

I loved the title *Bear to the Bone* but again was disappointed by the plot and players. Here we see some forgetful stud modeling on a table and being photographed. Within two minutes the photographed and photographer are kissing and grabbing genitals like they are making a pizza. Voyeurism is sensual, and they didn't do anything about it. I would have freeze-framed on still images of the tip of the penis with the pinky slightly in the asshole and another finger encircling it. I presume the bear had an unusual amount of hair. The male body is so *other* that all men seem like bears to me. All men in their types are just so different from me.

What was missing from the porn for me was the female touch: a subtlety of the space behind the ear, the neck, the pulse of the wrist—and to stroke the inside of the arm, the pit of the arm so sensitive. For me what is missing is the thinking dick, and the fact that a man can lose an erection at any moment—and he can't fake his arousal.

The dick has a brain. The dick has a heart. The dick has a soul. The dick is turned on by conflict, humor, anxiety. Nurturing is the real turn-on for me. But ultimately all fetishes, all preferences, are just unresolved childhood traumas connected to consciousness. Our personal kinky gives us a code toward individuation. To find the mother, be the mother, avoid the mother or the father; the provider, the punisher, the protector—abandonod, humiliated, and transferred in romantic intrigue to the liar, the cheat, the ex-lover. What's so lovely about porn is that it gets us off by turning off our obscene collection of personality disorders.

But enough of this history/herstory. When it comes down to it, I don't need a reason to cum. And I don't need a reason to desire a gay man.

It is summer and my clothes stick to me as I walk into 31 flavors and see this beautiful man working in an apron at the counter. He asks me what flavor and I say French Vanilla, and he turns around and reveals his naked buttocks. He brings out his mighty organ in his hands. I notice that everyone has dropped to their knees, so I do my bidding and suck the cold iced cock until I get a vanilla creme down my throat. It immediately cools me down.

Songs of Experience

by

Tom Healy

Songs of Experience

I. With A Man My Father's Age

Fiddlestick legs,
carpeted back,
garbage-bag belly,

he called himself
Count. Count
O'Brien of Ireland,

take off your clothes,
the knee-high socks
and double-breasted

blazer, the nelly
snigger of your brass
buttoned up. Bite

the pillow and close
your eyes. Your
belt is in my hands.

II. Sparks

Our bodies wouldn't sing electric.
We tried once or twice—

when you spat in my face
and I laughed, or you demanded

I call you sir, yes sir
and I kept forgetting.

The thrum of current
came when we lay reading,

and talk was our lust,
like gossip about Henry James.

III. The Anesthesiologist's Kiss

He was the first
man I knew
with hair on his face.
I remember
his beard

almost covering his
lips, then mine
which were
parted by
the thirteen fears

of a five-year-old.
He held
my chin and
pressed gently
like rainfall.

I was crying,
then drifting. But,
little rose, he said,
you'll feel so
much better soon.

The Order of Things

I never imagined a priest
had hair on his back.
I've always believed
in the order of things.

Disappointment is meant
to wear clothes. To see it naked
seemed too cheap a thrill. I love
cheap thrills, defining sin.

"Contradiction is Catholic,"
the young Father told me,
stretching out comfortably,
having briefly died.

"I think you should go,"
I said, handing him his collar,
 buttering my lie in a plural:
"This isn't what we wanted."

"Honey, it never is," he said.
"Say your prayers."
I did. And believed. Love
is godless, and good.

The Milk-Truck Driver

He looked like a dwarf,
but wasn't. He walked
like a goat, but
was hung like a horse.

He thought he spoke
with his eyes, but
they had him on a string.
for whatever they wanted.

He pissed in the gutter
shook his horse's gift,
handled like surprise
borrowed from a shelf.

He thought his eyes kept
calm, thought they said
how generous. He was
alone, with a gift, with me.

How full were his beard
and his hopeful heart,
his teeth flickering blue,
his eyes on their own.

How he danced in our barn.
I was twelve, I watched him.
Cows grazed elsewhere,
not there, not looking.

How time took notice
when his eyes took
to gleaming. They were bored
by the dance, the waiting.

He spoke. I remember
that summer was leaving.
And I thought well maybe.

I thought well yes.
I thought when I smiled
his eyes said thank you.
I said wait a minute.
I said I'll be back.

His eyes flashed trouble
but his beard contradicted.
Whoever I was, I took
little time to become.

Then I thought no when
my brother beat him.
It was a heavy shovel.
As he cried, there was blood.

Slither

by

Mark Russell

A n afternoon, a window.

"Just look out the window" you say and if it's been a pleasant afternoon, and maybe they've had a glass of wine and feel comfortable they will. Go over to the window and look out. And rest their hands on the windowsill and ever so slightly bend at the waist, a sensuous bending, a delicate angle.

Quite.

And you watch them there. They are waiting for you. To ask them to perform another task. Look at something. Get something. See something in particular. They are waiting.

And they know you are watching them.

They are looking out the window at a church, or an empty street, or a park, or a graveyard, or an ocean . . . depending on the location of your afternoon. They are looking out. Soaking in the day.

And finally you step up closer to them and kiss them at the base of their neck. A light kiss so they aren't distracted from the view. And you both gaze out the window.

And you embrace your loved one. Standing over them, you lean down, and embrace them and hold them there with a kiss.

After a moment, because they know you will and they know they must you begin to undo their clothing. The buttons, zippers, and clasps of our daily armor.

Slowly—making sure that they keep their hands on the windowsill at all times, unless something must be pulled over and dropped to the floor.

Start with the garment covering their torso, making sure that no one on the street is watching, especially if your love is of the "fairer sex" so that they don't see her breasts fall free—not that this matters—but now is not the time to cause a public display. Remove their pants, but not all the way and keep their shoes and socks on. Let the pants, or skirt, unzipped, fall to their ankles, gently immobilizing them. Soft convenient shackles of love.

If your love has not intuited yet what you are about, they now have a very good idea. They may resist—slightly—ask for or suggest a different location, etc. Firmly instruct them to stay absolutely still and to observe the world outside the window.

Give them a task to take their mind off their fears. Have them describe the scene to you. Carefully. Exactly. What people are outside? What are they doing? While they do so, step out of your robe and pajamas and savor the sight of your love arrayed thusly in the afternoon light.

Now things must get more serious.

Approach the loved one. Stroke their back. A dappling of massage and kisses. Pull the remaining undergarments down to become tangled with their ankles and the heels of their shoes.

Don't only focus on their naked back; the chest and or breasts, especially breasts are easily cupped—the nipples touched by fingertips. Once erect, the nipples of either sex can be flicked by fingers and lightly pinched to bring your love's attention forward. The slight pain presages what may come.

You are of course naked as well and the back of their thighs match with your legs. If the inclined plane of their lower spine is just right your sex can rest on its field, nestled between the twin mounds of their buttocks.

Your hands have of course full access to their sex, for their arms must at times support both of you as they hold onto the window. A light brushing and probing commences. You may kneel and lick and worship at the gate, breathing deep their fragrance.

Hobbled as they are—powerless and all powerful, radiant—begin again.

Soaked in the sun, small beads of perspiration lubricate all. The fingers find their home and preparations are fully begun, opening the gate with spit and if needed a little jelly warmed in the palm, smoothing any fears. Whispers of subtle instructions are mixed with small bites and wet and wetter kisses, their head bent back to yours.

Sheath your phallus, tear open the package with your teeth and put on the second skin, one hand always touching the loved one.

When your sex is properly aflame lean closer to your love. And breathing with them, your tongue tracing their earlobe, tell them to concentrate on the scene before them. Insist they ignore the old woman or workman across the way, whose curiosity is now quite piqued.

Nudge the small portal open and enter them.

This is a most divine feeling. No quick or unexpected movements, wait as they accept you into the tight confines of their sacred body.

This is often accompanied by a short gasp, for no matter how often your love has stood at this window with you, there is always a bit of surprise that certain parts can fit within certain parts.

And slide in, and in, pulling back just a little only to go deeper and then deeper. Yet again, pulling back and then deeper still. Your love, if they know what is right and required, is forcing their hind quarters back against you.

They are clinging for dear life against the windowsill, singing for you a deep throaty song speckled with pain and joy.

Soon you will be singing for them as well. Singing loudly for them, crying for them, as tempos increase, as both bodies gain a full understanding of what is happening here—and asking for more and more. Control becomes less of an objective. The world becomes about delightful tightness and friction. The membrane of the afternoon, once peaceful and languid, is torn open into raging abandon, raging raging raging flashing abandon. And finally after much work, your hands grasping their hips to impale them to the utmost your sex nudging the bottom of their heart, finally you spill in your love—your gift—such a sweet sting—your honor bestowed upon them.

Standing naked in the falling light against the window wrapped in each other's arms. Torrents of sweat and juice running down your legs. Breathing in and out still as one heart. The evening comes for you.

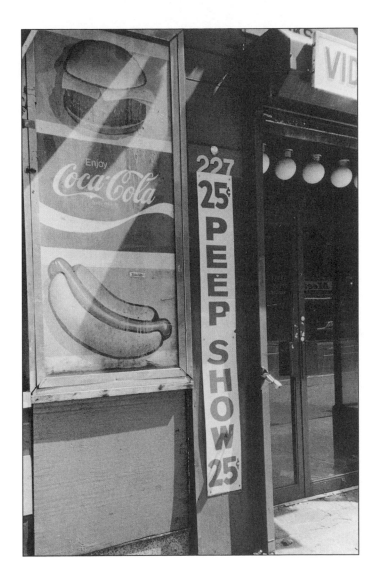

Cybersex

by

Leslie Baze

She logs on and punches in: **www.xxxlivesexchat.com.** Several seconds pass while she waits for the screen to download.

An instant message appears from LUVLEATHER: Nice name wanna fuck? She ignores it.

An instant message appears from dOGgYsTILe: GET PISSED! WATERSPORTS PICS CLICK www.goldshowers.com and she ignores it.

An ad appears.

THE FUKUOKU 9000 FINGER-SIZED VIBRATOR IS HERE! 3-SPEEDS, PORTABLE, GOES ANYWHERE YOUR FINGER CAN GO! CLICK WWW.BLOWFISH.COM

She already owns a Fukuoku 9000 finger-sized vibrator. She keeps it in its attractive green and deceptively coin-pursed-shaped carrying case with a few Handi-Wipes.

Not recommended for internal anal play. (If this little bugger gets stuck in your butt, you'll be one unhappy camper.)

She reads on.

WE HAVE INNERSPACE CONTOURED DILDOS

She does not own an Innerspace Contoured Dildo and considers clicking.

An instant message appears from TBradley: hi wanna chat? She types back, LAMEASS, then reconsiders and punches IGNORE.

She scans the room.

YOU HAVE ENTERED LIVEWIRE SEXCHAT AT XXXLIVESEXCHAT.COM.

MEMBERS: Ike4547, DivaQueen, HotBox23, VaMpYrE, PantiSnffr, Porter751, TBradley, 696969,

dragnbny, FairyAcid, PunkChik, KillrFarah, ErZuliE, SpyderFish, BigGayAl, BoobMan
GET INFO INSTANT MESSAGE IGNORE

He flashes a message out into her empty space: SUCK YOUR CLIT TILL YOU SCREAM??? It flashes lazily, blue-red-green-blue-red, in the right-hand corner of the screen.

She downloads his image. He has a pierced eyebrow and straight, white teeth like chalk lines. He downloads her image. She has large brownish nipples and blonde hair swept across her face in an alluring, freshly-raped sort of way.

DivaQueen: sugar I'll eat you till your eyes cross

Ike4547: BIG BALLS NEED HEAD

PunkChik: describe yourself Diva do you have a pic

HotBox23: KISS IT . . . SUCK IT . . . LICK IT . . . EAT ME TIL I'M RAW

DivaQueen: redhead beauty wide slick mouth IM me for JPG

BigGayA1: hardbody fantasy boy i know youre in here the wait is o

PunkChik: Diva you do girl on girl

BigGayAl: ver

PantiSnffr: DivaQueen is a MAN you ass

Ike4547: BIG BALLS NEED HEAD

She runs his image through Apple PhotoMuss 3.5 to determine what he really looks like. PhotoMuss is this month's hottest selling piece of commercial re-imaging software. It allows the user to un-retouch downloaded photos and is an invaluable online dating resource. Version 3.5 includes standard PhotoMuss features such as *restore wrinkles* and *stain teeth,* as well as the indispensable new *add pounds.* She activates *add pounds* and types 15 into the dialogue box. She accesses the *stain teeth* function and dims his tooth brightness by 35%.

He presses PLAY on the stereo remote. The speakers next to his desk blare "Of Bondage, Up Yours" by X-Ray Specs. He masturbates to the image of her breasts on his desktop while he waits for her reply.

She eats a Twinkie and downloads his financial portfolio for last quarter.

He experiments with a technique he read about in *Penthouse,* several quick strokes followed by two long ones. There was a specific numerical pattern recommended in the magazine and he struggles to remember it. "Five quick . . . two long . . . three quick . . . two long. . . ." When he cums he aims for the image of her nipples but shoots too far to the left and splatters jizz on his cat. The cat, asleep on the printer, wakes up and miaows.

Scilla289: 5′10′′ blonde hot bod lookin for action
Ike4547: BIG BALLS NEED HEAD
PunkChik: Scilla - do girls?
BoobMan: Scilla 289 whats your cup size
Ike4547: BIG BALLS NEED HEAD
HotBox23: hey Punk I'm pierced wanna eat me?
Scilla289: 36-C never done girls but might try
PantiSnffr: EATS CUNT

After several long minutes she sends him a copy of her dating profile. She is a graphic designer who used to be a supermodel. Financially solvent. Perfect sexual health. No kids.

He towels the cat and tries to imagine her face in 20 years.

He sends her a profile. He is a dirigible pilot turned Web designer. Financially solvent. Perfect sexual health. No kids.

They fuck twice online, then decide to meet.

He e-mails her a program:

Hello lover . . . glad to hear you can make it Friday . . . I have some preparing to do.

I pirated some Web-touring software I thought we could use. It should be self-installing, but if you're running system software of 98 or before you may have to install it manually. Put the file labeled "Cantigo Plug-Ins" in your Systems folder and the "Touring Prefs" folder in Preferences.

I checked out the Fredrick's page like you asked. My favorites are the red teddy (#GS-204) and the merry widow (#MW-622B).

Are you planning on wearing that Friday? I can have it shipped overnight.

On Friday at seven o'clock he opens up his Virtual Girlfriend file and downloads her image. She opens up her Virtual Boyfriend file and downloads his image. They meet, as arranged in **www.xxxlive-sexchat.com.**

RECORD THE TIME OF HER ENTRANCE AS REPORTED BY YOUR WATCH/LAPTOP/DIGITAL PHONE:

She is eight minutes late by his Quartz Indiglo with black leather band retailing for $59.95 at www.time.com. Waiting makes him nervous and he picks at a loose thread on his stained blue-plaid boxers. While he waits he opens a second browser window and downloads new photographs from www.armychicks.com/spankings.html.

LUVLEATHER: Farah which sex are you

MandysGift: deep blue velvet very soft lowcut

Ike4547: BIG BALLS NEED HEAD

PantiSnffr: BIGGEST FUCKING DICK IN UTAH

KillrFarah: LUV I'm whatever I fucking want cock or pussy you pick

LUVLEATHER: all-girl orgy everyone imagine I'm tonguing your clit

BoobMan: are your nipples big or small & what color

Ike4547: BIG BALLS NEED HEAD! BIG BALLS NEED HEAD! BIGBALLS NEED

KillrFarah: that's not saying much PantiSniffr arent you guys all mormons all

MandysGift: medium-sized dark pink like a rose color & hard

KillrFarah: inbred & shit probably married your sister fuckin retard

Ike4547: HEAD!!!

He sends her a message: DID YOU GET THE PACKAGE? OPEN IT NOW.

She opens the brown-wrapped package he sent via Federal Express. Inside she finds a chain-mail dress and lacy underwear, a heart-shaped box of chocolates, a porn video entitled *Splatman* on CD-ROM, and an electric stimulator commonly known as a "pocket rocket."

She mixes herself a vodka and cran. He mixes himself a martini. They drink.

He launches Cantigo WebTour 5.5 and clicks on PILOT.

She launches Cantigo WebTour 5.5 and clicks on PASSENGER. Screens appear.

GO TO: WEBUSERS.ANET-STL.COM/~CIVIL/ FREAK%20SHOW/FREAK AND ACCESS THE VIRTUAL FREAKSHOW.

"Shlitzee the Pinhead" has a cephalic dysfunction which

makes her brain small, and a pinhead stick out the back of her head. If you touch it, it is soft and moveable like soft, dry clay. Shlitzee appeared in freak shows and in movies. Now, she lives at the famous freak's trailer park in Florida where freaks winter from their freak work at the few venues open to them. Shlitzee wants you to help her by writing your Congressman and asking for "Rights for Freaks to Work in Freak Shows." After all, it is a free country. Or it was, before the liberals destroyed our way of life.

He sends her an instant message: PRETTY INTENSE STUFF HUH?

She sends back a message: THIS ONE HAS A BEAUTIFUL SMILE.

"The Nail Man" is an interesting freak. He still lives at the Freak's Trailer Court in Florida, and he performs his act to visitors several times per week. The Nail Man takes a nail and hammers it into his head for you. In addition, his body allows him to do many other things, because it is perfectly malleable and "gives way" in interesting contusions which are against normal logic.

She sends him a message: THAT'S HOT.

Help these Freaks return to the lives they love! EMAIL YOUR CONGRESSMAN advocating the rights of Freaks to perform in Freak Shows and make a productive living.

They click on EMAIL YOUR CONGRESSMAN and send out matching form e-mails.

Since it is still early he directs her browser to **INTERNET BUNGEE JUMP.** She watches as the videocamera guides her through a simulated Bungee experience. Romeo Void howl out a remix of "Never Say Never" from the speakers mounted on the ceiling. They each jump twice.

TO PARTICIPATE IN THE INTERNET BUNGEE JUMP YOU MUST TYPE IN YOUR VISA ACCOUNT NUMBER. IF YOU DO NOT HAVE A VISA ACCOUNT, GO TO http:\\www.visa.com AND AN ACCOUNT NUMBER WILL BE ASSIGNED TO YOU.

He takes her to **www.antagonists.com.** They play trivia games for an hour until they're both drunk and silly. He directs her browser to **Furniture Porn** and then **The Kama Sutra of Pooh.**

GO TO WWW.VGG.COM/FURNPORN TO VIEW FURNITURE PORNOGRAPHY ON THE WEB.
GO TO ORBITAL.PLANETX.COM/POOH/POSI-TIONS.PHTML TO VIEW WINNIE-THE-POOH PORNOGRAPHY ON THE WEB.

He e-mails her an interactive Japanaporn program by French Kiss, featuring animated S&M dolls of all styles and sexes. They go to the MainPage to watch other users have an animated virtual orgy. They patch in their images.

In thirty minutes a dialogue box appears: YOUR RESERVED TIME AT THIS SITE HAS ENDED. DO YOU WISH TO EXTEND? PLEASE ENTER AN ACCOUNT NUMBER.

Eventually they end up at an Asian sex site.

A dialogue box appears: **PLEASE WAIT . . . FREE ASIAN PUSSY LOADING**

He sends her a message: GOT YOUR POCKET ROCKET? and she answers, OF COURSE.

He sends another message: PUT YOUR FEET ON EITHER SIDE OF YOUR MONITOR.

She peels out of the lacy underwear he sent and activates the digital camera on top of her computer to send him images in real time.

A message flashes across their screens: **EXOTIC GEISHA SLUTS . . . YOUNG ASIAN SCHOOLGIRLS . . . SEE THE "BANG COCK GIRLS" IN ACTION! . . . 15000 HARDCORE PICS &24-HOUR LIVE ASIAN SEX SHOW . . .**

She pulls her dress over her head and it falls to the floor with a loud clank (Volume 8). She types, KISS. He types, KISS, UNHOOK BRA, LICK RIGHT NIPPLE . . .

A dialogue box appears: **WOULD YOU LIKE A TACTFUL FADE-OUT?** and she impatiently clicks, **NO, I WOULD NOT LIKE A TACTFUL FADE-OUT.**

The picture unscrambles.

RECORD YOUR OBSERVATIONS HERE:

The following week they meet again at **www.hornybuttlove.com.** He downloads a copy of *Vampire Hunter D* and they watch on their respective monitors while he types instructions: ONE FINGER . . . TWO FINGERS . . . THREE FINGERS . . .

This continues for four months.

His brother comes to visit, finds his Virtual Girlfriend program, downloads a virus. When they sign on he accidently transmits the virus to her. Now whenever they fuck online a flock of clucking penguins runs across the screen and obscures the picture.

This happens twice before she disconnects.

Weeks pass. Late one night he makes a run to the liquor store at 12th and Elm for some good scotch. She's buying a bottle of Sauvignon Blanc. They have no reason to recognize each other.

Over the next few days she takes a new series of digital photographs. They are posted on the World Wide Web at **www. girlsforhire.com.**

F

by

Jessica

Hagedorn

W hat you see is what you get.

Oh yeah, baby.

You gotta have rhythm, in your soul. The word SOUL. Something funky and torrid by James Brown, juxtaposed against a lush green landscape, manicured and mowed to perfection.

A jungle, jagged and forbidding, female and tropic.

Green perfume: the scent of mildew and rot. You can see your breath, like in a steam room or a Turkish bath. It is unbearably humid. Prehistoric birds are . . . squawking.

The word "bath" is subtly erotic. The marriage of "Turkish + bath" unbearably so.

A dead body lies in the midst of this lush green splendor.

Think of Antonioni's *Blow Up*. Think of a golf course. Think of me.

Always a dead body. Always a corpse. Always a surprise. But arranged beautifully; arranged to stun and shock and titillate. All things beautiful and mysterious, to the bitter end.

Death is my fetish.

And Saint Sebastian.

And God.

And get thee to a nunnery.

The word "nun" for example.

Death is ultimately at the bottom of this coy little rant (the word "coy," the word *coy* italicized). Not just any death, mind you. But a sense of foreboding, something ominous and looming in the background. Dissonant chords, the distant wail of a siren.

Sudden betrayal. *I've been made to feel like a fool.* Baby, baby. I have danced towards the edge of an abyss. On the edge of a razor blade. Ooh, baby. The word *abyss* itself. Onomatopoeia is my fetish, the word *onomatopoeia* itself. (I've always been able to spell it correctly, even as a child. Drawn to it like a magnet.)

Decaying beauty in architecture is another delight. Those faded green colonial mansions in the tropics, for example. Ravaged slowly from the inside and out by heat, rain, animals, and time itself. Faded, crumbling, peeling paint on the walls. Vegetation choking architecture: I could brood about that for days.

Rust.

Ruin has been cheapened nowadays, become a trend called "distressed."

Distressed jeans, distressed interior design. Pathetic.

Decay, like anything else of value, has to be earned.

I celebrate Havana slowly sinking into the sea. Manila slowly sinking into the fetid Pasig River. The boxer's broken nose, broken teeth, swollen eyes, and puffy lips. The convict's lovingly detailed tattoos.

The word *skeleton*, italicized, has possibilities.

My desires are inherently Catholic. The face of a fallen angel makes me hot. And mind you, angels exist in New York City. In Barcelona on the Ramblas, in Berlin in those squatter encampments, and in Manila almost anywhere. Probably in Bangkok too, though I've never been there. I'm not referring to sentimental, fat cherubs or beatific, asexual ethereal creatures. I'm naturally referring to Lucifer, fallen archangel, a major cliché, darkness as the other side of light.

Here's what I crave: salt, shoes made of buttery leather, and the power of certain words said aloud. Blood, for example. Fallen angel. Hunger.

A fallen angel, a young man with a bleeding, sinewy torso sticks his head into the garbage, foraging for food. A shirtless, barefoot young man lurching down a Greenwich Village sidewalk in a stoned stupor. He stinks: he is hungry and dirty and evil incarnate. He will die soon. His mind is gone. I fall in love with his face, the face of vice. The face of **F**: feral, feline, fucking, fallen.

If I had the balls I'd offer him a cup of java. Or a juicy burger, a milkshake and some fries. Then . . . nothing too graphic here. Nothing too obvious. I'm a good Catholic girl.

I understand taboo completely. The need for it.

Sex = death = divine = damned = heaven.

The word "taboo" is absolutely pornographic.

I like 'em young. But not too young. I like 'em when they're poised on the brink of the abyss, of manhood—past adolescence but not quite seasoned yet. Not ready for death but ready for the forbidden. Tattooed biceps, form, but . . . not too pumped up. In fact, I hate muscle boys. Much too obvious. I prefer a juicy burger every once in a while. I usually stick to vegetables and fish, but I can appreciate an expensive slab of meat. Well done. For someone who likes blood (the idea of blood, anyway) I don't care for rare meat.

I am the least visceral person I know.

I'm a bundle of infuriating contradictions.

An element of danger is always delicious.

Gardens gone to seed, black-and-white movies. It's no accident I'm a film noir buff. Black film. Dark film. Ominous, ambivalent film. A dead body, usually a woman's somewhere in the lush green landscape or in the gloomy lobby of an elegant, empty building.

When you least expect it.

The word "desire" is music to the ears. Desire: a fallen angel who knows how to kiss. A lithe demon who carries the memory of hell in his little black heart: that's heaven. A taste for expensive meat and the dank, green smell of rotting gardens.

Despair. The word "despair" excites me. The eerie cadences of high mass, sung in Latin. Dead languages. Pretty to the ears. The word *agony*. Close to death, but not quite yet. You keep me hangin' on.

F for fetish. **F** for father. Bless me **F**, for I have sinned.
F for futile. **F** for fact, **F** for fiction.

Sublime. There's no end to it.

Why Did He Cut Off That Man's Leg?

The Peculiar Practice of Dr. John Ronald Brown

by

Paul Ciotti

Twenty-five years ago, when I was a junior reporter and stringer for the San Francisco bureau of *Time* magazine, I came across the greatest story I never wrote, which was actually a pretty smart decision at the time, given that the story had no ending, I didn't know how to write such a story then, and even if I had written it, *Time* wouldn't have run it. It wasn't merely that the story was too bizarre. *Time* was a news magazine, and this wasn't news. It was, rather, a glimpse into the darker corners of the human spirit, the kind of thing you naturally gravitate to late in the evening, when, tired of films and politics, you'd say to your friends, "Do you want to hear something really sick?" And there'd be a silent, collective "ahhh," like that of children snuggling in for a bedtime story, knowing they were about to hear what they'd been waiting for all night.

I first came across the name John Ronald Brown in the late fall of 1973 in the *San Francisco Chronicle* when I saw an item in Herb Caen's column about a doctor down on Lombard Street who was "lopping" people's penises off. As it was my (self-appointed) job for *Time* in those days to cover the more raggedy edges of the ongoing paradigm shift, I called up the clinic and found myself talking to Brown's partner at the time, Dr. James Spence, who, despite some reservations, invited me to see him.

Silence struck me as a bit of a hustler, far less polished than one would expect of someone with a medical degree—if he had a medical degree. To some people he gave business cards reading "Dr. James Spence." But to me he said he'd earned his medical degree in Africa and thus couldn't practice here. (I later heard he was an ex-con who claimed to be a veterinarian, but that degree was phony, too.)

The clinic wasn't much—just a few rooms on a busy street, it seemed more like a real estate office than anything else. Sensing my skepticism, perhaps, Spence invited me to an upcoming formal dinner at his hilltop home in Burlingame, where he and his partner, the renowned plastic surgeon Dr. John Ronald Brown, would be explaining his new operation to a group of urologists, proctologists and internists, some of whom, Spence hoped, would join him and Dr. Brown in setting up the finest sex-change facility anywhere in the country.

A week later, I drove to Burlingame and discovered that Spence had a splendid home—if it was his home—overlooking the distant San Francisco Airport and, beyond, the bay. It was a surreal evening. Dinner was served by half a dozen attentive transsexuals who were undergoing hormone therapy while awaiting surgery.

At first, the other doctors seemed quite intrigued by Spence's proposal for a full-service sex-change clinic. I remember sitting at one end of a long dinner table, watching Spence cut up a pear with a pocket knife while another doctor earnestly asked how he would select candidates for surgery. "It takes one to know one," Spence told his startled guests. "We let other transsexuals make the decision. They can tell best when someone is a true transsexual—a woman trapped in a man's body."

After the fruit and cheese, we adjourned to the kitchen, where one of the waitresses lay back on a butcher-block table and casually flipped up her skirt. A gooseneck lamp was produced, and all the doctors proceeded to examine the kind of work currently being done by Dr. Brown's competition.

I'm no expert in female anatomy, but the waitress's genitalia didn't look like those of any woman I'd ever seen. There was no clitoris or anything resembling a vagina. It rather looked like someone had taken a pickax and neatly poked a small, square hole, an inch on a side, directly into her groin—either that or like an aerial photograph of a Manitoba iron-ore mine taken from 20,000 feet. In contrast, Spence maintained, Brown had developed a revolutionary technique that would give transsexuals fully orgasmic clitorises and aesthetically pleasing vaginas.

Later, Dr. Brown and I stood around the kitchen table while he displayed what to me were ghastly photographs of his surgical technique. One picture showed a gauze noose holding up the head of a bloody penis while Brown sliced away at the tendrils of unwanted erectile tissue (the *capora cavernosa*).

Unlike some other gender-reassignment surgeons, and contrary to what Herb Caen had written, Brown didn't exactly lop off the penis. At least in later years (his process was continually evolving), he carefully split the penis, then, after saving the nerves and blood supply, positioned the glans penis under a fleshy hood to create the clitoris. With the leftover penile skin he made the labia majora. Finally, after removing the fat and hair follicles, he used the scrotal skin as lining for the new vagina.

As a layman, I couldn't tell if Brown was a competent surgeon or not, but I must say he came across as genial, knowledgeable and obviously quite proud of his technique. There was a certain naiveté (and even passivity) about him that struck me as surprising in a surgeon, but compared to everything else I'd seen that night it didn't warrant a second thought.

Since this was hardly a story I could write for *Time,* I produced an appropriately dull and thoroughly bloodless article about the growing phenomenon of sexual-reassignment surgery: "Though the first modern medically supervised sex-change operation took place in Europe in 1930, transsexual surgery did not attract wide notice until the transformation of a former GI named George Jorgensen to Christine in 1952. . . ."

A month later, in early January 1974, just as my story was about to appear in print, Brown called in a near panic to beg that I not mention his name. The proposed new clinic had fallen through, and Spence, he said, was now saying all sorts of terrible things about him. As my story didn't mention Brown (or anything else about that night), I told him to relax. That was the last I heard of him until early this October, when I clicked on the Internet and the following story caught my eye:

> San Diego—A 77-year-old former doctor has been convicted of murder for fatally botching the surgery of a New York man who wanted his healthy leg amputated to satisfy a bizarre fetish.

The story gave the name of the fetish as apotemnophilia— "sexual gratification from limb removal." It said that "only 200 worldwide are known to suffer the fetish." It reported that the victim, 79-year-old Philip Bondy, had paid $10,000 for the operation, after which he died in a "suburban San Diego hotel" from "gangrene poisoning." It said that the unlicensed doctor who performed the surgery could get "life imprisonment for second-degree murder." Although the story gave the doctor's name as John Ronald Brown, at first it didn't ring a bell. But after downloading additional stories, I found myself looking at a photograph of a heavyset, pink-complexioned man with thinning, disheveled hair, and suddenly I realized, *Hey, I know this man.*

Driving up to San Diego County's George F. Bailey Detention Center, I feel as if I'm visiting some remote outpost in the mountains of Mars. The detention center is located on a desolate brown hilltop two miles north of the border with Mexico; off in the distance I can faintly see Tijuana, shimmering in the heat and haze. There are no people, no birds, and no wind. Two faded flags hang limply outside the visitor entrance, which is landscaped with cactus and crowned with long coils of razor wire.

Because Brown is staying in the jail's medical wing (he's diabetic), he's wearing what looks like a surgeon's standard blue operating smock (the difference is that his is splattered with fat gravy stains). Although cordial and deferential as we talk by phone through the wire-reinforced windows, Brown at times seems anguished, or at the very least distracted, gnawing on his fingernails or swirling his tongue around the corners of his mouth. Sometimes, he turns sideways and lets me talk to his profile while he leans wearily against the concrete wall.

Although I find it hard to hear Brown (a man in the adjacent visitor's chair is reading religious tracts into the phone), eventually I'm able to get to the heart of the matter: Why, against state law, the Hippocratic oath and, in my opinion, basic common sense, did he cut off that man's leg?

Brown replies that he was simply doing what doctors are supposed to do—meet the patient's needs. "In cosmetic surgery we do things all the time for which there is no need. We are constantly rearranging what God gave us."

"But what about your own liability?" I ask. The patient, I point out, was a frail old man, still recovering from pneumonia, with a history of heart disease and bypass surgery. Even in ideal circumstances, his post-operative prospects were far from great. "Weren't you worried that people would ask questions if he died?"

Brown shrugs. "I didn't spend much time thinking about it," he says.

Someone who did think about it was Gary Stovall, a homicide detective for the San Diego suburb of National City, who on May 11, 1998, was assigned to investigate the death of an elderly New York City resident found in Room 609 of the local Holiday Inn with his left leg missing and blood oozing from the stump.

Despite the bizarre circumstances, at first it wasn't completely clear to Stovall that a crime had been committed. A friend of Philip Bondy's had initially told the police that Bondy had been in a "taxi accident" in Mexico and had required immediate surgery in a clinic there.

But to Stovall that story didn't make sense. If Bondy had been in an accident, why didn't his body have any other injuries? If an American citizen had been badly injured in a traffic accident, why didn't the Tijuana police know anything about it? And strangest of all, why did Bondy have two $5,000 receipts in his room, one for "surgery" and the other for "hospitalization," both signed by a local man named John Brown?

Because Stovall was working on another murder case at the time, he couldn't immediately go see Brown in person. And besides, says Stovall, a baby-cheeked detective with a deceptively mild manner, "I was still under the impression that he was a good Samaritan."

But when Brown still hadn't returned any of Stovall's three phone messages by Wednesday morning, May 20, Stovall drove to Brown's San Ysidro apartment and banged on the door.

"Do you know why I'm here?" he asked.

"Yes," answered Brown, who had come to the door wearing a robe. "It's because of the man who died in the hotel room in National City."

Although Brown was "nonthreatening, polite, well-spoken, and obviously well-educated," says Stovall, it was also clear to him that Brown was not someone for whom "personal appearance was a high priority." When Stovall asked him to come down to the station, he put on a wrinkled shirt and a stained jacket. Not only did his apartment smell like "garbage," but the couch was bloodstained and the stuffing was falling out. The stove was "filthy" and the sink was stacked with dirty dishes. There were books, professional journals, travel bags, and medical supplies scattered about the floor. "If a child had been living there," Stovall says, "I'd have put him in a foster home."

Brown declined to say whether or not he'd amputated Bondy's leg, says Stovall, but he talked about virtually everything else, including driving Bondy to the clinic and visiting him at the Holiday Inn the following day to inspect the wound. (He saw some "minor red marks," Brown tells me, and "possibly" a pale-blue tint, indicative of emerging gangrene.)

At first Brown didn't want to make a statement, says Stovall. "Then he said, 'Okay, I'll make a little statement.' He ended up making a 29-page statement." Although Stovall still didn't know what had happened to Bondy, he was convinced that *something* illegal was going on. After 90 minutes, he left the interview room to tell his superiors that he was going to arrest Brown.

Brown, who tends to be oblivious to the psychic atmosphere, didn't even realize that he was in trouble. After waiting 45 minutes for Stovall to return, he says, he was bored and restless—"There was nothing to read." Deciding he had better things to do, he walked out of the station and headed home. He had gone two blocks and just turned a corner, he says, when suddenly two police cars and what seemed like 12 officers appeared.

It reminded Brown of the "Toonerville cops." Then, he says, "one pulled out a gun and pointed it at my head." Brown looked at the weapon in astonishment. "All I could think," he says, "was '*What a fucking big gun!*'"

If the gun amazed Brown, his arraignment dumbfounded him. The prosecutor, Deputy District Attorney Stacy Running, asked the judge to hold him without bail on the grounds that he was an "incredibly dangerous individual to the citizens both of the United States and Mexico."

To Brown, none of this made sense, either legally or morally. "I didn't think any laws had been violated on either side of the border," he says. "Or, from now on, is every surgeon who performs an operation where the patient later dies of infection going to be arrested for murder?"

Friends and former patients were outraged as well. It wasn't Brown's fault that Philip Bondy died, says Ann, whose sex-change surgery was a great success (but who asked to be identified only by her first name). "That old man was already sick. He just wanted his leg cut off so he could get a hard-on. Dr. Brown was just doing his job."

To Brown's ex-wife, Julie, and their two teenage sons, his arrest came as a devastating shock. "My oldest boy was going to spend the day [with him]," says Julie, a hearty, buoyant woman who has remained on close terms with Brown. "He called over there. 'Can I speak to my dad?' The police said, 'Your dad has been arrested for murder.'"

As soon as the police finished searching Brown's apartment—they took everything, including the garbage disposal, she says—they came over to search hers. "There were a bunch of guys in yellow jackets, like a SWAT team. They had a search warrant. They asked me to sit on the couch. The first thing they did was take pictures of my fish tank. I heard on the news that Brown had been arrested for cutting off the man's leg. What did they think—that I was keeping it in the fish tank?

"They were here for hours. They told me I was going to jail and that I would never see my kids again. I was crying. I begged them, I said, 'Please don't take my kids away.' They said Brown bought me from my father. 'Did he pay for you?' I said I wasn't a cow. 'Yes, it was an arranged marriage, but so what?'"

Julie, a native of the Caribbean island of St. Lucia, met Brown in 1981, when he opened a practice there. "He asked me if I would like to get married," she says. "I said, 'I don't know.' I was 17. He was 59."

Although the two were divorced in the early '90s, after Brown was sent to prison for practicing medicine without a license, Julie says she still loves him. "He raised me. He taught me to read and write. He's a really good man. If I had it to do again, I'd marry him in a heartbeat."

One thing I quickly discover is that there appears to be no broad middle ground in people's opinion of John Brown. Some former patients can't praise him highly enough. "He did exactly what I asked," says one young woman who asked Brown to increase her cup size from 34B to 36B. "He was always a gentleman, courteous, very considerate, thoughtful, intellectual, and calm."

To old friend and longtime admirer Patrice Baxter, Brown was "one of the best surgeons in the United States." Not only did he do Baxter's tummy tuck, face-lift, and breast implants, he also did her granddaughter's ears. "They stuck out. The kids on her track team called her Dumbo—'Why don't you just fly?' He did her nose, too." It turned out so well that she became a model.

At 66, Baxter has a trusting manner, pink, unblemished cheeks and, thanks to Brown, a generous uplifted bosom. She met Brown in Rosarito Beach in 1982, she tells me, and over the years he operated on so many of her friends and relatives that it became a running joke. One time when Brown was visiting Baxter's home, she ran out of bedrooms. "So my girlfriend says, 'Well, he can sleep in my room. He's *seen* everything I've got.' Then I said, 'Well, he can sleep in my room. He's *made* everything I've got.'"

Which isn't to say that Brown didn't have his faults, says Baxter. "He was brilliant, but he had no common sense. He would walk through plate-glass doors. He couldn't balance his checkbook." Sometimes in the middle of a conversation he'd just pick up a magazine and begin to read. His bedside manner was no great shakes, either. "He tended to mumble. He didn't hold your hand."

But so what? she asks. "He wasn't a general practitioner," he was a surgeon. He certainly wasn't in it for the money. "He only charged $2,500 [for a sex change]. Half the time they didn't even pay."

In the last 25 years, according to Brown's estimate, he did 600 male-to-female sex-change operations, most without benefit of a medical license. Even so, with at least some of them, the results could hardly have been better. One 33-year-old "manager for a major airline" tells me she had Brown do her gender-reassignment surgery in 1985, when she was only 19. It was so successful, she says, that when she later got married, her husband never guessed she'd been a male. (To simulate a period, she used to prick her finger to leave bloodstains on the sheets.) I also hear from Ann, a Cambodian refugee whose father was killed by the Khmer Rouge, that Brown changed her entire "suffering, painful life" from that of "an ugly worm to a beautiful butterfly." Furthermore, unlike that of some transsexuals, who have difficulty passing as women, her surgery turned out so well, she says, that she got a job as a stripper in Las Vegas's Chinatown.

At the same time, there are plenty of other people who tell me they won't rest until Brown is behind bars for life. UC San Diego plastic-surgery professor Jack Fisher has personally repaired 12 to 15 of what he calls Brown's "pelvic disasters." "He's a terrible, appalling technical surgeon," says Fisher. "There's just no other way to describe it. He doesn't know how to make a straight incision. He doesn't know how to hold a knife. He has no regard for limiting blood loss." Basically, says Fisher, the man "had been committing crimes against humanity for years."

Dallas Denny, an Atlanta-based transgender author and activist who periodically posts warnings about Brown on the Internet, says that among transsexuals he was known as "Table Top Brown" for his willingness to operate in kitchens, garages, and motel rooms. "Patients were waking up in parked cars or abandoned in hotel rooms. There was no screening and no aftercare. Anyone who walked in the room was a candidate."

And the results of the surgery, says Denny, were horrific. "Some of these people, expecting vaginoplasties, received simple penectomies, leaving them looking somewhat like a Barbie doll," she wrote in a 1995 attack on Brown's skills. "Others ended up with something which looked like a penis which had been split and sewn to their groin—which is essentially what had been done. Some ended up with vaginas which were lined with hair-bearing scrotal skin; these vaginas quickly filled up with pubic hair, becoming inflamed and infected. Some ended up with peritonitis, some with permanent colostomies. Some ran out of money and were dumped in back alleys and parking lots to live or die."

Cheree, a northern California businesswoman, went to Mexico in 1984 to have dual sexual-reassignment surgery with her brother at Brown's Tijuana clinic. "He ran specials—'bring a girlfriend, two for the price of one.'" But after Cheree saw the conditions there, she changed her mind. "The sewers overflowed once or twice a day." There was never enough running water or enough bathrooms. The operating room was just an ordinary bedroom with an OB-Gyn chair. Sometimes, says Cheree, "Brown would sip coffee while doing the operation."

But the thing that most bothered Cheree, she says, was Brown's "brusque" attitude. After surgery, he would grab the dried, blood-clotted bandages and rip them right off. He was always so disheveled, too. "His hair went in different directions. His shoes were scuffed and worn down. I remember him walking down the hall eating raw weenies right out of the package. *A fucking package of weenies!*"

In one case, says Cheree, who spent 11 days at Brown's clinic caring for her (new) sister, Brown operated on an HIV-positive patient who still had pins in her arm from an auto accident (she used the insurance settlement to pay for her surgery). In another, he used too much erectile tissue to construct genital outer lips. As a result, whenever the girl got excited "her labia got hard."

But despite Brown's flaws, says Cheree, there was a reason why so many "girls" went to him—"He gives you a vagina at a fair price." Whereas with other doctors you had to take hormones, wait up to six years, live as a woman, undergo psychological evaluations and then pay $12,000 to $20,000 or more, with Brown it was good old-fashioned capitalistic cash-and-carry. Anyone, says Cheree, could raise the necessary $2,000 or $3,000 Brown used to charge (in the '80s) by turning "a couple of tricks." The word would go out that Brown was coming to town. "He'd shoot silicone anywhere you wanted it. For $200 he'd do breast surgery. For $500 he'd do cheeks, breasts, and hips. After injections you had to lie flat on your back for three days so the silicone wouldn't go anywhere. He plugged the holes with Krazy Glue."

There wasn't any indication in Brown's early years that he'd one day end up as an itinerant peddler of silicone injections. The son of a Mormon physician, he found academics so easy that he graduated from high school before he turned 16. When he was drafted by the Army in World War II, he did so well on the General Classification Test (scoring higher, Brown says, than any of the previous 300,000 people who had gone through the Salt Lake Induction Center) that the Army pulled him out of the clerk-typist pool and sent him to medical school. He graduated from the University of Utah School of Medicine in August 1947. But after two decades as a general practitioner in California, Alaska, Hawaii, and the Marshall Islands (and after nearly losing a patient when he got in over his head during a thyroidectomy), Brown decided he needed formal surgical training. He spent two years at Newark City Hospital as chief resident, he says. Later, he attended a program in plastic surgery at New York's Colombia-Presbyterian Hospital, but in what would become the first great professional disappointment of his life, he was never able to achieve certification by the American Board of Plastic Surgery (and with it staff privileges at major hospitals).

"I passed the written part of the exam without cracking a book," he says. The problem was the orals. As a result of having grown up with a "domineering" father, he tended to fold when confronted by authority figures. "My brain turns to cottage cheese."

Ten years later, in 1977, in what was the second great disappointment of his life, the California Board of Medical Quality Assurance, in part as a result of his association with James Spence, revoked his medical license for "gross negligence, incompetence, and practicing unprofessional medicine in a manner which involved moral turpitude." Among other things, the board charged, Brown allowed Spence to hold himself out as an M.D.; he allowed unlicensed people, including other transsexual patients, to write prescriptions under his signature, diagnose patients, and provide medical care; he misrepresented sex-change surgery on insurance forms as corrective surgery for "the congenital absence of a vagina"; he exhibited "gross negligence" by failing to perform sex-change operations in an acute-care facility (Brown did them in his office on an outpatient basis); he unaccountably failed to hospitalize a patient who had a "life-endangering" and "pus-infected" wound the size of a softball where his penis used to be; he failed to take medical histories or do physical exams before surgery; and he did sex-change surgery on virtually anyone who asked for it, regardless of whether they were physically or emotionally stable enough to cope with it.

Despite the medical board's harsh denunciation of Brown, the administrative judge who recommended that his license be revoked apparently did so reluctantly, as he also filed a "memorandum opinion" on Brown's behalf, pointing out that the doctor, despite his "difficulties," appeared to be "a pioneer" who made "innovative contributions" to the emerging field of transsexual surgery. Perhaps a better resolution to the problem, wrote Judge Paul J. Doyle, would have been to limit Brown to doing surgery in a "medically recognized organization," while denying him any responsibility either for determining the eligibility of prospective patients or for their postoperative care.

Most doctors, when they have their licenses revoked, give up, leave the country, or find another line of work. At first Brown did try to work outside the continental United States. But after successively losing permission to practice in Hawaii, Alaska, and the island of St. Lucia ("I don't know what you have to do to lose your license in the Caribbean," says UCSD's Jack Fisher), Brown returned to Southern California, where he started what would eventually become an ambitious underground practice in gender-reassignment surgery, breast implants, face-lifts, liposuction, silicone injections, penile implants, and penile enlargement. To avoid legal problems, he lived in Chula Vista but did his surgery in Mexico. (In his advertising brochures, Brown referred to this as his "international practice.")

In 1986, *Penthouse Forum* magazine sent a writer to Tijuana to investigate Brown's claim that he could make penises an inch or two longer by cutting the suspensor ligament holding the penis root to the pubic bone. The article, published as "The Incredible Dick Doctor," portrayed Brown as a wildly inattentive driver who backed into other cars, an absent-minded dresser whose pants fell down in the operating room, and a blithe spirit of a surgeon who, when he accidentally made a cut in the penile shaft that sent blood spurting everywhere, casually declared, "I made a boo-boo."

A few years later, the television news magazine *Inside Edition* followed up on the *Forum* piece with an investigative story on "The Worst Doctor in America." In it, Brown, who apparently gave the camera crew free run of his clinic, is shown performing a scalp-flap operation to give a transsexual a more feminine hairline. Although the patient is supposedly under deep sedation, he moans and howls all through the procedure, a development Brown dismisses on camera as "nothing unusual."

It seemed unusual enough to the San Diego District Attorney's Office, however, that it launched an investigation that led to Brown's spending 19 months in jail for practicing medicine without a license (he'd previously been convicted of prescribing narcotics after his license had been revoked and practicing under a false name). The jail term didn't deter Brown. He'd decided to become a "rebel" long before. "I didn't like some of the things that organized doctors were doing, so I rebelled," he says. "Later I didn't like what the government was doing in support of the medical organizations, so I rebelled. I chose to ignore the laws." As soon as he could pull things together (he had to drive a taxi on Coronado Island for a year), he resumed his surgical practice, doing operations in Tijuana and living now in San Ysidro. It was there, in 1996, that he got that first tentative call from a New York therapist and apotemnophiliac by the name of Gregg Furth.

Furth was a Jungian analyst who in 1988 had published a well-regarded and often-cited book, *The Secret World of Drawings*, which analyzed the artwork of children dying of leukemia for clues to their subconscious (many apparently knew exactly when they were going to die). A handsome, personable man around 50, he was good friends with a much older man, Philip Bondy, a retired Loral (satellite) Corp. engineer and fellow apotemnophiliac who liked to collect photographs, slides, and videos of male amputees.

Despite his professional training (and years in analysis), Furth still had no idea where his and Bondy's apotemnophilia came from. Although Johns Hopkins psychologist John Money, who originated the term, had argued that apotemnophilia was "conceptually related to transsexualism, bisexuality, and Munchausen's syndrome (feigning illness to get medical care)," Furth believed it had less to do with sex and more to do with possession by an alien limb.

"The way he explained it to me," says Deputy D.A. Stacy Running, "is that it's as if 'Your leg is attached to my body, and once I get it off, my body is whole. You see me as being mutilated. I see myself as finally being whole. I live with it. I can't understand it. How the hell do I explain it to you?'"

Officially classified as a "paraphilia" (extreme or atypical sexual behavior or desire), apotemnophilia can be irresistibly intense. Some apotemnophiliacs, when they can't find a doctor to do the surgery, resort to removing unwanted limbs with chainsaws, shotguns, trains and, in one case, a homemade guillotine. Others spend their time looking for a surgeon who will take their desires seriously and not just patronize them with referrals to psychiatrists. In 1996, while passing through San Diego, Furth came across a newspaper article about John Ronald Brown, and suddenly he knew he'd found the man for whom he'd been searching his entire adult life—a competent "fringe" physician who wouldn't balk at cutting off a healthy leg.

Fearful that Brown would turn him down if he came right out and said he wanted his leg amputated—"I didn't want to hear 'no' over the phone," Furth would later testify—he flew to San Diego to plead his case in person.

It wasn't a hard sell. Brown says he found Furth likable and persuasive, while Furth thought Brown uncommonly open-minded about a would-be amputee's right to choose. Brown set the price of the procedure at $3,000, and in February 1997, Furth traveled to the Clinica Santa Isabel in Tijuana, where Brown did his surgery.

Unfortunately for Furth, Brown had neglected to tell the assisting doctor that they'd be cutting off a healthy leg. "He was Mexican, short and round," Furth testified. "He wanted to know what all this was about." When Furth told him, the doctor became enraged. "He kept saying, 'This isn't right! You don't want this!'" Finally, he stormed out of the building, forcing Brown to cancel the surgery.

A year later, Brown called Furth with "good news and bad news." The good news was he'd found another surgeon to help him. The bad news was the cost was now $10,000.

Although increasingly ambivalent about the surgery, Furth testified, he also felt he couldn't turn down such a rare opportunity. One reason: His good friend Philip Bondy planned to have his own leg cut off as soon as Furth had his done. So when Furth told him the day of the surgery that he was having second thoughts, Bondy "scolded" him, Furth testified, telling him that if he backed out now, "You'll regret this the rest of your life."

But on the taxi ride to the Clinica Santa Isabel, Furth found his attitude changing anyway. By the time he got there, he knew beyond any doubt that he did not want his leg removed. "It was over. It was finished. [My compulsion] had died. I went out and told Brown, 'Absolutely not.'"

Thinking perhaps that Furth was merely nervous, Brown offered him a sedative. But, Furth testified, he didn't want to be sedated. He wanted out of there. Before leaving, however, he suggested what he thought would be a win-win solution for everyone. Even though he no longer wanted the operation himself, he knew someone else who did. "Maybe we could switch it around," said Furth. "Philip [could] take my place."

Brown performed the operation on a Saturday morning. Bondy was happy at first, even though, as he would later tell Furth, he had felt Brown "sawing" on his leg. As it was just as illegal to amputate a healthy leg in Mexico as it is in the United States, right after the operation Brown drove 15 miles out into the desert on the old road to Ensenada and threw the leg out the window for the coyotes to eat. Then, before driving Bondy to the National City Holiday Inn, he gave his patient some lessons in walking with crutches. ("He kept falling down," Brown says in some exasperation. He couldn't seem to grasp the concept of a three-point stance—he'd put his remaining foot between the crutch tips, not in front of or behind them.)

By Sunday, Bondy was feeling hungry and dehydrated, and his

voice was sounding raspy. Furth, who was staying in an adjoining room, brought him food and water and sat up with him past midnight, talking about the surgery and what it all meant. Around eight Monday morning, Furth testified, he came back to see what Bondy wanted for breakfast and discovered a "horrible," "traumatic," and "chaotic" scene.

Bondy was lying half on the bed and half off, with blood oozing from a blackened and gangrenous stump. "I saw the phone tipped over," Furth said. "I saw the wheelchair upsided. I saw the sheets pulled out. I touched the top of his head. Rigor mortis had set in. This man did not have a peaceful death."

As the medical examiner determined, Bondy had died from *clostridia perfringens* (also known as gaseous gangrene), a fast-moving flesh-eating bacteria that lowers blood pressure and causes the heart to stop. According to Jack Fisher, the bluntly outspoken UC San Diego plastic surgeon hired by the prosecution to critique Brown's medical skills, Brown had failed to leave himself a large enough skin flap to cover the bone and stump. As a result, the skin was stretched too tight for any blood to flow. This killed the flap and allowed *clostridia perfringens* to feed on the dying flesh.

The photographs of Bondy on his deathbed reminded Stacy Running of an inmate at a concentration camp. "He was very thin, very emaciated. There was not an ounce of excess flesh. The skin on his face followed the skull. The mouth was open. It looked like he was screaming or crying when he died—to God or I don't know whom."

It was clear to Running that Brown had amputated Bondy's leg. It was equally clear that Bondy had paid him to do it. The question was *why*? Then she got a call from Gary Stovall, who was in New York searching Furth's apartment.

"I can remember to this day," says Running, a petite, articulate woman with an open, guileless manner that reminds me of Mary Richards from *The Mary Tyler Moore Show*. "I was working here. Gary calls. 'Stacy, are you sitting down? Listen to this.' And he started reading to me from a piece of literature [on apotemnophilia].

"That was when we first realized what we were dealing with— that Phil Bondy wanted his leg cut off for a reason we couldn't comprehend. We were in shock. And we are people who see the worst that humanity has to offer. We see people do horrible things to their wives, their husbands, their children and their friends. We've seen just about everything you can see. And then something like this comes up and knocks you for a loop."

Prosecutors have cases where they don't have enough evidence. They have cases where the evidence is contradictory. But rarely do they have a case where the evidence is abundant, bizarre, and thoroughly documented on videotape.

When Detective Stovall searched Brown's San Ysidro apartment, he found not only bloody shoes, bloody pillows, used needles, silicone vials, and two or three dozen empty tubes of Krazy Glue, but bloody towels in the bathtub soaking in bleach, bloody swabs in a travel bag, and dozens of returned advertising brochures (apparently the remnants of a recent mail campaign), which read in part:

> The prettiest pussies are John Brown pussies.
> The happiest patients are John Brown patients.
>
> Because . . .
>
> 1. Each has a sensitive clit.
> 2. All (99%) get orgasms.
> 3. Careful skin draping gives a natural appearance.
> 4. Men love the pretty pussies and the sexy response.

In what turned out to be a lucky break for the prosecution, Brown also owned videotapes of his operations. One of them, entitled "Jack Has a New Pisshole Behind His Balls," had been shot by a friend of the grateful patient and given to Brown as a gift. It showed Brown cutting an opening in Jack's urethra just behind his testicles so Jack could urinate sitting down. "The guy was tattooed from his head to his knees," says Running. "He had big flames coming out of his butthole. Just when you thiink you've seen it all. . . ."

But it was the video of transsexual surgery that most fired up the prosecution against Brown. "I've seen medical videos before," says Tom Basinski, an investigator in the D.A.'s office. "Usually the scalpel slices right in." But Brown's scalpel was so dull he had to push hard, saw back and forth. "I said to myself, 'Oh, my God. This is why this guy has to be stopped.'"

In the video's opening shot (which is reminiscent of that famous scene from *The Crying Game*), an attractive Asian girl—Ann, the soon-to-be Las Vegas stripper—is shown standing naked from the waist up, quietly chatting with Brown, who is off camera. She has nicely formed breasts, and abundant black hair that cascades down her shoulders. Then slowly the camera moves down her body—and suddenly you realize she has a penis.

When the actual surgery starts, I find it so unsettling I have to turn off the tape. "All the men had the same reaction," says Running. "The judge asked, 'Do I have to watch this surgery?' I said, 'Well, yes, you do. You're the judge.'"

Apparently Brown intended the tape to be an advertising or training video, as the second scene shows the doctor sitting in a chair, wearing a white coat and explaining the upcoming operation to the camera. "He has a microphone, and his hand is kind of shaking," says Running. "You see him reach up and grab his hand. And this is his dominant hand, the one he operates with. He holds up crude drawings, ripped out of a spiral notebook. He says, 'This is the corpa . . . the corpa . . .' He's stumped on the word. He finally says it, 'the capora cavernosa,' the spongy tissue on the underside of the penis. He goes on in this vein. You can see him waving [the cameraman] off when he loses a thought. The tape was so crude—you could hear dogs barking during the surgery and music playing. The scrotal skin was lying on a board. It had pushpins in it. It was so dirty and dried out, it looked like it had been run over by a tire."

To Brown's critics, in fact, it almost seemed as if he had seen too many Frankenstein movies. "Brown does an operation called an 'ileum loop,'" Running tells me, "in which he takes a piece of intestine, leaving it attached to the blood supply, and diverts it to make a vagina. The problem is, your intestines digest food, secrete enzymes, they smell. He almost killed a rebuttal witness in [a prior trial] by doing that to her. He pulls all your guts out of your stomach. Your intestines are connected to your vaginal lining. In many cases he stitches it back to your stomach, and you get peritonitis. He is quite the adventuresome surgeon. He uses human beings for guinea pigs. He is as close to [the Nazi doctor] Josef Mengele as you can get. But I couldn't say that in court. It would have been grounds for a mistrial."

Initially, says Running, the case against Brown "had come in as involuntary manslaughter," but after reviewing the evidence against him, she upgraded the charges to "implied malice murder in the second degree." This applies in cases where the defendant does something that is dangerous to human life, knowing it is dangerous to human life and doing it anyway. But it wasn't enough merely to show that Brown had botched Philip Bondy's surgery and then abandoned him in a hotel room. To make the murder charge stick, Running had to demonstrate that Brown had a history of being reckless throughout his career. And to do that, she had to find former patients to testify against him.

They weren't easy to come by. Some people told powerful, compelling stories, only to recant them a few weeks later. Some people clearly had hidden agendas. Others told stories that simply didn't jibe with the known facts. On top of this were the large number of women who didn't want it known that they once were men.

When D.A. investigator Basinski, a tall, outgoing former cop with a shaved head and big gray mustache, began calling the people on Brown's patient lists, a lot of them just hung up on him. "Some were hookers," he says. "Some thought they were in trouble. Some just didn't like the police. I called one woman, and an older woman answered. 'Why do you want my son?' she said. 'He committed suicide two weeks ago.'"

As Basinski later learned, Christina (formerly known as Eddie) had mortgaged her house to pay for a total of 10 surgeries by Brown. But according to legal documents filed by Running, the skin grafts that Brown used to line Christina's vaginal walls were so thin that they tore during intercourse. When Brown removed Christina's lower ribs to give her a narrower and more feminine waist, she subsequently developed an abscess as big as a basketball. Christina's nose job turned out so poorly that she ended up with different-sized nostrils, one of which turned up like that of a pig. Christina complained to Brown that he'd made her vaginal entrance too small. But when Brown enlarged it, Christina felt he'd "ruined" her.

Today, Brown says he feels badly that he didn't better explain the procedure to Christina. But when he called to tell her he was refunding $500, her mother told him that her son had just hanged himself in the garage. (According to Running, Brown took the news quite calmly, noting merely that "transsexuals had a high suicide rate.")

There was another patient, a genetic female named Mona, who had gone to Brown for breast implants and a face-lift. But Brown, says Running, accidentally cut a nerve in Mona's face, leaving her with a crooked smile. Her implants also failed, causing her breasts to rot, turn black, and leak a fluid that her boyfriend said smelled like "cat piss." Everything was so bizarre. Sometimes, says Running, when Brown dropped by to inject Mona with pain killers, he'd be wearing only one shoe.

Running's most effective witness, perhaps, was Camille Locke, a bright and forceful woman who at times can be quite contentious. (Basinski says he got so mad at her in an argument over O.J. Simpson that he "wanted to punch her out.") Despite her strong personality, Camille is quite modest in her language and demeanor (when referring to a penis, she demurely calls it a "phallus").

Before her sex-change surgery, Camille had once been an insurance underwriter with clients like Caterpillar and International Harvester. But after surgery, she tells me, she was lucky to find a $5-an-hour job teaching brokers telephone sales.

When Brown did Camille's sex-change surgery in November 1997, the operation took two hours. "He gave me an epidural," says Camille. "I woke up 10 minutes prior to the end of the operation. We started talking. Brown said, 'We're almost done.' I wasn't scared. I was happy as hell. I was finally getting what I wanted. When you are climbing Mount Everest, you don't worry about a little frostbite on the top."

To keep her vaginal opening from growing shut while it healed, Brown gave Camille a phallus-shaped stent made of the same kind of foam used to cushion furniture. "He told me to put a condom on it. I had to hold it in place with little white bra straps. Otherwise it would fall out when I stood up."

After several days, Camille returned to her home in the San Fernando Valley to recuperate. There, to her horror, she developed a recto-vaginal fistula that caused feces to pour out of her vagina. "My bladder was blocked, my lymph glands swelled up and my skin turned yellow," she says. She was hiccuping constantly, unable to stand, and near death. "Black stuff was pouring out of my lungs, all my systems were shutting down. All I would have had to do is take one breath and let go." After five days, a friend found her lying in her own feces and drove her to the hospital, where the doctors took one look and said, "What the hell is this?"

The pain was so bad, says Camille, she was screaming at the top of her lungs for 24 hours straight. "They were giving me morphine every 15 minutes. I had an MRI and CAT scan. Six doctors were operating on me simultaneously. I had to have a [temporary] colostomy. They were ready to body-bag and toe-tag me."

Running knew such stories would have enormous impact with a jury—if she could only get the witnesses to court. "We were dealing with people who were very needy, very high-maintenance and sometimes petulant. Many were terrified that the community in which they live and work would find out. Carrie [another witness against Brown] once came to court wearing two wigs, sunglasses, and her hair down over her face. "Gary [Stovall] leaned over to me—'Your witness looks like a sheepdog.'"

Defense attorneys have an old saying: When the facts are on your side, argue the facts. When you don't have the facts, argue the law. And when you have neither the facts nor the law, pound the table.

And that's exactly what Brown's attorney, Sheldon Sherman, did, says Running: "He slammed his hand on my table at least 17 times. He screamed and slammed his hand, and spittle flew and caught me under my right eye. And he is frothing at the mouth at these *'God-like doctors who won't let Brown be a part of their club!'*"

"It was a tough case," says Sherman, a blunt-talking, no-nonsense attorney. "The evidence, facts, and the law were all against us."

Having no really good defense options, Sherman chose to portray Brown as a brave and caring man who tended to a segment of society no one cared about. "No one else would deal with transsexuals," he said in his closing argument. "John Brown said, 'I'll deal with them.' Did he do this for money? No. He did it because he cared. And if you don't believe that, then you have my permission—as if you needed it—to find him guilty of murder."

Unfortunately for Brown, after a day of deliberations that is exactly what the jury did.

Sherman, who is planning to appeal the verdict, says he still can't understand how any California court ever get the authority to try Brown for murder. "Brown is guilty of practicing medicine without a license," he says. "I could also go with the notion that he was guilty of manslaughter. But murder? Come on. How does California even get jurisdiction? If you shot someone in Mexico and he died in California, could you be charged with shooting him in California? Of course not. It's the same principle."

Besides, he says, it was never Brown's intention to murder anyone. He was trying to help Philip Bondy. "He believed that if you are a consenting adult you should be allowed to do what you want to do. Who is not to say the 48 hours [that Bondy lived after the surgery] weren't the happiest 48 hours of his life?"

Brown's sentencing is now set for December 17. Given the small latitude open to the judge in such matters, says Sherman, Brown will most likely get 22 years to life.

Which to Gerry McClellan, an investigator for the California medical licensing board who has followed Brown's career for nearly 25 years, is very good news indeed. Brown, says McClellan, is one of those people who, because he lives his life almost entirely in his own mind, is impervious to reality. "He has no social conscience. He really believes in what he does. That's what makes him so dangerous. He is a sociopath, a sincere sociopath. Jail is a momentary hindrance to him. He's been burned before—he keeps putting his hand on the stove. There is some kind of grander scheme he is fulfilling. I just don't know what it is."

Actually, as Brown tells me in a series of late-night collect calls from prison, it isn't his scheme. It's God's scheme. And there isn't just one, there are many. In the main scenario, Brown is released from jail, raises money, and finishes development of a "hyperthermia chamber" that, he says, will cure cancer, AIDS, and genital herpes. As Brown explains it, the patient would be placed in a chamber with an IV drip to replace lost fluid, swathed in bandages and sprayed with hot water to induce a healing fever.

Brown has also developed a prototype of an asphalt removal machine that uses chisels set at a 45-degree angle in a rotating drum, which would cut the cost of such removal from $2 to $4 a linear foot to a mere 50 cents. He has designed an aerodynamic attachment for the rear of trailer trucks that he says will reduce fuel costs by one third. He has plans to write four books: an autobiography based on his medical career; a full explanation of the movement of tectonic plates; a proof of the existence of God based on gaps in evolutionary theory; and most important of all to Brown, a novel about the life of Jesus based on little-known facts in the historical record. This last book, which causes Brown to sob whenever he talks about it, will tell the story of what he believes was Jesus's youthful betrothal to Mary Magdalene, his uncle's crucifixion in an earlier Roman terror campaign, and Jesus's role in orchestrating his own crucifixion.

In the meantime, Brown is pursuing what he calls the "Doc Holliday" scenario. Before he was arrested, Brown had written to a dozen states, asking if they would consider giving him a license if he would agree to work as a general practitioner in some small rural setting without a resident physician.

The problem at the moment, of course, is that he's locked up in jail. But even that, Brown believes, is not necessarily an insurmountable obstacle. After he lost his license in 1977, he says, he went to live on a 550-acre Mexican ranch. As he was walking up a hill one night carrying a kerosene lantern, God spoke to him, clearly and distinctly. "Words started pushing into my mind," says Brown. "The words kept coming up for two days. The message began, 'Why do you kick against the traces?' It went on: 'You should know that the details of your life have been arranged so that you would be where you are now, doing what you are doing.' I knew that meant working with the transsexuals. It went on: 'What you are doing is appreciated, because these are my children, too.'"

By the time the conversation was over, says Brown, he knew he'd been given a mission—to take care of the surgical needs of God's "children," the transsexuals, for the next 20 years. Now, he says, God is guiding his steps again, this time to finish his hyperthermia chamber for curing congenital AIDS. In case He forgets, says Brown, every day he "reminds" God of the "special program I plan for AIDS babies, and I pray every night He will release me soon."

But if God has some other plan for him, Brown says, "I'll be content to be here as long as He wants me here."

The Nibbler

by

Adam Levy

I arrived at a maximum correctional facility in upstate New York on a brutally hot Sunday afternoon. My assignment was to convince the Nibbler, a convicted murderer and cannibal, to agree to an interview for a television documentary about aggression. The producers had explained to me the fine points of legality, loopholes, discretion, deniability. I wasn't to talk about money, but money was what it was really all about. Money and sex. I would have to open myself to him, build trust. Listen and nod and encourage. And then, once he felt that he was in control, once he had been stroked and calmed, my job would be to seduce him, get him to put out, to talk.

The guard arrived. He led me into a small antechamber, pressed a buzzer on the wall, and a big gray door slid slowly on its electric rail until it shut with a thump. He then walked across the room and pushed another button and a similar gray door buzzed open on its tracks and we stepped outside into the prison courtyard. The sun was high overhead. As we walked, the guard's keys played against his hips in a slow tambourine rhythm. I said, "He's known for his mood swings, isn't he?"

The guard looked at me with utter contempt. Finally he said, "Don't worry. I'll keep an eye on you."

I had envisioned meeting the Nibbler in a small, private room with a glass divider and a guard standing there, just as you see in the movies. But the room we entered was chaotic and informal. The guards sat behind a desk on a raised platform and they were talking among themselves. I didn't see any security cameras. The guard led me to the desk and handed over a piece of paper. A female guard read the paper and picked up the phone. "Tell number 11490 that he's got a visitor," she said. She listened for a moment then said, "I see" and hung up. "He's here already waiting for you. Back there, by the microwave."

After I had given him my best smile, we shook hands. The Nibbler brushed a kernel of popcorn off his lip and stared at me. He didn't look anything like I had expected. I had pictured a sinewy, evil, flinty, hard man. Instead, he looked avuncular and sweet, with a big distended belly, cauliflower nose, flapping jowls, and dark spaniel eyes. He looked like Bill Murray with 30 more pounds and a few years in lockup.

I followed him across the room. He walked to a small desk positioned behind a two-foot-wide concrete column and totally obscured the view from the guard's desk some thirty feet away. I knew I couldn't hesitate when he graciously indicated that I should take a seat. It was important to show that I trusted him. I pulled out the chair and sat down. He sat down in the chair next to me, not across from me, and leaned back. I began by telling him that I was an emissary between the producers and himself. My job was to broker the deal, to get him to talk, and to make sure that his expectations were met.

He gently interrupted me at that point.

"You know," he said, "I don't do Geraldo. He's been trying to get an interview for years. He just sensationalizes everything. Serial killers have standards, too."

I told him that the producers wanted to know if he would talk about the murders, the cannibalism, the sex, in graphic detail. I also explained that this was a legitimate science program that it dealt with the chemistry and neurology of his brain rather than sensationalism. I said we could talk money but only in certain prescribed ways.

"So," said the Nibbler, "you're the flunky."

"Yeah I'm the flunky," I said, noting the bounce and play of his conversation, his touch of ironic wit. "And I'm paying court." He liked that. Leaned back in his chair again, stretched his legs. And then he began to tell me about his family, the fact that he was related to an important line of Englishmen. A cousin had served under Churchill in World War Two. That man's son was a famous writer and journalist, who had written about the Middle East, books that the Nibbler had read in the prison library. Fascinated, he had begun searching out his roots and had written the family in England long letters, and had even traced their coat of arms onto his prison stationery. But he'd never received a reply. He seemed baffled and hurt by this.

Talking about this disappointment reminded him of a February afternoon in 1963 when he was a boy and the snow had fallen for three days straight and the wind had blown steadily for an entire week. The snow had piled up in drifts as high as the eaves of the house and it was impossible to open the back door. If you looked out of the kitchen window, he said, all you could see was a white expanse. On that exceptional day, his mother had come out of her bedroom at noon in a terrycloth robe, and the robe had clung to her provocatively, outlining her pendulate form underneath. Someone else, someone he didn't know, was in her room and his mother had ignored him. Later, he went upstairs and opened one of the dormer windows in the attic and slid down the roof and jumped from there onto the pillowy buildup of snow on the top of the garage and climbed in through a window where, in the cavelike cold, he found some snowshoes and clambered back out of the window and walked for five miles through the snow to the shack of a night watchman he knew. He kept his direction by following a telephone wire which was normally fifteen feet in the air but which he could now nearly reach up and touch. He recalled how he walked in the total silence for what seemed like hours with just the stars and the telephone wire to guide him.

I asked him if he had been scared and he laughed and said he was never scared in the out-of-doors.

He said if I could talk with one person from his past then I would understand the things that he would later grow up to do.

"Who's that?" I asked.

"I'm not saying," he said.

He went on to talk about his father. When the Nibbler was nine, his mother found out that his father had a second wife and family. She was furious with him but they didn't split up. Instead, she punished him by not letting him go out of the house on his own and by not allowing him to watch TV. This sounded suspiciously like a punishment that a child would receive. Was he mixing up his father and himself?

"Basically," said The Nibbler, "my father was pussywhipped."

"How did that make you feel?" I asked.

"Like I never wanted that to happen to me," he said, and laughed. "And as you know, I made sure that never was the case."

He rolled his eyes in an exaggerated way like a movie madman. He was referring to his propensity to chew the vaginas of his victims. He was also indicating that he knew that I knew what he had done to the women, and by making a joke about it, and sharing the joke, he was drawing me in.

Suddenly, for no apparent reason, the Nibbler switched the subject to gardening, a hobby of mine. We were quickly into a discussion of the best variety of the flower *rudbeckia*. He had very detailed knowledge about specific plants. He took great pleasure in grafting, he said and had once taken a cantaloupe and grafted it onto a watermelon vine and then crossed the resulting plant with a cucumber. This experiment took him the better part of a summer and by the last week in August he had an odd-looking fruit, which tasted delicious. He then went on to tell me about some rosebushes a landscape gardener planted one April in front of the apartment building he was living in shortly after he was paroled from Attica. The gardener had turned up one day and began to aerate and then prepare the soil and unwrap the almost fully grown bushes from their protective burlap sacks. The Nibbler went out to watch. He asked the gardener when he thought the bushes were going to bloom. "Give it a year or two," he said, "they need time to get established." The Nibbler thought for a moment, and then said to the gardener, "If you come back here at the end of October, I'll show you something surprising."

That was around the time he borrowed his girlfriend's car and began visiting the prostitutes in the rundown industrial part of town, and met Sophie Peel. She had leaned in through the car window and said with a smile, "What can I do for you today, Mitch?" Later, when he couldn't get it up and she had laughed at him, he had pressed his thumbs into her trachea and held on tight as she struggled like a fish on a line. Back at his apartment, he added colossal amounts of Miracle Grow to the water when he went out to tend to the plants. In the autumn he rigged up a complicated electrical system of wires under the soil; the wires kept the roots of the plants warm through the first frosts. By mid October the roses began to bud and by Halloween they had turned into immense and vivid flowers, looking otherworldly and strange, surrounded as they were by the muted colors of fall. The gardener returned, as he had promised, and was amazed, as were the neighbors when, a few weeks later, the first winter storms arrived and powdered the magenta and vermilion petals with snow.

This odd and haunting image put him in mind of one of his favorite meals. Friends had invited him to their house one Thanksgiving; in appreciation he told them he would prepare a special dish. He bought the largest turkey he could find and stuffed it with a chicken. Inside the chicken, he placed a pheasant and inside the pheasant he stuffed a very small pigeon. When he removed this great hulking Russian doll of meat from the oven, where it had been cooking for a great number of hours, and brought it to the table, his fellow diners watched in hushed amazement as he slowly extracted each bird from the belly of its host.

As he continued to talk about this meal, I realized that we were having a very pleasant, getting-to-know-you chat about gardening, cooking, and family memories, but that each story was rippled with some strange distortion. He had been conversationally scanning me, finding footholds where he could latch on and bond. He seemed intent on depicting himself as special and distinctive; I was trying to show empathy and a certain degree of communality while remaining personally distant. It occurred to me that he was doing a much better job of things than I was.

The first time the Nibbler killed and ate human flesh, he said, was in Vietnam. "I was the perfect soldier; I never felt remorse." He described how he was on patrol in the border region between Vietnam and Cambodia, a place where the mountains seemed perpetually shrouded in mist. The fog line was distinct, he recalled. You could approach it and practically put your hand across the line— one part of your arm in the damp, the other part in the clear warmth of the sun. One day while he was on solo patrol he came across two Vietnamese women making grenades. They had piles of cartridges in front of them and metal springs and they were emptying the gunpowder from the cartridges, mixing it in a bowl and then loading it into casings. He opened fire, hit and killed one of the women and wounded the other. He then strung the wounded woman up in the manner that he had learned while hunting deer in the woods near his home. When she spat at him, he plunged his knife into her insides and twisted. He opened her up. Soon she was limp and compliant, just hanging there. In the aftermath of his fear, he explored her with tongue and finger. And then he beheaded her. And then he cut off one of her legs and roasted it over an open fire.

After he told me this, I looked out across the visiting room, needing to stabilize my sense of reality. Three kids, high on sugary snacks and soda, spun like tops in the corner of the room. I didn't know what to believe, didn't really care. A wave of deadening fatigue swept over me. I eyed the vending machines. "Do you want anything to drink or eat?" I asked and immediately regretted it. The Nibbler looked around the room, gave me his mock-maniacal stare and said, "I'll pass. I don't see any good-looking women."

When I returned to the table holding an ice cream bar and a soda, he was scratching his arm. He was chummy, convivial. "People are weird," he said. "They write to me all the time."

"What kind of people?" I asked.

A woman from Indianapolis who had her uterus removed, he replied, two girls from Paris with tattoos in circles around their necks. "I know that because they sent me pictures," he said. "You wouldn't believe the stuff people send me." He used to get photographs of naked women all the time before the prison put a halt to it. "Oh, yeah, lots of snatch. Sometimes boyfriends and husbands would send the pictures but mostly it was the women. All these photographs of women and their pussies—hairy, shaved, pierced— you name it. I put them all in a book. I kept it under my bed."

He then returned to Sophie Peel. After she had stopped twitching, the Nibbler propped her up in the front seat of the car and drove her around town for a few hours, her head lolling back and forth across her naked torso. She had laughed at his vulnerability but now she was quiet. He had made her into his ideal: an available cunt that didn't talk back.

He then suddenly announced that he would do the interview. I could tell the producers that he would talk about the sex, the killing, the cannibalism in graphic detail. A doctor had recently done an MRI scan on his brain, and the Nibbler gave me the doctor's name. The producers could use this information, he said; they could show the scans. We talked about money in the circumspect and rigorously legal way that I had been schooled in. It was all going to be okay. He put his arm around me. "Adam, now you can tell your friends you've met a man who really has eaten pussy," he said, and laughed.

Later, on the drive back to New York City, I stopped at a drive-through car wash and punched in the most expensive treatment on the panel. Full power surges of water cascaded around and above and below the car, the drone of jet spray splashed off the hubcaps, the rocking of the buffing wheels and the slap slap slap of the rubber ribbons followed by the hot hum of the drying machines—they all failed to do the trick. I couldn't get him out of my head. I pulled the shimmering car out of the lot, drove 500 feet down the highway, and then pulled a dangerous U-turn and drove back to the car wash to do it again. The afternoon had turned overcast, with a summer thunderstorm brewing on the horizon. I got strange looks from the gas station attendants as I put the car through the wash again and again and again.

So You Like Dante
Poem
It's All True
from Go Now
Across the Years

by

Richard Hell

So You Like Dante

a sonnet

> Dante and Beatrice didn't have this, did they:
> penis, tongue, and fingers piercing
> clinging rings of muscle lips? I do,
> I want to kill you with it
> so you'll want it always. Thus I hope
> to compose concerning you
> what has never been written
> in rhyme of any woman.
> You're sitting on the chair
> and I fuck you there.
> I fuck you in the mouth,
> I fuck you in the ass.
> I pull on my cock while I stare in your eyes.
> "Ass" and "eyes" are a very good rhyme.

Poem

Do you know what's my favorite book? Your butt.

It's All True

To Orson Welles, Knut Hamsun, and Edgar Allan Poe

The train I arrived on that early Autumn night might as well have been a bicycle—I was the only passenger getting off, I felt anxious and awkward as I would have on a bike, and, most of all, I've always had a strong sense of fantasy.

It was very late at night, though comfortably warm, and I began walking away from the center of the small village toward the hilly forest that surrounded it. I wasn't exactly afraid in the unfamiliar darkness but my senses felt extraordinarily acute. Actually I was never so happy to be completely alone and a stranger. I'd taken the ride from New York on an inspired whim and didn't know where I'd gotten to. Tears came to my eyes once or twice simply because there was nothing to prevent them from doing so. I was glad to be still capable of sensitivity.

I was following a grassy path in the open misty woods. The moon was very bright. Ahead of me I saw an animal. It was a young doe but it actually had antlers! And it was white. Sexually mutated and albino as well! I want with all my heart for you to believe that this is really true. A thoughtful and sophisticated human mind or one that's utterly naive realizes that anything it can conceive must exist. (The universe is certainly as large as a human mind.)* But I won't humiliate myself any further with pleas for your confidence. The highest art form is the meditative joke.

I fell for that doe the minute I laid eyes on it. I've never been able to fall in love in public or with a creature that can talk. This is my innermost self . . . but it doesn't take much courage to reveal inasmuch as I admit I realize you're not likely to take it very seriously. I approached the pale doe with eyes half closed and with very weak-feeling knees, as if I were gliding, and the only other muscles moving were in the rise and fall of my chest. The deer gazed at me motionlessly. It gazed at me devoid of tension as if it were invulnerable. Did its brain get the wrong genes too? No, it could never have survived the slightest mental deficiency on top of all the rest. I looked her over and she seemed practically aglow with alert intelligence. Considering

---

*Could be said to be untrue. There are more "states" of the brain than there are atoms in the universe.

the handicap of her glaring visibility, not to mention the sad and confusing effect her possession of antlers must have had on all the other deer, the apparently excellent condition of her health suggested she probably possessed quite *superior* intelligence.

How long shall I dwell on this incident? So many things happened that night. I was never so happy. I gently put my arms around the creamy neck of the calm animal and my head against the soft fur of its side. I stroked it, hardly breathing. I felt completely abstract, as if my being were a force of desire to please the doe. Paradoxically, this feeling increased my own excitement as I found myself automatically further elaborating my act of tenderness toward the exquisite animal with a gentle sexual caress certainly known only among deer until discovered by me in those moments spent engulfed in the dreamy billows of utter sensuality that seemed to clothe the white doe, blurring the boundaries between us and combining and replacing our surfaces with mist. . . . We came at the same time. The doe's vagina would taste like warm folds of liquifying bubblegum and then like lobster-meat drenched in lemon butter sauce. The alternating flavors shifted like shafts of light reflected from the facets of a giant pink diamond. I was never so grateful. I was a flood of gratitude, pleasure, and happiness.

As I lay in the grass with the stars overhead, the doe wandered away. Soon after, I arose and continued my walk.

from *Go Now*

Chrissa wants to see New Mexico so we are driving south and despite all, I get to doing pretty well at enjoying my high. After a while I'm too drowsy and I return the wheel to her. My head against the window, eyelids drooping, the goopy tides of pleasure take me and I nod and nap for hours.

When I wake up we are back in dense piney mountains, a little smaller-scale than in Colorado, on a twisting two-lane road. Chrissa says we've been in New Mexico for an hour, approaching Taos.

I take over driving again and I do everything I can to buy into the opportunities for peace of mind promised by the dope.

The trees thin out as we twist down out of the steep hills into the desert. Behind the wheel on the narrow back roads we take through the wildness I am in love again. I want to kiss everything, I want to eat the light, I want to inhale it all, everything I see, through my nose and eyes and ears and mouth. The barren land with its occasional weatherbeaten roadside stops—diners and junkshops and half-assed Indian trading posts—isolated, dug-in, conforming to the immense indifference, corresponds perfectly to my inner state and makes me happy.

Even though there is something inherently selfish in doing the drug—playing to my feeling of apartness and craving for ego protection—it also fills me with this expansive affection. I have my flesh back and my confidence boosted, and Chrissa over by the window in the big front seat lights me up. I feel lucky and I feel manly and I get the idea of fucking her in the desert. I want to fuck her cleanly and thoroughly and I have the feeling she wants to be fucked. She's been mothering me for days and giving me all the benefits of the doubts and now for a while the doubts are swept under the rug, it's a vacation, home from work, time off, a reprieve, I am all outward confidence and tenderness and she is glad for the break from nursing me, glad to give up the responsibilities of caretaking, and all the coyness is gone between us and I know that the drug will let me fuck for hours and nothing would please me more than to take her where everyone wants to go, and just fuck and fuck her.

The swells of lightheaded, big-dicked impulse surge in spells and build, until late in the afternoon it comes to a head and I pull over and stop beside a little desert road. In this act it is hardly even personal, or it is meta-personal, it is a man and a woman. The mannish man feels like fucking a woman and the womanly girl feels like being fucked by a man and they both know it and that's all there is to it. Carrying an Indian blanket I'd picked up in a junkshop I lead her across a roadside stream by its tattered screen of trees and we walk into the desert until we feel sufficiently engulfed in it and distant from the car and the dead-quiet road, like it's a kind of darkness, and I fuck her brains out. Nothing has ever felt so sexy. It does matter of course that it is her, Chrissa, who has her will and her self-possession and her varying stances regarding me and whom I thirst for and whose response to me has always mattered, Chrissa, that face and proud naked body become purely given up to my ragingly hard dick on the grainy hard-packed desert floor. And she wants me to feel that power, even anger, blood lust, conquering drive, fuckly aggression, she doesn't care, she laughs in the middle of it with delight to allow it done upon her, to get its benefits, and ride it and embrace it and the ultra-intense abandon that doesn't exclude skill and strategy. It is her giving over of herself that makes her pleasure possible because it is rare and scary, dangerous to her and exciting to me and it is my excitement that makes the whole thing possible, because that is how dicks get hard and we both laugh. And it doesn't let up and she just gets wetter and wetter and more and more astonished and her cheekbones burning red and she hacks and screams in orgasms and I slow for a minute and then it reaches the top again and then goes over it. I look down at my cock coming in and out of her and that seems anonymous and I want it to be her and I tell her it is me, it's Billy, and she opens her eyes and her glassy-eyed glazed face gets this feral watchful triumphant look like a cat about to pounce and she says I'm Chrissa and you're fucking me out of my mind and her eyes close and her face goes beatific and spaced again and the rhythm changes a little bit, rising, and we both laugh from all the way inside, hoarsely, and in a second she comes some more. I don't have it let up. There comes a point after two or three series of her orgasms where she makes as if to have me stop but I resist and jam her through once more to where you really can't tell if she is being killed and her cunt is erupting all around my cock and it's like she is getting electro-shock and noises like farts and spurts of mucous are splashing up into my pubic hair and it is just as it should be, everything all broken down and dissolved and shattered and exhausted and I lie on her, my dick still hard as a rock inside that gulping melted slush, throbbing till it settles like we sink to the bottom and rest there, nestling beneath it all.

When I pull out and slide to the side, oblivious to the grating smudging dirt, and wrap my arm and knee across her, head bowed to hers, she whimpers tinily because she's enclosing me in that resting place. In a little while we get up and get dressed like coal miners or oil field roughnecks at the end of the day. The desert air and simple blown open vista have a sinewy sting of the persistent reduction to the irreducible necessities that seems all the richer by it. It feels as if that fuck has linked us back to our beginnings seven years ago. I take a breath and this one reaches all the way down and clicks and fully catches as none have for days and days as if I am whole in the world again and belong. But of course the feeling is a fragment of a larger broken thing.

Across the Years

Flavored paper dumps rocks over the other side
splintering like a waterfall onto an
island in the half light. It resembles
handwriting. A hand stretching until its
nearly translucent, transatlantic

* * *

Reaches across the years to me
as when, alone, I held my own (hand)
Imagining it yours. You helped to make me that kind
   of great
awful poet whom I exploit here
the way
I'd like to fuck you in the ass
so much.

Penis Passion
and
Gimme Some Dick

by

bell hooks

Penis Passion

Working on a poem inspired by the joys of having sex in the world's smallest study seated on an old-fashioned straight-back chair painted red where I spend much of my time writing, I seek for words to describe the sensation of sitting in the lap of sweet lust moving my body back and forth against the deliciously hot moist penis of my off-and-on-again lover A. Among the penises I have looked upon and touched in this world his gives me the greatest sense of delight. Yet finding words to describe the pleasure I feel, words that do not perpetuate coventional sexist thinking about the penis are hard to come by.

Females finding and expressing delight in the male body was for such a long time utterly taboo. Before the contemporary feminist movement and sexual liberation, women did not say much in print about our feelings about the penis. No wonder then that when we finally gave ourselves permission to say whatever we wanted to say about the male body—about male sexuality—we were either silent or merely echoed narratives that were already in place. At that time heterosexual women active in the feminist movement often boldly and boastfully talked about the penis using the same language of conquest sexist men used when talking about sexual pursuits. In those days in feminist consciousness-raising groups we not only talked about how women had to become more comfortable with words like pussy and cunt so that men could not terrify or shame us by wielding these words as weapons, we had to be able to talk about cock and dick with the same ease. Sexual liberation had already told us that if we wanted to please a man we had to become comfortable with blow jobs, with going down, with the dick in our throat—so far down it hurt. Surrendering our sexual agency we had to swallow the pain and pretend it was really pleasure.

Feminist interventions on the issue of sexuality along with sophisticated birth control changed all that; it said to women who wanted to be with men that we had a right to define the place of pleasure for us and the will to claim our sexual rights. It let us know we did not have to consent to force or pretend to like pain. It let us know that the penis was not "a one-eyed trouser snake" in the garden of sexual bliss threatening to turn our bodies into a place where pain defines, penetrates, and punishes. And that we did not need to see any penis as the enemy.

Like many young women who came of age in that intense ecstatic moment when sexual liberation and feminist movement converged, I let go all the fear of the penis that had haunted my girlhood. Fears that were rooted not in envy of the penis and the male body as a whole but rage that it had to be feared. In those days the message about the male body that females received loud and clear was that whether wanted or unwanted, penis penetration could change a girl's life forever. She would never be the same; she would never be good again. I can remember the sheer bliss sound birth control offered us. For it meant we did not have to fear the chosen penis. We could embrace our curiosity about it, our wonder and our passion.

Then there was the dread of the unchosen penis, raping against one's will and desire. That penis we were endlessly told was always out there somewhere waiting to search and destroy. The one-time violating violence that could leave one changed forever. That dreaded penis has to be put in its proper place before females can enjoy the penis either from a distance or close-up.

As a small girl I thought of the penis as a magic wand. Magical because it could move and change its shape, because seeds could come from it that would come to life in a woman's body. I had only seen the penis of a boy baby; it was not envy I felt but wonder. I feared for him and his magical wand so exposed, so easy to wound and hurt. And as so many girls have testified I was relieved that my girl genitals were not out there, exposed, were not visible. That sense of girlhoood fascination and appreciation of the penis changed when I received warnings about sexual danger and the threat that the male body would destroy female innocence. In those days there was no discussion of female passion. In my sexual imagination the wand became a weapon, something males used to bring us down, to destroy us.

No wonder females rejoiced when birth control and feminist insistence on female sexual agency made it possible for us to think about the penis in new ways. We could see it as an instrument of power and/or delight. We could go down between male legs, abandon ourselves to mystery, and rise up satisfied, pleased with our knowledge that we could give and receive sexual delight. We could express our annoyance at expressions like blow jobs which implied that anytime we sucked dick it was service work we did to pleasure men, and proclaim our freedom in the sucking and the coming and the sticky semen. The pretense was over, females who enjoyed sucking dick could name and express that joy, could name it as an act of power which required males to trust in the sexual integrity of the female—to trust that at his most vulnerable moment she will give pleasure and not pain, that she will nurture, nourish, and not diminish and destroy.

A generation later females living in the new culture of freedom that feminism and sexual liberation produced would from the start approach the penis without fear. Writing about coming to sexual power in her teens in *Promiscuities,* Naomi Wolf recalls how quickly she and her girlhood friends moved from thinking dick sucking was silly to passionate interest: "Within a year, we were obsessed. Not so much with what penises did . . . But rather with what they were—the improbability of them, the beautiful weirdness, the way they oddly rose of their own volition and oddly defied gravity, their unfathomable responsiveness." Female talk about fascination with the penis often stops at girlhood and teen reminiscences. Not because it ceased to marvel but because the marvelous aspects of the penis lose their charm when linked with strategies of male domination.

Even though contemporary feminists worked hard in the 70s to come up with new ways of talking about female sexual agency in relation to the penis, new words did not come into general usage. Individual women gave the penis of male partners witty cute names, but overall there was not a widely accepted re-visioning of how we all might see and experience the penis. Then and now women talk about how the words used to describe female genitalia are much more varied and compelling than those used to describe male genitals. Reading lots of erotica, both gay and straight, I was dismayed to find that overall the penis is still primarily represented as a weapon, as an instrument of indelicate and painful penetration. Talked about in terms of force, whether in descriptions of pleasurable consensual sex or forced sex and bondage, no one seems to have much to say about the penis that challenges and changes sexist representation. To identify the penis always and only with force, with being a tool of power, a weapon first and foremost, is to participate in the worship and perpetuation of patriarchy. Fundamentally, it is a celebration of male domination.

No wonder then that as feminism progressed many anti-sexist women feel there is no way to engage the penis that does not reinforce male domination. While many who claim feminism, as a political act, have chosen lesbianism or celibacy as a way to resist sexist sexual subordination and have no interest in the penis, those of us who enjoy penis passion often find ourselves silenced by the assumption that mere naming of our pleasure is traitorous and supports the tyranny of patriarchy. This is simply false logic. Submitting to silencing makes us complicit. Naming how we sexually engage male bodies, and most particularly the penis in ways that affirm gender equality and further feminist liberation of males and females is the essential act of sexual freedom and agency.

When women and men can celebrate the beauty and power of the phallus in ways that do not uphold male domination our erotic lives are enhanced. In an essay published in the anthology *Transforming A Rape Culture,* I wrote about how I had to change my sexist thinking about the penis, letting go my erotic fetishization of the hard penetrating dick, to embrace an eroticization of the penis that was more wholistic. My penis passion was enhanced when I stopped thinking of it solely in relation to performance, to penetration. I enjoyed learning how to be sexually aroused by the sight of a non-erect penis. Continuing in the tradition of the first contemporary feminists who were also advocates of sexual freedom, I believe we still need to see more visual images of the penis in everyday life. In a context of mutual sexual pleasure rooted in equality of desire there is room for a politics of sexuality that is varied, that can include hard dicks, rough sex, penetration as gesture of power and submission, because in a liberatory context these acts are not intended to reinforce male domination. But without this progressive sexual context we end up always creating a world where the penis is synomous with negativity and threat.

The presence of life-threatening sexually transmitted diseases has been used by sexual conservatives to reinforce anti-penis sentiments. Many women have returned to a fear of the penis that is practically Victorian. Despite the sexual revolution and the prevalence of feminist thinking, it has not taken long for sexist social mores to triumph over the new ways of thinking about sexuality introduced by the feminist movement and gay rights. The vision of the phallus as always and only an instrument of force is conservative and lacking. Yet it still reigns supreme. When I read lesbian erotica where all the symbolic phalluses used in sexual play are described using sexist vernacular, reinforcing the sense of the phallus whether real or symbolic as a weapon, I feel dismay. Clearly, we must continue the work to create liberatory sexual frontiers, places where the penis is precious and can be cherished.

Changing how we talk about the penis is a powerful intervention that can challenge patriarchal thinking. Many men fear that their bodies lose meaning if we value penises for the sacredness of their being rather than their capacity to perform. After a romantic meal with a man who captivated my sexual interest, as we sat in my living room listening to music, I asked him to show me his penis. He responded with alarm. We were fully dressed. We were not engaged in sexual foreplay. The mood was erotic. He appeared alarmed at the thought of his penis being looked at apart from a context of performance and wanted to know why I wanted to see it. I responded that I wanted to see if I liked it. He asked: "Will you know if you like it by looking at it?" I responded: "I will know that I like looking at it."

I shared this story with friends. And again and again males and females responded as though I had threatened his masculinity. I believe that the sense of threat arose simply because I was asserting the primacy of the female gaze, a female sexual agency not informed by sexist conditioning, one separating pleasure in the male body from penis performance.

Returning to a bliss sense of the sacredness of the body, of sexual pleasure, we acknowledge the penis as a positive symbol of life. Whether erect or still, the penis can always be a marvel, a wonder, a magic wand. Or it can be likened to a caterpillar, as Emily Dickinson tenderly declares: "How soft a Caterpillar steps—/I find one on my Hand/ From such a velvet world it come."

Gimme Some Dick

Sexual imprints begin in childhood. that's certainly where it started for me—my fascination with the penis. then i just imagined seeing and touching them all. i wanted to go up to every male in sight and urge him to just show it to me, just let me squeeze, touch, and watch it do its thing. in those days everybody thought those tall lanky brown-skinned basketball players had the dicks any male in his right mind would die for—lean smooth hard ever ready dicks. as a girl i was less concerned with the ever ready and more with just the magic of touch and what touch could do. it was just mere accident that i chose a basketball playing boy, younger than me, wearing jeans that were just baggy enough for my hand to go on a search and seize mission and feel the thrill of that hard on coming. whether it took seconds or minutes i was thrilled by the feel. just a mere touch would make my pussy wet then wetter each step of the way. like a boy meets girl thing, it was a pussy gets ready for dick thing. and even as a girl i liked to be in charge, to direct the sexual traffic.

by the time i reached mature womanhood i was getting bored with dicks, almost all of them (and the men who brought them to my attention were just not that alluring). yeah i was one of those feminist broads who wore the button (so many men so many reasons not to sleep with any of them). the main man of my sexual life at the time had a long uncut dick that could stay hard for hours but after a while, once i got over being curious, i found the too long too thick dick in the hand felt good, but the pound the pussy into oblivion got tiring quick, that the big dick in the mouth was cumbersome (like who enjoys the feeling that you are chokin) and no woman who's really into dick wants to feel like she's working (blow jobs are strictly for workers who are being paid, laborers on the sexual plantation) so i let it go and went on searchin, hoping to find the dick of my sexual dreams a lean smooth eager to give the pleasure by any means necessary—ever ready dick.

from the moment we laid eyes on one another i knew. i had gone to spend the weekend at a friend's house. for some time she had been telling me about her sport fucking way younger than me male roommate but we had never met. after a quick introduction and greeting he went on to his room. she caught the gleam in my eye, seeing that i have looked him over and like what i see gaze—she could only say "don't you dare—he's just a baby." i took that to be her way of telling me i was too old cause he was nobody's child.

later sitting on the living-room floor eating indian food with our fingers, licking and laughing he gave me the "i'm ready for what you got silent come on down" which i nicely translated as "i got just the thing for you to lick." made me hear taj mahal singing that song about the candy man in my head—"all you ladies gather round cause the good sweet candyman is in town—this here candy don't melt away, it just gets better so the ladies say" cause i'm into the sweet and sticky, a definite lollipop queen.

late that night we talked but then he went into his room and closed the door. leaving me wide awake, wet, and wondering. time just slowly passed. i lay there afraid to make a move and scared that if i didn't bust a move i would just be missing out. i had to take the chance, to do the do.

not wanting to be caught in the dark naked and needing to explain i grabbed my thin silk blouse and my short elastic in the waist skirt, all easy to put on and take off (thinking if nothing else i could plead i heard a noise and was just checking it out). my knock on the door went unanswered. i opened the door a crack and still no signs of life, streetlight glare helped me see there he was asleep helpless sprawled among a tangled sheet legs wide open his hand close to his penis. i could not resist moving that hand and reaching through open boxer shorts to touch his private parts, warm to the touch. slowly his dick began to swell and as it swelled, my hands began to stroke it to fullness, making him feel my presence with my hands i felt the wetness in my vagina as he begin to quietly moan.

emerging as if from a dream startled that the mouth moving back and forth in soothing rhythm was proving be all too real he begin to speak. in sultry tones i got it all under control. i ordered him to hush, lay back and dream, and i begin to suck first slow, then harder taking his dick deep into my throat, letting the moisture in my mouth make it slick and wet, sucking until his long lean penis was jetting outward hard hot and ready. my pussy sloppy wet i wanted to mount his flesh and ride but i held and let the intensity of the yearning strengthen my desire to lick, suck, and take it all in— smelling the sweet funky scent of his sweat and his juice, gently prying open the tip of his dick with my tongue, caressing the shaft, while holding tight with one hand moving. i gave him a wake up nibble, playfully biting.

while he moved and moaned i demanded "give me some dick, all of it" but i teased "not until i'm ready." i wanted to fuck him just a bit first, to do a little dance on his penis, wetting it with all my juices, licking, then sucking again, then letting him cum in my mouth, spitting it back and licking him clean, till we were spent and satisfied. and i could fall asleep hands on his crotch with the lyrics "you must be stuck on the candyman's stick" playing in my head like an all night lullaby.

Scene IV *from the play*
Carson McCullers

by

Sarah

Schulman

I n New York. Small apartment filled with boxes. Streetlight in through the window. Carson and Reeves are sleeping in the dark. He wakes up, lights a candle by the bed. He starts caressing her under the sheets. She moans.)

REEVES

Do you want me to touch you or do you want to go to sleep?

CARSON

Both.

REEVES

Come here, Carson. It's been so long. You've been away all summer. I miss you. I'm been sweating here in New York, while you've been lounging in Vermont. Now I want my calm, my peace. My piece of paradise.

CARSON

My mind is full.

REEVES

Of what?

CARSON

Of the summer of famous writers, of Louis Untermeyer. Of my reviews, of my second book, what will people think? I asked Louis to sleep with me, he said he was too tired. That's what happens when you're fifty-five.

REEVES

I'm not fifty-five.

CARSON

Cocktails at quarter to six until sun-up and chatting with Robert Frost. Breadloaf was just the first slice of where I belong, Reeves. Where I'm going. This is the way it's going to be.

REEVES

You're not so famous now that you can't take love from your husband, are you?

CARSON

Well, give me an image of something I can hold on to. Fill my head with it. With sex.

REEVES

Oh, *(unsure),* all right. Let's see. . . . You mean like. . . . Ok, we're in a cinema, in a small town. Back by Charleston. Hardly anyone is in the theater. We're watching a funny, dumb romantic comedy, it's as though we are alone. Then you put your arm around me in the theater and start stroking my head, my neck, my shoulders. Then you reach over and unbutton my shirt, stroke the hair on my chest. All the love in your heart is open to me and coming at me and I'm getting very aroused, very. I'm longing for you and you're giving me everything in your arms and in your two hands, which are now molesting me. Holding me between my thighs. You whisper in my ear "Reeves, I love you." We walk out of the theater, excited, beaming. It is a beautiful night. Warm and cool at the same time. Down at the pier, the longshoremen on the night shift are loading and unloading their ships, sailors strolling, playing cards and smoking. We come to an old rotting pier and crawl over the NO TRESPASS sign, out onto the thick, spare beams over the shining water, all that activity on the boats behind us, and I unbutton your blouse and take the full weight of your breasts in my mouth, press myself against you, Carson and we're so filled with love.

CARSON

That's not really working.

REEVES

What would you like?

CARSON

Can I offer another image?

REEVES

Please.

CARSON

You undress me in a barn and lay me down across the hay. Louis

Untermeyer is watching. You tie my hands over my head and my legs to an old heavy wooden table's legs and you . . . you demean me in front of him.

REEVES

Whore, slut, that sort of thing?

CARSON

Yes.

REEVES

I'll tie you to the table and you won't be able to do anything about it. Mister Untermeyer, limp dick in hand, will probably start snoring. It will all be up to me. And, um, little girl, you . . . little slut. I'll give you a thrashing, that's what I'll do. And you deserve it for treating me this way. I'll whup you with my belt and I'll cram my cock into your . . . anus, your asshole.

CARSON

I don't want real pain. I just want a little surprise.

REEVES

Oh, Okay. I'll slap you, then. I'll. . . . I'll. *(He slaps her, we hear the crack.)*

CARSON

Oh.

REEVES

Little girl. . . . Slut.
(He slaps her.)

CARSON

Reeves, my mind is so full, I have to go to sleep now.

REEVES

Why did this happen? Was it because I asked you to put your arm around me in the movies? To take me in your arms and say "I love you?" Is that why you're being so awful?

CARSON

That's a good question but I'm too tired to discuss it now.

REEVES

Just tell me, Carson. Do you want to care about me, or don't you? I won't punish you, just tell me the truth, do you want to?

CARSON

(Softly, in a baby voice)
Reeves. You slapped me.

REEVES

You asked me for it.

CARSON

I need to live somewhere else. I'll go move in with Auden in Brooklyn Heights. *(Looks at him. Gets out of bed.)*

REEVES

Leave here?

CARSON

It's a house full of artists, Reeves. Auden and Benjamin Britten and Peter Pears. We'll be better off.
(Pulls out suitcase and opens it.)

REEVES

Don't run away.

CARSON

What's the alternative?
(Starts putting manuscripts in her suitcase.)

REEVES

Don't be afraid to need me. Just tell me the truth. Do you want to or don't you? If you want to, I'll help you.

CARSON

Why do you even care for me?
(Puts typewriter in her suitcase.)

REEVES

Because you're the kind of woman who can do anything she wishes but you have to want to. If you want to love me, you will love me. Even from Brooklyn Heights. Do you want to?

CARSON

Not when I'm this tired. Good night dear. I should have never let you touch me. I should have gone to sleep.
(Exits.)

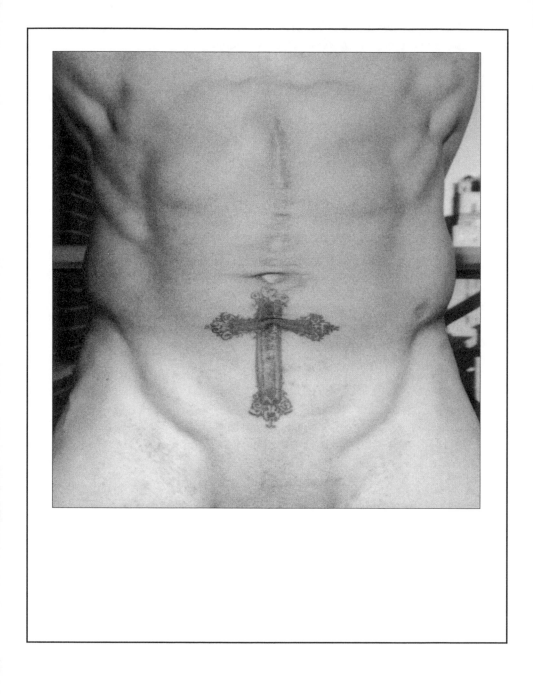

3 Specimens

by

Ishmael

Houston-Jones

SPECIMEN 1

FACE

The nose is crooked. Discoloration at the tip. Lips curve up. He closes his eyes.

Single earring, loop? Hoop? Whatever. Perfectly formed ears.

What do you call that grouping of stray hairs under the center of the lower lip?

Pockmarked temple.

Fingers touch.

Eyebrows almost taper at the ends. They scrunch together in the center of his forehead.

***

Beginnings of some kind of mustache. His feet are moving in dirty, wet socks.

***

Stud earring in the other ear.

Hair. Mostly dark brown. Looks greasy.

He crinkles his brow as he looks around my room.

***

Face red. There's a smirk. Weak chin. The feminine inside of him intrigues me.

Bored. He looks bored

His eyes are tearing. No nose hair. Lips part.

Swallow.

Crumpled face. Really ugly folds under the eyelids when he closes them tightly.

Slight smile. Remembering what? Egg shaped brow. Nervous flutter of eyelid. White teeth—surprising since he smokes.

Mouthing the words of the Pet Shop Boys song on my CD player.

"Love comes quickly, whatever you do/you can't stop falling, ooh-ooh, ooh"

***

SHIRT OFF
Redder from the neck up than the chest.
Nipples: oval—they're like oval quarters—that's not quite it. "Dusty Rose," darker than the chest skin—
Not pink
Blue/green veins under the skin in the pits. About 20 hairs under each arm. Protrusion of ribs.

***

Back to the nose. I can't quite get it.
Nervous swallow.

***

Breathing in the belly. Weirdly small belly button. Faint hairs start in the valley of the ribs.
Mole, off to the right, mid-chest.
Moles around belly button. Random hairs.
The navel itself looks like a knot didn't create it. It's almost nonexistent. A mere indentation. Slightly brown and then a slit. Some dark hairs—a few long ones growing from the center. Looks like an asshole.
His pits are almost scentless. No deodorant. No soap. No sweat. Strange.

***

BACK:
Dent marks from clothes or sheets. Upper back looks almost tanned.
Scattering of moles.

***

THIGHS:
Heavier than I imagined. A few scars on legs. A tiny birthmark on the back of his left thigh.

***

FEET:
Long.
Long bony toes. Clean under the nails. Hairs on top of arch. Well formed.
His legs are tanned up to the mid-thigh. He looks really bored.
Feet are cold and without smell.

Boo-boo on ankle.
He's fiddling with his hair.
Where does he want to be?

**

IN MY BATHROOM:
He's pee-shy. He holds his cock underhanded—thumb over top.
He pees. Yippee!
He's peeing a lot.

**

BACK IN MY BEDROOM, HE'S NAKED.
Drops of piss on his thigh. Penis is small and unthreatening. There's a drop of pee hanging off the head.
Pubic hair is dark brown and straight. Ball sac is loose and red underneath. He has a rash that he thought he had to explain. He's circumcised. A brown circle rings him mid-dick. White spots on the scrotum.
Even his pubes smell clean. There's something almost medicinal about the odor.

**

He's smelling his hair.

**

ON HIS BELLY.
Tiny, White-boy butt. Red blotch at the top of the crack.
Unmuscular back.
Shiny scrotum.
Right leg straight, left bent.
Birthmark mid-back on the left.
I can't get the soles of the feet.

**

OK, THE ASSHOLE.
The buns are hairless but in the crack straight brown hairs radiate outward. The slit is near perfect. No "roids." Pink and wrinkled. No sign of brown.
Holding it open—There's a blue/purple vein encircling the pucker. Remarkably—or maybe not—there's no smell.

**

Gray stretch marks over the buns.

**

Cold feet. Skin peeling off the soles.

**

Goose flesh on the buns.

***

(*"I want to fuck him really hard."*)

***

WATCHING VIDEOTAPE. "Le Desir en Ballade" by JD Cadinot
Fold under the eyes. Droopy eyes, murky-brown. Muddy. Stray hair
over forehead. Stretch marks in front of the armpits. Is he blushing,
or just naturally red?

***

Shallow breathing through his large nose.
Hands the same size as mine but look much bonier, longer.
Open pores on forehead.
Blue/green veins down the length of his arms

***

Slight smile. Somewhat immobile. Flinch.
Eyes brighten. Then darken at the sight of an enormous black cock
in the video.
His penis stays the same. As does his scrotum. No movement.
Soles of feet clasp each other in prayer.
Right arm crooked behind him around a pillow. Thumbnail worries
against pad of middle finger.
Left hand holds the edge of the mattress.
Breathing in belly. Slanted eyes. Moons in the fingernails. Almost a
sneer.

***

Penis is growing.
[Men are fucking on-screen]
Scrotum tightening.
Eyes are slitting.
Almost no movement.

***

[I have to pee.]

***

His balls glisten.
He touches his right nipple.
He looks like a handsome young girl.
He brushes his nipple with his fingernail.
He strums his flanks.
When he stands he's nearly buttless.
I must find a new way of saying "buttless."

***

LISTENING TO NEW-AGE AUDIOTAPE "Male Multiple Orgasm, Step by Step."

He's wearing my wool socks. He asked. His feet were cold.

He's smirking; so am I.

Swallow.

Highway of veins mapped across his torso. What's the exact size of his nipples?

Hands behind his head.

That nose: A bump in the middle, big pores, small hook.

***

What is he thinking?

Where did he come from?

How was he spawned?

In what position did his parents fuck?

He's biting his lower lip. Holding his left hand over his head. His feet were cold.

***

("I want to hit him.")

Why doesn't he smell?

Frown. Vertical lines at the bridge of his nose.

***

Why is he here?

I mean, why am I paying to have him here?

Is this the only way I can have someone like him here?

I want him; but I don't know what I mean by that.

***

He's following the instructions on the audiotape.

Roar, tiger, roar!

***

I'm attached to his coldness. His warmth surprises me.

I can't believe he's doing this.

I can't believe I'm here.

He's got the beginnings of pecs.

Sitting: Back deeply furrowed at the spine.

Prominent Adam's apple.

Clavicles look breakable.

***

His fingers are strolling down the path from his anus to the base of his scrotum.

I can't get the nipple shape and color right.

Gym biceps. He likes roaring. He's using his left hand. This is so
. . . . goofy.
Yay!
The tape distracts me.
I hadn't really looked at his body. I thought he was skinny. Actually
he has a very hot body. This is cool.
He's going for it.

***

His collarbones jut out. My wool socks are sexy on his feet. He has
bony knees.
He's touching himself. He's doing this. He's "feeling for his
pleasure." He's hard. His hole *is* perfect. He wears the ring he
bought in Thailand on the third finger of his right hand. His asshole is sucking. He's becoming splotchy red all over. The area
between his anus and scrotum is becoming swollen. The hole in his
erect penis is on the underside. His eyes are closed. He holds his
dick with all the fingers of his left hand. The head is purpling. He's
rubbing his "clit."

***

Swallow
One hand clutches his balls.
The Dalton School class of '88 did he say?
He says he has a girlfriend out of state.
He says he's never done anything like this before.
He's fisting himself tighter. He's smiling wistfully.
Swallow.
The cock head is pearlized gray.
I don't care if he comes.
I think he's closer.
I see his upper teeth.
Big Adam's apple.
Lips parted.
That smacking sound of his greased dick being pumped.

***

("I could strangle him.")

***

Knees up and parted.

Is he becoming "multi-orgasmic" as the tape says he should? He's chest breathing. His little buns are thrusting. His hair is lank. Abs are washboarding. Head turned away from me. Eyes have been closed for a long time.
Hard swallow.
Left hand pumps.
Right gropes his scrotum.
I'm becoming bored. I want to turn on the TV.

***

("I want him to sit on my face.")

***

I want to taste his cum.
Dot of nipple standing out, erect.
Swallow and change of breathing.

***

MEMORY FLASH FROM 1971
[So to do this and not do this/
to fall/ to wallow/
pig wallow/ shit/
pig shit/
English Peter walked barefoot through the pig shit in pen # 8.]

***

Left hand stroking.
Shudder.
Purple/gray head.
He has grown. He growls.
I want him but I'll never have him. $100 to watch him get off by himself. Hmm? That's cool (in all senses of the word.)
Is he still doing that "valley breathing?"
I want him to cum and leave so I can masturbate alone.
I want.
I want.
I don't know what I want.
Rape? I don't really think so; besides I couldn't get away with it. I still carry guilt from that thing with the girl next door when I was 10 or 11.

***

I wish I could masturbate in the "traditional" way—using hands instead of mattress humping. I'd whip out my cock and jerk off with him.

Maybe.

***

This tape is too much.
Too new age touchy-feely for this situation.
Turn it off.

***

Watching him is cool—in all senses. He's working so hard. Is my presence turning *him* off?
I wonder what my neighbors are doing? Or the guy across the street who walks around naked?
It never. . . .
Shit.
Don't start complaining.
Donna Summer—"She works hard for her money"—pops into my head.
Is he doing this for me? It's after midnight. All god's children should be in bed—ALONE.
I hope he's forgotten me.

***

HE CUMS

***

Hooray!
Finally.
Substantial amount of fluid. Didn't shoot far.

***

Penis pulses by itself. A thread of semen connects it to his thigh.
Gleam of sperm on forearm.
Red eyes. Dreamy. Distant. Looking toward the ceiling.

***

He's mopping up really well.
His red dick, soft, points up and to the left.
His eyes and mouth are closed.
He clutches the towel to his chest.
Fingers his clavicles.
He's puny and non-ominous again.
Swallow.
It's so quiet. Rain outside. Occasional traffic. Not even breathing.
I want to smell his hands.

***

("Patrician face. Or White trash. The desire to mess it up is redundant.")

He's coming back. He's breathing. Eyes opening. Toes moving inside my socks. A gesture of hand then back to the collarbone.

***

I have a chubby.

***

His dick is becoming its former self.

On some level I want to embrace him.

On most levels I'm too far away.

I wish this were his place so I could put the money on the table and leave.

Bony knees jut out in front of calves. Twisted legs.

I assume he wants to go now and is negotiating a graceful and profitable exit.

I can't tell if he'll ever be a good whore. I want to fuck him someday—at least on a political theoretical level.

Shit. He's going to smoke in my apartment.

He's so cold blooded.

$.

SPECIMEN 2

"What should I do, do you want me to strip right away?"

"No, wait, just sit down and relax on the couch. Your e-mail said you'd been fisted. So, tell me about being fisted, Rickie."

"I've only done it a few times."

"How did you decide to do it?"

"Well, my ass has always been a turn on for me. It feels good having something up there."

"How many times have you tried it?"

"Twice."

"Where did you do it?"

"I saw an ad for a guy up on 125th Street in Harlem who gives colonics."

"What did it feel like?"

"Nice."

"Did you trust the guy?"

"Now that's an important part of it. This guy, I didn't really trust

him, and he tried to go further than I was prepared to go."
"Further?"
"Yeah. He wanted to keep going further up there, and I wanted him
to stop."

He wears glasses.
He has vertical creases down his nose.
His glasses are wireless.
He has heavy, heavy eyebrows.
He wears a blue and green striped shirt. And a watch.

Speckled gray beard.

He swallows.

He has deep furrows around the mouth, a blunt nose, Semitic. The
Beard is neat.
Hair pouffy.
Jeans.
Light brown Bass shoes.

"Could you please take your glasses off?"
"Sure, I need to lay them down somewhere where I can find
them."
"Are you blind without them?"
"No not blind, just very nearsighted. I need them to drive."

He has bushy arched eyebrows.
Crow's-feet.
Laugh lines.
No holes in ears.
"No, I could never take that kind of pain."
Mole in the palace of anxiety.
Expensive-looking cheap watch.

Eyes—brown, kinda murky. Uneven.
His facial hair gives him that "evil Hebe" look like in the Nazi anti-
Jewish propaganda cartoons.
He has a softer look.
He looks nervous and apprehensive.

He looks around my room then back to me.
He's maybe 50 years old.

His hair is styled into a fluffy almost Pompadour.
If he were an animal, what would he be?
Some kind of big sad dog. But wiry.
Dark red lips from under heavy 'stache.

"Go ahead and take your shirt off."

Tan skin, but sallow at the same time.

"Do you shave your chest?"
"My friend does it for me. He gets a kick out of doing it."
Stubble. Saggy breasts. Soft gut distended. Folds of belly.

No piercings anywhere.
He couldn't stand the pain.
Flesh hangs over waistline.
For a minute I get chilled because I think he has no navel.

"Do you not have a navel?"

He shows it to me. It was hidden in a narrow crease of belly skin.

"You chew your nails."
"Down to the nubs."

He wrings his hands; intertwines fingers.
He could be a killer.
Hands the same size as mine but thicker. Wrinkled fingers covered
in fur; veiny and blunt with ragged nails.
Cut on the middle finger of the right hand.
No rings. No moons.

"You can undress now."

He does so quickly.
White, white feet.
Hard-on.

Thick thighs, shaved thighs.
Thick dick, shaved pubes, but not entirely. Halo of brown fuzz arcs
around base of his penis.
Mole on dick.

"Usually I get hard as a rock right away. I must be nervous."

You must be.

Thighs—blue veins and stretch marks. Circumcised. Fat balls.
Stubble.

"My friend shaves me, I don't know, he just seems to be into that."
"Do you ever shave him?"
"No. Well once I did, but I had to do it on the sly, so his wife
wouldn't notice."
"Your friend is married then."
"Yeah, for many years. I think she must know. I mean she has to. He
says he only stays with her for the kids. You can't break up a marriage.
But he never has sex with her. He can only have sex with men."
Feet turned out. Nubby toenails. Does he chew them too?

Lying on his stomach. Is he going to fall asleep?
Thin but mostly formless.
No back hair.
Some black moles dot his back. Three large and some smaller ones.

The crack—
Light brown edges; faint butt pimples probably from shaving.

He looks like a sleepy corpse.

Heavy calves, white.
No buns. Face reddening.
I want him out of here.
Twitches. Is he gonna fall asleep?
He rolls over.
I don't want to smell him.
The stubble on his stomach is disconcerting.
Nipples medium-sized, like nickels, rosy pink.

Stubble on the underside of his dick.

Loose fat balls; mouth dumbly open, index finger moving against thigh.

"Uh, how old are you, Rickie?" I kinda startle him awake.

"Forty-four." God! We're the same age.

"You don't have very many scars."

"Should I have more?" Slight chuckle.

Well-formed feet. Dick moves on its own. No nose hair. Eyes are not aligned perfectly.

Sort of classic study of "The Male Nude" from turn of the century art books. And I, the blackamoor, sit clothed beside him writing, like in some strange kind of all-male "Olympia."

He's the anemic Odalisque rendered by Rodin.

A million Black men marched in D.C. yesterday and here I am today serving orange juice to a naked Jewish clinic administrator in the East Village.

A million Black men and my Queer self not among them.

He doesn't want to look at me. He looks bored and alert at the same time. He looks around. He's sitting. He holds his ankle.

"Do you live alone?"

Bumpy mottled knees. Clean on the underside of feet. No corns or bunions.

Rolls empty glass between hands. Looks sad, wistful. I think he wants to have sex with me.

I get this gooney grin whenever he catches me looking at him. He darts his eyes away. I wish I could make him into a serial killer. Or sadist.

Caved in chest.

I wish. . . .

He startled me with a quick move to put the glass down.

He's lying down; feeling his cock; eyes closed; kneading his balls, gently stroking the underside of the shaft. It grows. Lotions up. Prefers aloe hand lotion to K.Y.

Sliding hand-over-hand.
Tension in turned out legs.
Hand-over-hand.
Fat cock of medium length reddens. Ball sac tightens. Eyes close.
"Do you care if I do this?"
"No, it's good, keep going."

Do I care?
Tension in his thighs. I can see his belly button now.
Eyes scrunched together.
Short tight strokes, righthanded. Jerk of head. Twitch of full body.
Fast, it's over. Cum had yellowish tinge. No sound hardly at all.

"Do you have something I can wipe off with?"

I'm an ill-prepared host and have to scurry into the bathroom to
find a cleanish towel.
He rests. More relaxed.

"What were you thinking?"
"I wasn't thinking of anything except maybe how good it felt."

Oh.
Looks like he's gonna fall asleep again.
Brown skin around scrotum. Deep navel. Still touching his cock as
it shrinks.
Lonely, he looks lonely.

"I get away on weekends. I have a house in Western Massachusetts.
No, I was born in the Bronx."

His little blue bikinis are on my other chair. Blue jeans. White
socks.
He fingers his balls. He fingers his cock. He rings that ledge around
the head.
I can see him in his office being defensively unpleasant to co-
workers.
Is he going to have another go? I think he's getting off on the
scrutiny. He's "fiddling" with himself.
As he gets dressed:

"Is that it? I thought you'd ask more questions."
"Really? So what haven't I asked that you want to answer?"

Longish pause.

"Well . . . what turns me on?"
"Well, Rickie, what turns you on?"
"Oh, I don't know, being naked with my friend."
"Hmmm."
"Yeah. We're almost a perfect fit. It's almost too perfect. We've been seeing each other twice a week for almost six months. We're from different ethnic backgrounds. He likes to shave me, and to tie me up. He doesn't do anything once he ties me up, but he gets off on just doing it. But you know he doesn't like any of that stuff done back to him. He doesn't like to be touched. We met over the Internet too but we got together in person for the first time at the Marriott. You know, I didn't really think he would show up. But he did and like I said it was perfect. Except for the wife. And the kids. We made an agreement not to know anything about each other but we broke that one almost right away. He called me from work one day and told me to call him that night at his home on Long Island. He invited me out there. His wife was very nice while I was there but he told me she threw a fit once I left. She must know, right? He takes me out to dinner. I've taken him to my place in Western Mass because there aren't any nosy neighbors nearby; but I'd never let him come up to White Plains. He calls me sometimes three times a day from work, and you know it's weird that he finds the time to do it because he's a high school principal."

His teeth are crooked and unevenly spaced.

"Let's see, that was an hour and half. Here you are. Good-bye, Rickie."
$.

SPECIMEN 3

He's shorter than I am.

He sits facing me.
He's wearing gray shorts,
His white T-shirt has a pink square with a green triangle inside over his left breast.

Sips water.
It's a humid gray day.
Looks down at the floor.

Hiking boots.
Clean/white socks.

He's stocky and solid.

Strong jaw.

Puts the glass down.

Leans forward on elbows, hands gently hold themselves.

Fresh haircut.

Looks at my artwork.

Sparse hair on legs.

Driving music on CD player.

Looks around.

Quiet—we're being quiet.

He focuses like an animal.

Leans back on his hands.

Looks out of side of his eyes.

Checks out the books on my shelf.

Actively scopes out the place.

I'll sit next to him to get the face.

He does not look at me.

He's never been to this part of town.

He scratches his back.

Inspects a box of porn videos on the floor.

Tries to look behind me.

Largish thighs.

Ankles crossed.

Head tilted to one side.

Palms spread at either side of him, supporting him on the bed.

It's so quiet between us.
Easy quiet,
Gentle quiet,
Too quiet.

He could beat me up if he wanted to.

Smoothes his hair and gets some loose ones in his hand—he has to brush them away.

Picks up, examines, and puts down blindfold.

I don't know what he just thought.

I think he's trying to see what I write.

He does *not* look bored.

Real active looking around but also takes time to study things, like CDs, books.

Is he casing the joint or just curious?

I want to sit next to him to zoom in closer on his face, but I feel shy.

He tries to see into next room through the French doors.

I should move in closer.

He picks up the back massager from under my bed.

I tell him it's a present from my mother.

He flicks it on/off/on. Changes speeds.

He looks bemused.

He looks like an anthropologist.

He feels the vibrations.

Tries to interpret the situation.

Tries the vibrator on his muscular calves. His back. His upper back.

He asks if it's OK to use it.

I say it's fine.

It's fine.

"Do you work out every day?"

"I used to until two to three weeks ago—after midsemester things got hectic; I don't get to go as much as I want."

He asks if I work out.

"Are you tense a lot?" he asks me. "Is that why your mother gave you this?"

What was that face?

He's enjoying the back massage. Now back to the calves.

I'm assuming he has a short fat cock.

Now on the thigh.

I'm assuming virtually hairless except the usual spots.

Turns off the vibrator.

Am I still in the room?

Seems to be really listening to the Glenn Branca CD.

Sit close.

No holes in ears. Light stubble. Looks like a goatee in the making.

He looks at me writing. Looks away.

I need to calm down.

Good ears.

I should stop mentioning moles. It seems everyone has them. One in the fold of his upper left eyelid.

Light acne scarring at the temple.

Pouty lower lip.

Heavy fold over eyes. Dark brown eyes. Clear.

Square jaw. Set. Looks determined.

Straight nose at too severe of a downward angle.

The fresh haircut shows skin at the side.

He's so calm and I'm all over the place.

Maybe it's the drive of the music.

The newly cut black hair is tousled. Fringe covers his forehead.

What do I want to know from him?

He studies Architecture.

Anyway.

Smile. Talk about Texas. Blah, blah, blah.

Shirt off.

He was so awkward. It was almost as though he'd never done it before. First tugging at the tail. Then crossing his hands at the collar and pulling.

He'd told me of his birthmark in an e-mail.

Mauve nipples. Perfect circles. Chest is large but not "cut," as they say.

The birthmark is under his right tit and is large and messy.

He flexes and looks at his reflection in the blank TV screen.

Is he sucking in his tummy?

He leans back on his hands.

No hair on arms or chest.

Thick neck.

Breasts, while not saggy, not tight to the chest when he leans forward. Pointy. No gut, but not washboard either.

Not pale. Not brown. Is this what is meant by yellow?

A couple of chest zits.

A few stray hairs just below the deep navel peek above the waistband.

Drawstring shorts with "PENN" in red and blue letters on one leg.

Raises arm for me. The way he's doing it he looks like an amputee. The black pit hairs are wiry and a little thicker than I had imagined.

Starts untying boots. Careful about where he puts things. Undoes drawstring. Shorts and jockeys off in one jerk. Socks last. Puts each in its boot.

Dick has a shiny raspberry head. Uncut with foreskin rolled back. A splay of black pubic hair fans up toward his navel. Sits with his short legs spread. Shaft of dick is a lot darker than the rest of him. Massages his left foot.

"BLUR" on CD. "Boys and Girls."

Squarish, blocky feet. Almost no soleprints.

Lies down—hand behind head.

Dark shiny scrotum.

The birthmark is a brown mottle over the right ribcage.

Crosses ankles. Cock leans to his left. One testicle keeps contracting and relaxing.

Dick is stiffening. Pointing upward. He holds it. Examines the peehole. Gropes balls. Fingers its shiny head. He's gentle with it. Thumbs the head in a circular motion over the ledge. Looks down at it. It's pointing directly up at him. I'm getting a little turned on. It's longer and not as thick as I thought it would be. He's rubbing his ankles together. I want to get out of the present tense.

He bends his dick to the side and presses it to his left thigh. Now he's fingering it like a recorder. No hair on the scrotum itself. Begins worrying with a strand of pre-cum. Rubs it between his thumb and forefinger.

Spreads legs. Squeezes balls. Tension in thighs.

He looks at his dick as though he's never seen it before. Pats it as if it were a pet hamster.

I tell him to roll onto his stomach.

Cute butt. Hairless. Zitless. Some black hairs in the crack.

Some stretch marks at the bikini line. Buns lighter than back and legs.

Real barrel upper body.

Don't know if I can touch him. I want to see inside the crack. I don't need to. I can imagine.

The inside of the crack is darker brown . . .

He wiggles his ass. Flex.

Again it's too quiet.

Dents of socks around the ankles.

One dark spot at the top of the crack.

Satiny, hairless back.

He goes to the bathroom.

He's back.

He sits cross-ankled on the bed

"When I wrote, 'What's the most deviant sexual act you'll admit to,' you e-mailed back that you'd masturbated with the American flag. Tell me about masturbating with the American flag."

"Oh my God. I guess it was like third or fourth grade. I, um . . . (giggle). It was definitely a turning point in my history of masturbation.
I first discovered the good feeling in the playground trying to climb the pole of the jungle gym. After several attempts I noticed that it felt really good.
After that I'd pretend to climb that pole every recess.

"Then by complete accident I was left all alone in a classroom and I wanted to take stuff. There were two flags—one California, one U.S. So at that young age I stole state property. I had to hide it at home.

"I noticed the feel of the fabric. I happened to be naked and started to rub myself with it. I was just at the age when I began to be able to shoot fluid."

"I hid it under my mattress. After eight or nine months it started to get stained. There was a hard crust. It was like it wasn't the same material. It felt more like plastic. It had lost its original silkiness. It was like crystal paper. It even changed colors. I threw it out.

"The thing is, my mom's an immigrant and she always told me to revere the American flag; that if you ever let it touch the ground you should then burn it. I remember that I had no concept that what I was doing was wrong. What was funny, I never let that flag touch the carpet in my room."

Chat, chat, chat.

"I've had bondage fantasies since I was a little kid. Ever since I saw

Charlton Heston in *Planet of the Apes,* I wanted to be Charlton Heston being chased by the Apemen."

I try to imagine Mr. Heston as a short little Chinese kid with a cum-stained American flag under his bed.

Chat, chat, chat.

His balls still periodically contract.

"I acted out these fantasies once. I got tied up with a fuck buddy. I went with some guy and got some rope but then he says 'Lick my boots.' And I said 'No way, I'm not going to do that.' "

Chat, chat some more.

"Is it OK that I didn't jerk off?"

"It's fine."

It's fine.

$.

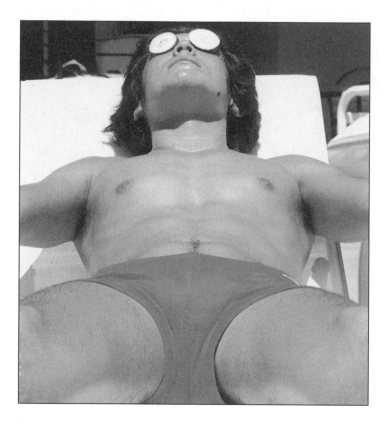

The Everlasting Secret
First Family of Fuck,
An Expose

by

Vaginal Davis

Warning to mothers everywhere! Lock up your stinky feet skateboard-sexy sons! The First Family of Fuck is hootchie for them, and they're a greedy gaggle of fat-titty bitches, whose oozing fuck mounds stirfry trouble.

The First Family of Fuck, also known as The Everlasting Secret Family of Fuck, is a loose knit ring of sex-crazed strumpets who terrorize young, dumb, and full of pimply cum skatefucks with their every hungry double-barrel hatchet pussies.

Their New York City-based leader is Patty Powers—she insists on using her real name. She wants the world to know that her cooze is so drippy and fidgety that she needs it filled at all times, and is hoping this article will bring her more fucktees.

Patty is also known in the filthy underground sex world she inhabits as "Clamps." That's right, this selfish libertine can leap through the air with a single bound and clamp her raw-action pussy (like that in-utero monster in *Aliens*) on any unsuspecting face. She's proud that her cunty juices are acidic, burning sex scars on those she claims as helpless victims of her grifty lust.

Patty may look 22, with her touched-by-an-angel face, petite frame, voluptuous curves, and Jane Wiedlin of the Go-Go's voice, but this blond scrampa actually is a ripe and seasoned 37.

Is she a sexual predator? Eh, maybe. She's definitely a major cock trap.

Patty doesn't spend any fool time analyzing her desires. She has been into skater-thrash dudes since the skateboard was invented, not exclusively mind you, skaters just happen to be her fav flavor treat, she says it's like mixing pesto sauce with splooge.

"What can I say?" she cackles, "I'm cuckoo for caucasian cock.

White skater cock is hot! So I'm not being politically correct, I'm still an equal opportunity hose monster."

Patty started The First Family in Manhattan with a core group of her best girlfriends, who she also bumps bush with from time to time.

She and her friends all dig crunching on younger men. When they started comparing notes and exchanging e-mugs they found out that they shared the same obsession for skaters. Patty readily admits she was the first to tumble down the ramp.

"The Family isn't a cult, we're not that mysterious. Everything we do is out in the open. I'm the worse offender, I can really be shameless when it comes to sex with these schmucks. They taste good. I'll even pay for it."

Which is exactly what she did recently with one kid who was skating with his friends in Tompkins Square Park in New York's bohemian enclave of the East Village.

"I spent a half an hour sizing him up." Patty continues, "I could tell even though he was wearing baggy pants that he had a hefty floppy between his legs. Big-dick arrogance is a total turn on. I marched up to the fledgling, and in front of his skate pack told him I'd give him 20 bucks if he dropped the board and came home with me right now. Back at my apartment he was really excited and couldn't believe his luck. He was trying hard to act cool. It sort of makes you want to giggle out loud, because at his age, they're not good at hiding how they feel. It's a big deal for a kid to have an older woman give him attention like that."

Patty wound up giving him more than attention, bathing him and drenching Kiehl products on his adolescent acne. She wrapped a supersize prophylactic on his peterfication and let him plug away.

"These young bucks are all rigor mortisy even when they're unconscious!" Patty screamed.

Her motto: If you're going to have something in you, it might as well be hard. That's never a worry with her skaters.

"They have switchblades for dicks," Patty whispered breathlessly.

After she properly drained her latest conquest of all possible emissions, she fixed him a sandwich, and sent him on his merry way.

Minka, 35, is a critical care nurse living in the San Gabriel Valley with a gigantic pet hedgehog that bites.

She has pre-Raphaelite skin, natural red hair, is buxom, and still gets carded at bars. She and Patty went to college together in their native Toronto, Canada. Minka was married for nine years and lived with another guy for six. She has always been a relationship person, never into casual sex. One day she e-mailed Patty seeking this cute box boy at Trader Joe's doing board tricks in the parking lot on his break. Patty told her she'd kick her ass if she didn't give him her number and make him fucking skateboard all the way to her house in La Crescenta. Now Minka is juggling several skateboarder lovers.

"When my last long relationship ended I just wanted to have some fun. My job at the hospital is very stressful. I'm like one of those nurses you see on *ER* that yell, "Clear!" and put 200 joules through somebody. I deal in high-trauma situations, I work with cardiac arrests and people on life support," she said.

Minka is the kind of Nurse Betty that takes care of you during and after an emergency. When she first started seeing Damian (the skater bad boy that also got her preggers), he introduced her to the rave party scene. She'd get into these intense party situations with Damian and his crew.

"I'd have a boy beauty on each tit nursing, and another one doing the puppy chow down under my dress," Minka recalled.

Suddenly someone overdoes the partying and Minka winds up giving him mouth-to-mouth when he ODs. It happened to her a week ago for the second time. One boy stopped breathing on her twice while she was sucking his dick on a crowded rave dance floor. She would have killed him if he had died without first giving her a pud facial.

"Damian was laughing saying that the party promoters should be paying me for keeping their customers alive."

Don't tell Minka she's practicing community medicine. She's not having it. "Not to sound selfish or anything," she said, "but when I go out I've got my whole party action on, I'm soaking a very expensive high, I wanna get fucked at least six times by skaters or surfers, and I really hate it when I have to be in that space where I totally have to focus, and take care of somebody. I do that at the hospital. When I've got a killer buzz going, I'm on bone time, and I'm really there to dance and have fun."

"The skating phenomenon is something relatively new in Europe," says internationally acclaimed visual artist and long-time Family member Kitty Duchamp. This progressive Greek active beauty, who was born in Athens, teaches at the Kunstgewerbe-Schule in Zurich and keeps a stable of boy interns whom she mixes up potent coffee and frappucino enemas for. "Not only do my young men ride skateboards but they also snowboard and are generally quite athletic with a healthy desire to sexually experiment with an older, nurturing lover. From my enema and high colonic sessions with my students I am able to mix incredible colors from their feces, urine, smegma, and semen. A wonderful series I created is in the permanent collection at the Whitney. These masterpieces hold special significance for me of course."

Kitty is slightly versatile in that she is also French passive. She mentioned to me that the giddy abandon of the gang bang is merely a harmless rite of passage for young males and is a necessary and natural phenomenon. "I can either feign outrage or pretend to be helpless as these crazed, testosterone-infested boys work me into an ecstatic frenzy," she said. "If things get a little rough, like they start biting at my nipples so hard that they tear them open or if ounces of blood are shed, that's par for the course, and should be expected. The rabid intensity of the sex is worth any discomfort and or long-term pain associated with this form of expression. Sex is war, and the body is its natural battlefield. In Europe we don't equate violent sex play with abuse. We consider it foreplay."

"Those young skaters are so inexperienced that anything you come up with they say, 'OK!' They want to learn, so you can train them and somewhere along the line you're turning them into better lovers." So sayeth Cuntry Camille, the midwest Family member looking a little long in the tooth. Camille has mousy brown hair, is a bit snaggle-toothed, but has a nice hard body and natural double-D cups. She works as a waitress at the Uptown Cafe in Bloomington, Indiana. The small college town was made famous years ago by the movie *Breaking Away.*

"After you fuck them a few times, they start looking real puppy dog and you want to bitch slap them, because it's really not attractive," Camille said.

Whenever she has to work a double shift she takes a sex break and walks down to People's Park in the town square where she has her pick of the humpiest heshen skaters. All the townies make their money selling Cat, which is the local 22-cent equivalent of Crystal

Meth. When she's in the mood she'll let the boys pull a train on her right in the park bushes. When a boy is on Cat he can fuck for hours without coming. It bums them out, but she loves it.

"The kids that are drug addicts try so hard to play it cool, but they are totally beside themselves getting hot free pussy, and the ones that aren't drug addicts are doing handstands in your living room," Patty revealed.

Patty started to get all psychological on me, saying that she likes the skaters that are drug messes.

"If they couldn't care less, and start to act like they're doing you a favor, that's the type that's usually better in bed," she said.

Patty prides herself for being the horndoggiest woman alive. She's beautiful, with large breasts that are real, not store-bought. She is even married to a famous rock star who has never been able to keep up with her sexual appetite. He doesn't even try, he just lets her do as she pleases knowing that sometimes he'll get to join in. He's really pussywhipped and corn knobbed. Last summer Patty accompanied him on tour in Europe, where he played big outdoor festivals. After one gig they picked up two young groupie girls and had a hot buttered fourgy. Patty art directed. She said it was fun, with lots of pert pussy grazing, and playing jump rope with squiggly vulvas, but it wasn't nasty enough to get Patty off, so she had the girls round up their boyfriends who were German skate Nazis with cruel club endowments. She choreographed herself and her husband getting deep tissue melts by the Krauts. The scene ended with the girls urinating all over everything and everybody and making quite a mess. Patty made the German hooligans clean it up with their tongues.

Patty works as a stripper, not because she needs the money, but because she's a writer and it gives her plenty of fodder. She's also a low-maintenance nymphomaniac. "I could probably get $100 for lap dances every night from the skaters that come to the club in New Jersey where I work, but I'd feel weird if I took money from boys I'd rather fuck later."

Patty is a pioneer in the field of bagging skater rats; none of her girlfriends had gone this route before her not-so-subtle indoctrination. She had a lot of disasters in the early days, because her heart would be broken or she'd hang on some word or phrase like there was a deeper connection than sex. She hadn't figured out that these kids were just acting their age. Now she knows them and their age group so in-side-out, she knows what to expect and she's always dead on. It makes the other girls in The Family crack up.

Patty let me in on a secret. "A guy can be as dumb as a brick, but if he fucks good, a girl will fall madly in love with him." She says she has statistics and graphs to back up all of her unorthodox theories.

Camille used to live in Orange County. That's where she first met Patty. They were both wild punk rock gals working the nudie bar circuit. She realized they were gnarly kindred spirits when Patty started talking about how she had itchy knuckles and loved fisting her boyfriends.

Until meeting Patty, Camille didn't know too many women who like to fist and get fisted. Of course she and Patty had sex—*a lot*. Patty even shrimp-fisted* Camille's twittering pussy making her pass out four times.

After a series of sordid relationships and substance abuse problems Camille moved back home to Indiana. When she first arrived she'd hang at the one disco in town in Bullwinkle's or go to shows at the rock club above it, Second Story. That's where she'd meet a lot of randy frat boys and wound up giving them as she calls it, "high skank sessions." She got bored doing fraternity brothers; they were too vanilla extract. One day she was trolling the student union and met her first skater boy who was also in a local band called The Erections.

"With young boys they never have problems getting it up, even if they're drunk. A guy in his thirties who is tired, his dick gets all spongy and he'll lose it halfway through. But with skaters, the first fuck, they come real quick then they're hard again in as long as it takes to smoke a cigarette. That's when they titty fuck you, and leave you a reservoir-sized pearl necklace. Then you can get four or five more fucks from them in several different styles and positions. Why do doggie style when you can have I Pomeranian or Papusa, and who needs the missionary position when you can get righteous in Grunion position—yahoo!" Camille screeched.

"I'm a Gemini," says Minka, "and we like to live a double life."

I'm here with her and two of her skater beaus, Baby Daddy Chips

*Editors Note (for the uninitiated shrimp fisting is sticking one's whole foot up a cunt or butthole)

and Suffer, at this awful rave party in the high desert called Release. The music is too loud for me, and everyone is dancing with these silly colored light sticks, like fan dancing at discos in the 70s. I want to leave, but I'm stuck because I made the mistake of riding with them.

"It's like having a split personality!" shrieks Minka, who is wearing a macrame halter top and see-through micro-mini. Her look is called "from coon to can't." "I was at work for twelve hours taking care of people who are dying, I came home, changed clothes and we'll be here raving for fourteen hours. I'm all hardcore."

Baby Daddy Chips moved to LA from Florida, where he was part of the rave scene in Gainesville and Jacksonville. He met Minka at the Dunes in the Desert party. He's 18, still in high school, about six feet tall, and is Dominican, German, and French. He's attractive in a sort of dopey boy stoner way. When Minka first met him he wanted to come back to her house, but he had a friend with him and couldn't sleep over because his mom needed her car back. When they first started to fuck she made it clear to him that just because he can fuck her with no strings or grief doesn't mean he's allowed to treat her like a doormat. Her makeshift ground rules are: 1. Sex is replaceable, if you don't show the expected excitement (like wanting to spend some time with her as a pet/friend since romance is too ridiculous) you are easily replaced. 2. If you want to drop by, fuck, and leave, it has to be done before 4:00 A.M. 3. Calls after 4:00 A.M. must be sleepovers with plenty of time the next day for sex. 4. No bringing friends along to sleep on the couch *unless* said friend is cute, and all parties are going to have sex. Bottom line: These kids don't behave badly out of rudeness or lack of respect. They just don't know any better and have to be taught.

"As an art project I orchestrated a live sex show with me and my students," brags Kitty.

"To participate the boys needed my vaginal prerequisite," she laughs. "I called Patty to tell her about it, and she said I'd better have the show videotaped and transferred to NTSC so that she can masturbate to it."

Kitty borrowed special lighting from the school's film department. It was quite a production and culminated with a coed circle jerk and everyone drinking each other's piss in these giant faux platinum goblets. One black American exchange student who had recently given birth started lactating, and got the bright idea to mix her breast milk with the urine and Nestle's Quik—the chocolate not the strawberry.

"Some people are just not organically interested in sex. With them penetration or a blow job is more than enough. They will never eat pussy, and come up with lame excuses why. Skater boys will do anything. When I'm sitting on their sweet faces they are like labrador retrievers. They have the energy, but not the focus," Patty reflects. "I guess that comes with age."

Patty has sex with a lot of different kinds of skater boys. Some are hustlers and others are FITs (Fags-In-Training). "Fags always want to fuck me, god knows why." She shrugs. "I guess because I'm a femme top. Those of us who came of age when punk rock formed, you had to make a choice to be gay or straight. I've been sleeping with girls since I've been having sex, yet lesbians wouldn't take me seriously, I would have to hear that I'm on the fence blah blah, and I'm sure it was the same for guys. But now with these skate kids, they listen to industrial music, disco, punk, it's all mixed together now, and everyone is openly bi. They are not forced to take a side."

"When I used to be a stripper," said Camille, "I slept with a lot of girls I worked with. My generation broke all the barriers and opened it up for these kids. When I visited Patty in New York she took me to this big club with all these cute 18-year-old boys. So much eye candy. They had a gay and straight entrance and all the Guidos were holding hands so they could have access to all the cool parts of the club. And I met two redheaded twins who are big dick thickerous and I went home with them. They take turns fucking my pussy to death with brutal accuracy for hours, then getting bashful when I tell them I want to watch them do each other. I accidentally-on-purpose shove my fist up one. Semen is flying everywhere, both twins are still hard and keep finding new holes to fuck me in, and just when the ultra seriousness of the brother-to-brother shit hits the fan, we start busting up laughing, and it's morning. They have to go to school so I meet their parents (who are my age) at the breakfast table, and I'm getting moist again wondering if their hot dad has a dick as succulent as his sons'."

"You have to come home and fuck me," Patty said to this skater at

Curfew, the big rave club in downtown Manhattan. He couldn't say no because she caught him by surprise. Patty's famous DJ friends had procured a bevy of young and very good-looking boys for her pleasure, but for whatever reason she wasn't into any of them.

"I'm not one of those l'il girls in the pop tops with no hips," Patty says pointing a finger. "I'm working a mighty voluptuous woman thing. I strip at this club in Jersey and it's one-stop shopping for me there. Suburban boys are so cute and people don't believe me when I tell them that. Hard, tight bodies and a willingness to please. What more could you want?"

Patty's all-time favorite type of skater boys are the ones who have melon-shaped bubble butts you can set a champagne glass on. Patty loves to rim. She goes crazy feasting on little nappy dugouts (as it's referred to on the East Coast). "One night this kid named Nelson brought up anal sex, and I ask him, 'Me or you?'" she says. He goes, 'Whatever.' So I finger him, and he sits on my face as I scarf a pink loaf."

Patty grabs some lube and covers her hand in it and sticks it up his hole. "Not bad for a straight boy," she said to him. She then shoved both hands in him until it made a whooshing sound. Patty creamed right on the spot. Then she whips out a Gidra (triple-headed black dildo) and starts fucking him with all three heads. He gets into it, and asks for something bigger. With a John Wayne Gacy grin she showcases this dildo that is so big that she can sit it on the floor and fuck it, which she does as a warmup. Then she fucks Nelson for 45 minutes and he's quietly hunching, letting her do whatever she wants, and not complaining. His penis is unlike any other. It's big and has a weird velvet-smooth texture like a camel's nose. Finally he goes, "Ow!" and Patty says, "Stop because I'm hurting you, or because you've had enough?" And he says, "A bit of both."

Patty figures that if she was a real guy she would have come so long ago, that this scene must be a *Last Exit to Brooklyn*–style gang bang and that she is number seven in line. Then he says something that was like icing on the cake: "Imagine you were in jail and someone with a cock that big wanted to fuck you all the time, wouldn't that be awful?"

Patty is crazy for this boy, even though he's catatonic. She rolls her eyes and says to him, "Yeah motherfucker, it would be so awful you'd never let anyone with a small cock near you again."

I asked Patty if Nelson was a sloppy bottom, prone to mudslides, and she said that he was meticulously clean. "At that age all they do is eat and shit." He's not much fun to have around when you're not fucking him, though, she said, adding that he's now in some lock-down, court-ordered rehab.

Patty fucked another boy who was a little dirty on the inside and she asked him if he'd like a daiquiri enema. Patty is the queen of exotic enemas. And he says, "Why don't I just go to the bathroom?" And she looked at him and said, "You can do that on cue?" and he goes, "Yeah, can't you?" And frowning she says, "No, that stops after thirty. I'm lucky if I have a bowel movement every day." Then she pissed on him because she was not sure if he was being a smart-ass.

"Not every young boy will let me plow him, but skaters are more into it than anyone else," Patty testified with religious fervor in her voice.

"I spent all of last year sowing my wild oats with teenage skater boys," sighed Minka. "Now I'm taking a hiatus from it. I'm casually dating a guy who is a little older at twenty-two. He designs web pages for Disney and is working on his Ph.D. in philosophy. He's set the new standard for any man who wants to see me on a more serious level, and he enjoys drinking my urine."

Minka may feel like she has slowed down a bit, but as of last week she went to a party called BurnAss and picked up two 19-year-old tweekers. They took turns jackhammering her twatkin. The tweek with the overzealous thrombone wound up scraping the walls of her uterus. After fixing some mushroom tea, Minka DP-ed, leaving them gagging on the lovely extravaganza of it all. "One of the boys with a pecan stubbied dick, had a bigger chest than me," she exclaimed. "He sure got a kick out of me calling him a dirty faggot bitch with Lee's Press On Tits. They sure took their sweet time in drinking the remainder of my piss, and my ego couldn't take that so I made them go home. The next day I felt funny and discovered that one of them had ripped the lining of my rectum and inflamed my hemorrhoids!"

Minka started having sex again with her original skater boy Damian, though she swore not to after he got her pregnant for the second time. "Damien's semen really tastes good," she admitted. "I guess I'm nothing but a pathetic dick pig. He churned that nasty cob down my throat so fiercely, I was coughing up blood. But I got my revenge when I raped his crater-faced ass with a garlic press as our fat neighbor watched through an open window beating off. Thank god I used my leather sheets, I easily wiped off the mess from Damien's two bloody stools with some Armorol."

"I can really turn boys out in a way nobody can," Patty proclaims. Even if they're lame in bed like Louis, a professional skater and surfer with Quicksilver. He's twenty with a perfect face and body. He's a premature ejaculator, but is so serene that I know after being with me he feels a little robbed. I don't care, I like his energy and he smells all shiny and new, his skin is like butter, his breath is always fresh and he has this delightful body odor and dewy jiss that brings back memories of the first blow jobs I gave in the fifth grade. I don't want to get all smarmy and sentimental but I just realized that I'm twenty years older than these guys I have sex with, and it's weird because I've lived more of a life than these kids ever live.

"Before I was in middle school I was hanging out at drag clubs taking tons of drugs and staying out all night, and then I quit school altogether, went to Amsterdam and London, became a prostitute doing the Shah of Iran, then I got hooked up with The Clash when they made *London Calling,* went to the States, started hanging out with Johnny Thunders. Moved back to Canada with this huge heroin problem. Got my shit together and finished school, and married a rock star. I lived through all this. So as doey-eyed as these kids get over me I know it's not going to be lasting because there just isn't anything to build from, but when I get one that can fuck me from behind and slaps my ass just the way I like and he climbs on me and gets epileptic when he's cumming and I'm covered in so much of it that I can't move from the bed, I know that as the czarina of the First Family of Fuck I've done a good job."

Picturing Porn: A Photographic Deconstruction

by

Carlo McCormick

Regarding Dirty Pictures

Foregoing any ruling here on that endless legal morass as to what constitutes obscenity, and conceding that any sort of aesthetic criteria one may bring to this is highly subjective and suspect perspective, let us just assume that there is such a thing as dirty pictures. Just consider how certain images can excite a kind of arousal that others can't. When my as-yet-unweaned baby boy comes across one of our "art books" he takes great joy in looking at all those breasts, so big they must seem like overflowing cornucopias of milk. Now whether we decide to keep the books around or eventually hide them, we can be certain that at a certain point in his development he may indeed look at those same pictures in a very different way. That's all we mean here, it's just that innocent.

That said, a picture (dirty or not) is subject to certain very useful tools in terms of describing it. Visual pleasure, be it abstract, spiritual, intellectual, or carnal, is a particularly individual response. The multivarious constituents of what goes into a picture to induce such a response are perhaps a little more certain. Trying to figure out how these different components might be defined and thought out when it comes to photographs of a more prurient nature, we asked five very different photographers to talk to us about a very specific element in their work. Because there are few readers equally familiar with art and flesh magazines, I must assert that all five artists here, regardless of their creative venues, are exceptional craftsmen, erotic visionaries, and each at a level of career and critical success that adds considerable credence to their thoughts on this matter. These are artists whose work is much more complex than the simplistic terms we have asked them to address. Perhaps the selection of photographers and subjects here is directed by what we find most interesting in their work, or what it is that it would be most interesting here to have them explain. Then again, maybe it's simply a way for us to construct our own dirty picture out of the best component visual strategies of five singularly outstanding contemporary photographers.

Jack Pierson on the Frame

Coming to international attention in the 80s as one of a circle of photographers (including Nan Goldin and Mark Morrisroe) loosely called the Boston School, Jack Pierson has continued to show his work in some of the world's most prestigious galleries and museums. Beyond his acclaim as among the more prominent of photographers to be embraced by the art world, Pierson has also delved into those practices that are demeaningly considered commercial photography. Having just collected these more anonymous and ephemeral photographs in a limited edition art book he titled *Pictures We Take For Money*, it would seem that Jack Pierson has a better understanding of the ironically fine line separating our comprehension and judgment of photography according to context. Unmistakably a work of art, on par with any project he's done for the fine art establishment, Pierson's *Pictures* is an unashamed exposure of the kind of ventures similarly successful photographers undertake to keep a working studio going. Without credit of any sort for models, clothing, editorial content, or commissioning publication, Pierson seamlessly assembles fashion photographs, celebrity portraits (from Courtney Love to Brad Pitt), and pictures for the skin trade where he's published in the likes of *Beefcake* and *Honcho*.

The frame, as we put it to Pierson then, is not so much the assembly of wood, matting, and glass that we put around some pictures while others are less carefully taped inside our lockers: The frame is context. Finding a common ground among fashion, celebrity, porn, and art photos to "excite and inspire," Pierson maintains a definition of porn as an illicit medium that "gets disposed of or hidden." Acknowledging a certain "timing" in having lived in the East Village in the early 80s when "every day the streets were being flooded with porn, with old-time vintage collections alongside the equally fascinating private amateur Polaroids," Pierson maintains that photography, by being printed and distributed is given authority—that a book and a magazine each constitute a different kind of weight.

Untitled, 1989

Yet within Pierson's democratic sense of equivalence there is a darker irony in that these pictures we pay for never really made him much, especially compared to his art. "I'm not good at it," he explains. "I'm ultimately too melancholy, too unexplainably sad. You may want to see a young-boy-I-could-have, but mine make you feel 'I wish I were young again, and can never be.' Instead of hero worshiping, you get that creepy feeling of something being done to them, coerced or violated, so that's what you have to whack off to."

The context of art versus commerce, he reminds us, is only a frame, but it is art that has always functioned to open the door for us to consider things in new ways. Just as one generation of artists like Koons and Halley made "New York's punk rock wild avant-garde, that sublimity of kitsch, a ready made," Pierson reminds us, "people have been looking at porn forever, and art will also change the way they do that."

Richard Kerrn on the Models

A leading figure in New York's underground Cinema of Transgression, Richard Kern became so inspired by the lesser-known pinup photographs of director Russ Meyer, that by the late 80s he abandoned super-8 film for still photography. Since then, he has enjoyed a growing reputation in the art world, regularly exhibiting his photos in galleries across America, Europe, and Japan, and publishing a number of well received photo monographs including *New York Girls* and *Model Release*. From his roots, where the models he worked with once came directly out of an underground scene he shared with them, he has now moved into a more professional relationship with the subjects he shoots for magazines like *Honcho, Barely Legal, Leg Show, Leg World,* and *Tight,* and the right chemistry and spirit to make his art has become increasingly elusive. As Kern's work has focused so much on the everyday personalities and idiosyncrasies of his subjects, his insights into the dynamic between photographer and model are particularly relevant. At the heart of this lies a degree of respect, or, conversely, the inability to work with models who are "dumb, doing it for the wrong reasons, or sleazy." Admitting that he will ultimately "like the photo more if I like the model," Kern offers a more formal clue to this chemistry: "If you don't see their faces, it usually means I didn't like their personality." On a more practical note, Kern offers the same advice for porn as with art photography: keep it business-like. "As soon as you cross that line, as many do, it muddies the waters." He adds, "It has to be extremely clear what you're doing, why, and how much you're getting paid."

If there is a visual and psychological anatomy to beauty, the very personal plays an important role. "Everyone has their type," he

Opposite page: Lucy with Scissors, 1996

explains, "and all I've learned is that whomever you photograph, no matter how beautiful they may appear, everyone has imperfections." It would seem that much of our sense of a model's real beauty is as dependent on these imperfections as any consensus ideal. As for the dynamic of a photo shoot, Kern offers a basic observation: "One thing people are missing when they look at photographs is the smell. Under all the lights of a shoot, with a bunch of naked people, there's all kinds of smells." On a perhaps less mundane note, Kern describes his process as "action painting—you start with a basic idea of what you want to do, put your subjects in that general area, let them move around, and shoot until you end up somewhere you like." Pose is a prerequisite of the medium, so essential and specific that when Kern runs down a list of standard poses needed— "bending over forward, ass in the air, feet spread, looking back at you, tight close-up of stretched pussy and butthole with rest of body out of focus . . ."—it's like a guidebook of carnal choreography.

Eric Kroll on the Wardrobe

Starting his career in the early 70s as a photojournalist, it wasn't until much later, when a particular vision of beauty triggered his earliest sexual experiences of the sensuality of women's clothing, that Erik Kroll's work took the leap from documentation to fantasy that marks him as an artist today. Since then, Kroll has established himself as among the great contemporary masters of classic fetish photography, with books like *Fetish Girls, Beauty Parade,* and *The Transformations of Gwen.* Having also edited major historical books on some of the greatest forefathers of fetish art like Elmer Batters, Eric Stanton, John Willie, and Bill Ward, Kroll is something of a walking encyclopedia on the subject. As the entire topography of the human form, as well as just about any accessory, pose, garment, circumstance, and body modification imaginable, has become the subject of elaborate fetish-fantasy worlds, Kroll could probably explain the specific frisson of anything from medical braces on crippled accident victims to the punishment shave. However, as with all such obsessions, Kroll's object of desire is exceptionally specific. "I won't take a picture of a nude woman," he explains, "but I remain completely enamored of adorning the body."

Lovingly describing an image of extreme heels, leather eye binder

Eric Kroll

and any number of items from his extensive vintage girdle and bra collection, Kroll's pictures are for him the equivalent of "a visual hardon." He can articulate the particular visual and tactile differences between leather, latex (rubber), PVC, and something like colored Saran wrap, but hasn't the slightest interest in something as popular as bondage ropes. But of course what they wear, be it the mummifactions of plastic wrap or the constraints of undergarments, offers its own architecture of containment. "I lost my virginity to a girl in a girdle, high heels, hosiery, and a beehive hairdo," Kroll recalls, "and I'm still responding to that now." With his mother a shoe model and his father's business the popular 50s textile and upholstery company, Boris Kroll Fabric, Eric's fascination is for a kind of sexualized fashion. Inspired by the early work of photographers like Irving Klaw and John Willie, Kroll is seeking a pure iconography of design—from the Bullet Bras of the early 60s through boots ("it's the lacing"), spike heels ("the thinner the better"), and stockings ("not pantyhose, that's another fetish"). And as much as what women wear has always been a cultural signifier for each era's concept of the ideal feminine form, Kroll's photography remains conscious of the body manipulation inherent in such costume. Inasmuch as he can assert that "high heels define the legs," he can reveal through pictures the erotic alchemy of corsets and girdles, as a combination of textures and reformations, from the satin around the crotch to the redefined waist and accentuated figure-eight body as archetypes of "extreme femininity."

Jeff Burton on the Landscape

Jeff Burton began as a painting student while at art school in Texas, but it wasn't until he moved to southern California that he found his professional and artistic medium in photography. Employed for many years as a still photographer for the Hollywood porn industry, Burton's work in galleries, recently collected in his book, *Dreamland,* stems not only from the pictures he takes while working at porn movie sets, but most significantly, from the stilted sun-bleached, chlorinated, breast-augmented and smog congested artificial paradise of Hollywood itself. Jeff Burton may shoot smut in the lowest grade-B video sense of the term, but his art offers a transcendental understanding of place—a conjecture of flesh and plastic, sex and alienation, dreams and the darkness that not even a perpetual sunshine can illuminate—that is the nomadic arc of sexploitation film sets lying between the Hollywood Hills and Sunset Strip. Full of humor, fun, disarray, and uncertainty, Burton's pictures are an exotica of the mundane, an erotica of space as much as body. Finding that the lower economic stakes of the porn industry offer "a lot more room for chance," Burton maintains, "I thrive on all those situational variables that are much more interesting." But at heart, for Burton it is more "than just the Surrealist notions of photography, it's the documentation of an installation. It's thinking of Los Angeles as a found object, because LA is even more of a found object than the movie sets."

Seeing Hollywood itself as "a visually powerful set of constructions" that he can "eroticize," Burton's pictures, filled with porn stars in idle repose, getting hard and fluffed for the next shot or engaged in visually absurdist play, turn the whole faux world of signifiers and superficiality on its end in multiple and fragmented shards of dissociative and psychologically recontextualized visual anecdote. Describing the land by its "signage, and fleeting, fractured images that offer less obvious connections," Burton's fantasy dream factory of carnal impostures "tells a different kind of story that's hopefully more open and loose." Working at this same material as a low-end hack-paid gig, Burton's interest with his art is more personal poetics than documentary reportage. His erotic "peripheral visuals" as well as his love for "the mythic and physical landscape of LA [as] amazing tableaus," is the art here, or what Jeff Burton describes as "different ways of looking at this stuff."

Charles Gatewood on the Lifestyle

In a long and forbidden journey from the emerging sexual underground of the mid 60s to its contemporary flowering in myriad forms of sexual ritual and spiritualism, Charles Gatewood has lensed the most viscerally disturbing physical extremes and sublime emotional ecstasies of modern sexpressionism in a body of work whose historical depth and intimate knowledge is quite unmatched. Whether we may choose to call it an industry or an art, a perversion or an enlightenment, a crime against—or a collaboration with— nature, for many different communities largely hidden within our population, sexual exploration is more than just a job or a pastime, it is a lifestyle: a religion. Whether he's describing what he did just that morning, or recalling the phenomenon that was the opening of New York's legendary Hellfire Club, Gatewood is more than a passive observer, he is someone truly living the life. With roots that go deep into the germinal underbelly of the 60s free love movement, where Gatewood along with porn star/performance artists Annie

Katie, from Charles Gatewood Photographs: The Body and Beyond

Sprinkle and Veronica Vera, tattoo artist Spider Webb, and writers Marco Vassi and Michael Perkins (author of *Deep Throat*) formed the nexus of R. Mutt Press, this man has witnessed and photographed acts that defy the imagination. At that inexplicable point in the zeitgeist where voyeurism is the defining frame of all activity, Gatewood's camera has been one of the most enduring and astute participants in the lifestyle of sexual adventure.

Author of the 1975 classic *Sidetripping*, with text by William Burroughs, and the deeply influential *Modern Primitives*, Gatewood understands the diversity and unity in what he calls "the radical sex community." Trained as an anthropologist, and out "in the trenches of S&M, B&D, Vampire Goth, Blood Sports, and the whole body arts community of tattoos, branding, scarification, and piercing," Gatewood's documentary intent is coupled with "the intoxication of the experience, the aesthetic and sexual high" itself. The boundaries of ritual and play that Gatewood and his subjects explore is both a total raison d'être and a path (say, the left-hand road) to ecstatic enlightenment. "I go into trance states, drawing on the creative energies of my subjects in an intuitive, visceral way," Gatewood explains. "It's through a deep interaction with the model that transcendental images occur in a magical process." That itself involves something more than the intensity of the artist. What Charles Gatewood is photographing is not well-composed art tableaus or outré commercial pictures; rather, he is capturing the Wiccan spirituality, pre-Christian ritual, and pagan sex that has reared its primal godhead in this disembodied age, like some atavistic legacy from the deepest, darkest well of our collective conscience.

Joanne pierces Anabel, from

Once Upon a Time

by

Linda M

Montano

Time was running out. Brian returned not only to his upstate, hometown, village life and prelude to retirement but to the religion of his youth, Roman Catholicism. Age, lost innocence, near fatalities, health crises, poor judgment and harsh wake-up calls had forced a surrender that only his art had known until then. In obedience he traveled back, not ahead, on his own trail, but back to the sights, smells, rituals, and sacraments; back to a physical posturing, an early, learned stance and awe-filled reticence that helped him survive his first 17 years in that town of watching and loose-tongued gossip over the clothesline. Remember, it was the 50s.

> *BHAJI*
> 1 cabbage sliced thin
> 3 large potatoes cut small
> 1 jalapeno, take seeds out if you want mild
> 1 tablespoon mustard seed
> 1/4 teaspoon turmeric
> 1 tablespoon coriander powder
> lemon juice to taste

Heat ghee. When hot, add mustard, chili, turmeric. When mustard pops add potatoes. Stir, cook 8 minutes. Medium heat. Add cabbage. Cook both until tender. Add coriander, lemon to taste. Eat with yogurt.

Scrutiny by others was a small price to pay for *The Return* because in going back he contacted a physical kinesthesia, an uncontrollable bodily response to mystery and presence which was swoonlike, ecstasylike, liminallike; back to a spontaneous desire to not move, rather *be* moved from within. Brian's first "experience" when 10 resulted in what seemed to be a fainting from hunger or overheating. It happened simultaneously with the Consecration of the Wine at Mass but after that one time, he hid the feeling deep inside, modeling the Zen-quiet equanimity of the nuns who closely watched their flock, mentoring stillness both in church and the classroom.

BASMATI RICE
1 1/2 cups basmati rice
2 tablespoons ghee
2 inch cinnamon stick
2 cloves
2 green cardamom crushed

Wash rice in cold water until clear. Cover with water and soak 30 minutes. Heat ghee, add rice, stir on medium, one minute. Add water, spices, and boil. Cover, put on low with lid and simmer about 20 minutes. When done, let stand 5 miutes. Eat with yogurt.

Once back in the same village, Brian's hypothalamus, reptilian brain, inner child, and drama-trained skills re-emerged and he attempted to construct himself as he had once been. Given the task of incorporating tremendous surges of energy into cells habituated to his own proclivities, he found the tug of war fascinating. With scientific observation he noted how he coped those first 15 years; voices then were punitive, repeating mantralike, "Hold it in," "Deny," "Don't show off," "Don't tell," and when the ecstatic force of Visitation washed over his soul-hunger at Mass or during prayer in public he heard, "Tighten up so the kids kneeling next to you don't have a clue what's happening. Only saints faint with love."

CHANNA KARI
2 cans chickpeas
1 tablespoon curry powder
1/4 teaspoon cumin
1 onion
ginger
garlic
2 cloves

Fry onions, garlic and all spices in oil. Add drained chickpeas. Lemon juice to taste. Sprinkle 1/4 cup fresh coriander on top.

For 40 years he had been away in lands and mental states of permission and creativity and free intimacy and desire. As a result he was terribly spoiled. Inclusion of *everything* as permissible had provided him with a playground for his secularized metaphysical flights. Orchestrating things so well, he actually made a living from doing what he wanted—at least that's what it seemed; days were an unending banquet, an art cruise, an uninterrupted ride into alpha and on the way back, he rearranged the muse's messages, sharing the wealth.

CASHEW RICE WITH PEAS
1 cup leftover basmati rice
1/2 cup roasted cashew pieces
1/2 cup frozen peas thawed in hot water
2 tablespoons ghee
pinch of hing, turmeric

In pan put spices and cashews. Stir. Add rice. Stir and heat. Garnish with coriander.

That was then. Encased in shame, the Prodigal Son crashed, came home to the same bed, same house, same kitchen table but this time something was different. Glued to the TV, he watched reruns of animal programs on the Discovery Channel and was heart-softened by one about wild ponies trained to be used differently. Actually, it made him cry—the ropes, the hoofs in the air, the handlers talking the wildness out until a saddle and bridle and bit, then rider won over the animal's will. Horse eyes went from flaming red to sweet surrender. Brian identified and Grace was the rider.

CHAPATI
1 cup flour
1 tablespoon oil
water

Combine all ingredients. Knead and form a ball. Place in bowl, 30 minutes. Knead again and form about 7 small balls. Roll into a 5-inch circle. Use flour if too sticky. Heat in nonstick pan until it bubbles and turn cooking the other side until it puffs.

Co-trainers there were many; critiques by blood family, his own uncontested memories and an amazingly wise and semi-cloistered monk who became his spiritual director. Father Gerald had been in India 35 years and his international experience had karmically prepared him to understand Brian's soul which was conversant with and practiced in eastern theologies. So when Brian said Kundalini, Father Gerald translated it as Gifts of the Spirit; Brian said Vedanta, Father Gerald said Transubstantiation; Brian said Nirvikalpa Samadhi, Father said Centering Prayer; Brian said Tantra, Father Gerald said Reconciliation; Brian said Makyo, Father said neurotic hallucinations. And on and on, spiritually echoing each other. It was much like a religious Berlitz course, a recipe for return and re-theologizing of Brian's ride back to Presence.

KEER
7 cups milk
1 cup rice
1/2 teaspoon cardamom powder
1 bay leaf
sugar to taste
raisins/sliced almonds optional

Combine rice, milk, bay leaf. Cook to boil, stirring constantly. When thick remove bay leaf. Add cardamom, sugar, raisins, almonds.
A year into his return home, it began again:
He was tossed to the floor—just like before.
The walls whispered messages—just like before.
He floated to the ceiling and beyond—just like before.
He fainted when the Host was raised at Mass—just like before.
To compensate he did three things:
    1. He asked, am I dreaming? Having a bioelectrical/neurological misfiring?
    2. He overate, became heavier and used the logic that said more pounds, less levitation.
    3. He met with Father Gerald and they talked for hours about the difference between demonic oppression and demonic possession. Once the difference was understood, Brian was encouraged to repeat Hail Marys, or the Memorare, or command the disturbance to leave in the name of the Blood of Jesus! Possession needed exorcism, oppression needed prayer. Father counseled further: "Learn to

pray, Brian, that is your greatest weapon and don't get attached to any of this. I want to read you something written by St. John of the Cross."

The pure, cautious, simple and humble soul should resist and reject revelation and other visions with as much effort and care as it would extremely dangerous temptations, for in order to reach the UNION OF LOVE there is no need of desiring them, but rather of rejecting them. Solomon meant this when he exclaimed: "What need has a man to desire and seek what is above his natural capacity?" This means that to be perfect there is no need to desire or receive goods in a way that is supernatural and beyond one's capability. THE ASCENT

CHAI
7 cups water
7 cups milk
1 cinnamon stick
3 cloves
ginger, cut or whole
6 green cardamom, crushed
few black peppercorns
sugar to taste
12–14 full teaspoons black tea or tea bags

Heat milk, spices and water to boil. Let sit 5 minutes. Add tea. Boil again on low for 5 minutes. If in a hurry, boil and stir for 5 minutes, strain, and serve.

Years of fearless body art was good training because now his 630 muscles relaxed when attacked; the 400 trillion cells of his body exuded light when bothered; his cerebrum, cerebellum, cerebral cortex, and hypothalamus were no longer overpowered by chaos. Humbled by all the newness and the simplicity of obedience, he let go of his tensions, forgot about his tortured conscience, and gave up his old appetite for the extraordinary. Life quieted itself.

And then, while in prayer one chilly March dawn, he surrendered, submitted, obeyed, received, and merged when a feather-winged lightforce wrapped him in a warmth beyond touch, piercing his side, his hands, his feet, with an invisible knife-tipped arrow.

This is not, THE END

MEDICINAL KICHEREE
1 cup rice
1 cup mung beans
4 cups water
Boil all together. Cover and simmer for 30 minutes until finished.

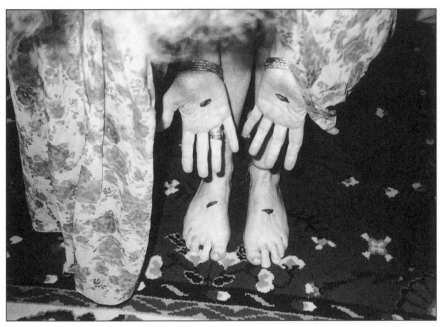

Hands and Feet Stigmata

A Month of Sundays

by

Tessa

Hughes-Freeland

After spending a number of years working in clubs, I unexpectedly found myself without a job. One night, while I was bartending, an apparently drunken woman staggered behind the bar, pulled out a badge, and told me to stop serving drinks. It was the beginning of the end. The following rigamarole, involving endless red tape and the lack of a certificate of occupancy to boot, meant that my favorite funky and decrepitly raw basement club on Eighth between B and C closed and I was out of a job. My lifestyle being what it was, my severance pay lasted a hot minute. After working a few temporary bartending gigs here and there, which all proved to be nonstarters, I found myself in a familiar spot; lying on my bed wondering how to get some steady cash. No sooner had my roommate come back with news of a job, than I was on the phone. A few days later I found myself answering five of them.

Crammed into a small windowless room in a midtown apartment, my days of training were trying and rigorous. It was brothel boot camp. I was screamed at and abused: told I was useless, an idiot, and never going to be able to do the job. I was told to code numbers and without warning was ordered to tear up a sheet of yellow lined paper into small pieces and to eat it as quickly as possible. What I couldn't consume I was instructed to burn. One of these days I was talking to a girl poured into a mint green dress. As she pulled her straps off her shoulders, she introduced herself to me. "They're real, don't you want to see them?" she asked, continuing to pull her dress down to expose her enormous breasts. She squeezed them together between her arms showing them off to me. "They're my twins," she added. She called herself Camille and looked like Snow White. That is if Snow White let her hair down, pumped up her mammary glands, and wore a skintight mini-dress. She was young and funny. She loved Marilyn Monroe and Madonna and, wanting to be an icon of beauty herself, was at this point dedicated to fixing up her smile. After knowing me a while, she told me that she and her boyfriend were into threesomes. She proudly presented me with a Polaroid close-up shot of his isolated dick, then asked me if I was interested. "How would you explain our knowing each other to him?" I inquired, amused. "Oh, I'd tell him that we met at the health club," she replied. It would have been better had she shown me more of him than his dick, then I might have recognized him on the day he came looking for her, through his thin disguise of an eye patch.

Now this was a job my friend had described as being easy. "You just sit around and read the Sunday *Times*," she had said. I later learned, after the paper had been read, along with everything and anything else that required only minimal concentration—all that could be afforded between fleeting glances at surveillance monitors and talking to men on the phone—that this was a job which fluctuated between unrelenting, unendurable boredom, edgy expectant paranoia, and busy rushes of adrenaline-charged energy. I ended up on the Sunday shift, presumably replacing my friend.

I switched on the surveillance camera monitors, plugged in the phones, and rubbed the handpieces with a soapy sponge. I hoped that none of them would ring before I'd had a chance to wipe them dry. The feeling of a wet ear full of amplified bubbles popping mingling with the familiar tones of a horny morning caller sounding through was not one I looked forward to at ten in the morning. I followed instructions left for me to order bagels. It was a misspelled and phonetically written note. I deciphered it by mouth: co-worker Luis. His written English was far from perfect, but this was actually unimportant since he had a completely convincing act. He was a Brazilian fag who answered the phones with the deep husky accented tones of a sexy older Romanian lady. At first watching and listening to him flirt with customers on the phone was farcical beyond belief; later it seemed more appropriate than ever. We were the people behind the curtain keeping the machine going. Perpetuating the illusion of sexiness in an unalluring workaday job.

Linda filled out numbers on the page well past 18. She believed that this was magic and I believed her. Maria was already dressed. She was marching around in her stocking feet, swiping the air with a rolled up magazine as she greeted us all with a loud "Hello babes!" which came out of a large smiling mouth set below a pair of piercingly blue eyes. She carried with her a large bottle of water to help with her diet, talked incessantly about the fights, and always referred to Mike Tyson affectionately as her "little Pup." If there were ever anyone she didn't like she would describe how she would ask the boys from her neighborhood to take them for a drive. Since we didn't get along, I usually felt a little threatened and unnerved by this, but decided not to think about it. Soon enough her eleven o'clock regular arrived. She opened the door, laid the charm on extra thick and accompanied him to a room. His name was Philip. He was a Benedictine monk who worked in the Bronx and lived with his mother upstate. He came every Sunday and stayed for two hours, and always saw Maria.

Today there was a residual drama left over from the events of the previous week. The question now was whether or not the cops would be back for further investigation or to bust us. It was definitely hot! Some things just cannot happen in a place like this and go unnoticed. Ten days previously Sam arrived at about 9:40. While he was parking his car he had been fantasizing about the busty girls described to him on the phone. He felt his heart rate go up. He was getting excited at the thought of it all. "Is she zaftig?" He had asked "I like them zaftig," he repeated.

Repetition was an unavoidable fact of answering the phones. Repeat the same information. Talk to the same guys over and over again. Reading characters through voices and being able to recognise them later was a necessary craft. Is the man I'm talking to a cop or a robber? Is he a freak or normal? Does he want to fuck me (usually), rob me, bust me, play with my mind, or just ask me the same questions 15 times a day? How old is he? Who is he and what does he like? Can I turn him on enough to interest him in coming over, yet get him off the line before he cums? All of this in addition to knowing how to make snap judgments and accurate on-the-spot decisions were of crucial importance when you were sitting at the desk. I was holding my life and other people's in my hands.

Veronica looked through the peephole and opened the door for Sam. They said hello. She showed him the sofa and offered him a drink. Linda, Imogene, Carla, and Dorothy sat around the coffee table. For a while they maintained light conversation about the weather, sports, and a smattering of celebrity gossip, which, with

Dorothy around, usually assumed *Enquirer*-like proportions. They introduced themselves in turn "I'm Melanie," "Linda," "Veronica," "Dorothy, just call me Dot," "and I'm Carla." Dorothy squirmed in exaggerated manner as she introduced herself, pushing her breasts together and up, at the same time shaking her head down, then throwing her hair back. Sam was transfixed. She was just the type he liked. He picked Dorothy. She picked up his drink for him, led him up a couple of steps and disappeared into a room. Twenty minutes later Dot burst out of the room in a state of utter hysterics. Unable to speak she pointed frantically toward the room. Linda rushed in. Sam was lying on the floor by the bed naked and motionless. Immediately she knelt beside him in an attempt to revive him through mouth to mouth resuscitation. She heard the death rattle and gave up. The 911 call had already gone out. The ambulance was on its way. Linda decided to dress Sam's corpse to maintain some dignity.

Enlisting Melanie's help they dressed him as fast and as efficiently as possible and put his wallet in his back trouser pocket. The cops spent hours interrogating everyone present to be sure there was no hint of homicide. Dot was overcome. For weeks afterward she would recall the event to everybody like a broken record. "He was sitting on the bed. I was in the middle of telling him a story. Then he must've started gasping for breath but I thought he was laughing. Then I realized it was serious and he fell down onto the floor. Linda and Melanie got him dressed before the cops arrived. I know I'm fatally attractive and I've sent men to heaven." She would talk dramatically, wobbling her head a little. She sat with her arms bent upwards at the elbows allowing her hands to fall outward, as if in a gesture of mock innocence. "But I've never killed a man before." Sam's brother came to pick up the keys to his gold Mercedes, which was parked outside. The police somehow managed to implement some tact by informing Sam's wife that they had found him dead in his car.

Melanie was just about to enter into a detailed description of what it was like to dress a corpse when a customer arrived. How disappointing. Melanie was a wild girl who looked extremely straight. She had moved into the building next door so she was never too far from work. She'd had a few businesses of her own including a diner and an escort service with five blonds working for her. All five of them were her. She would describe a variety of girls and go out on every call herself.

The doorbell rang and everybody went out into the living room. Jackie would be finishing her session soon, but right now there were only two girls available. I checked the time and realized that Zara and Kim were really late as usual. They were called the downtown girls because, like me, they lived downtown, wore black, went to clubs and got high a lot. I was supposed to be more responsible than them, but I wasn't. Though at this moment I was, since I was awake and they were asleep and I was going to wake them up. First I called Kim's apartment and left a message, then I called Zara. She sounded groggy when she answered. They lived in the same building so I asked Zara to go and wake Kim. Kim was a notorious deep sleeper. Zara said okay and that she would be at work soon. I knew she was lying. When you're doing heroin, the only thing that really sets Sunday apart from any other day of the week is that it's harder to cop. I knew she would take care of that first, I also knew that she would offer me a bag to chill me out about what by that point would be their extreme lateness.

When they arrived their transformation was slow yet miraculous. Zara had green hair. She wore girdles and corsets as outerwear— anything that buckled or tied. Kim had a shaved head and tons of piercings, long before they became fashionable. For Zara a change of clothes, an expertly executed makeup job, and a platinum wig turned her into a tall, sexy blond femme fatale who exuded such a sensual vibe that she had men falling under her spell without question. By the time she arrived two of her appointments were waiting. She was unperturbed. She reassured one and went to visit the other. Kim, on the contrary, had an athletic energy, which combined with her drug mania meant that she was, although well-intentioned, uncontrollably clumsy. It upset her that she kept breaking things. Tall, wearing a dramatic red wig with the stature of a superheroine, she was never so focused as she was when she was carefully arranging a selection of nails on a ceramic plate, or choosing some other tools in preparation for a session for one of her S/M novices. Turning a guy onto this was always a triumph for her.

The office was quiet. The smell of perfume mixed with smoke hung in the air of the unventilated room. The shrill ring of a phone pulled me back from the arms of Morpheus. I awoke, slumped on the desk. I extended my arm to reach for the phone and pulled my head and torso back up into the chair as I put it to my ear. "Hello," I said with artificial cheeriness. "Hello this is Howard. I'd like to find out who's there today," he said. I described the girls who were there that day." Can I tell you my fantasy?" Before I could stop him he continued. "We're on a desert island. We've been there for three days alone." I hung up the phone. On Sundays the freak calls seemed to stand out more from the others. There was one particular phone freak who only called on a Sunday. He was irritating and demanding beyond belief. Jeff, who called incessantly looking for someone with "dragonlady nails," didn't hold a candle to the freak-iness of Frankie. When Frankie called he persisted. At first he would let out these deafening burps in my ear. I'd hang up and he'd call back. He would call tirelessly for hours and hours. It was a true test of patience. I had none. From the burps he progressed onto cheap abusive mantras like the classic "your mother's a whore," or "your mother sucks cock in hell," alternating with "you big fat stupid bitch." When he called shouting, "you eat big jelly donuts!" I worked out that he was into food. Gone were the burps until the next time. It took about an hour of solid conversation before he was talked out and ceased calling. He liked movies, food, and girls of course. He told me all about his first date with a girl at his school. "She was real ugly," he said in a rough deep voice, "yeah, she was fat and she had sticking up hair." Occasionally he would come and spy on the building. Later he'd call and tell me all about it. Whenever he didn't feel like talking he would revert to his routine of calling and hanging up. So it would go on. Frankie called, I answered, Frankie hung up, so did I. It was infinite tedium.

No wonder I did a lot of drugs! If I wasn't using drugs to cheer me up, I certainly needed them to calm me down. That's where the Valium prescription for my "backache" came in useful. Unfortunately, the more Valium I took, the more I needed to lie down. The more I needed to lie down, the more my back seemed to ache. Heroin was the cure-all. Ecstasy was good for a groove but made it hard to concentrate. Coke was always available and filled those late-night hours, gazing through a camera into the vacant hallway of a small, modernized building, and further through the glass doors to the black night outside, with a portentous yet elusive existentialism. I was never alone.

Where there were drugs, there was always company. We all pre-tended that we were straight, even if we'd bumped into each other copping the previous night, or had even got high together. We being myself, the downtown chicks, and Jackie, the permanently crashed-out junkie. She lay behind me on the bench snoring. Her filth-ingrained feet were sticking out of the end of a sheet she'd wrapped herself in. She hated her Long Island parents intensely for their harsh criticisms and their abandonment of her in favor of her fault-less younger brother. When describing their wealth she would become excited and animated, then loud and angry. Mixed up on heroin with a methadone base, she exhausted herself and crashed. On the ebb of her nod she could be heard muttering phrases and stray words. "matter . . . care anymore . . . me . . . yeah." This was the nature of her rebellion. Her refusal to wash her feet or cut her toenails, and her need to lie about it, obscured the obvious with a petty distraction. Oddly enough it sort of worked. I'd glance back at her reflection in the mirror occasionally to make sure she was still alive and breathing especially whenever there was an elongated pause in her snoring.

June had arrived early for the evening shift when Tom, the owner of the bordello, dropped in. Tom dyed his hair and favored an Ivy League look. Ever since a pot-dealing speed freak friend of mine told me that he chose the same look as a disguise, as a mask for his depraved soul, I had become suspicious of it. Whenever I encoun-tered Tom I thought of this, as a way of mustering some degree of compassion toward him and his deficient social skills. He presented himself as a distinctly unlikeable person. He was imperious, bul-lying, and chauvinistic. His comments were filled with such hos-tility that it was obvious that he was a dissatisfied person who had gone to extreme lengths to get what he wanted. Here, it was sex. This was his world. Tom had started a bordello so he could have a girl at any time he wished. This was his domain and he ruled in a despotic manner.

He came into the room without saying hello. He talked with June awhile. They started to flirt heavily, then he walked out of the room. June, a very petite brunette, was one of the mature girls. She was just over 40. When Tom left the room, she explained to me that she had come to work for Tom because a long time ago he had saved her from a rotten boyfriend who turned out to be a pimp. She had a sweet nature, and laughed a lot. She was saving up to open her own antique store. Tom returned and immediately started to flirt with June again. He began undressing her. "I feel embarrassed doing this right behind the phone girl," she protested. They were behind me. I just continued staring at the surveillance screens. "Come on now, she doesn't mind, I'll blindfold her in a minute anyway. Then you can give me a blow job." "If you do that, I won't be able to watch the monitors," I interrupted. I was not looking forward to this. "You don't need to be able to see to answer the phones," responded Tom.

He approached the desk from behind me. I was fully expecting him to tie some dark fabric over my eyes right then, but he didn't. He leaned over me and poked around in among a number of small containers and papers at one end of the desk. "Dammit," he said, irritated. "You haven't seen a little brown paper bag around here have you?" "Do you mean the one with all the poppers in it?" I almost accidentally asked. Remembering in the nick of time not to. They were *his secret* poppers. As far as I was concerned they didn't exist. "Oh, no I haven't," I replied innocently. "Just one moment June, I'll be right back," he said and left to go and poke around in his storeroom down the hall from the apartment.

Right then the doorbell rang. It was Phil. Thank God! Phil never came alone. He always brought his "chauffeur" with him. Phil was into coke and usually stayed for a few hours. His chauffeur, Harry, waited in the living room where he drank and amused himself by talking to the girls. There was a knock on the door. Tom was back with his poppers. June went to the door and spoke through it. "I'm sorry, can you come back later please." She giggled a little. Both of us knew that Tom would never come into the apartment when there was a man in the living room. He tried again a little later, then again, then again much later, but Harry was still sitting there. Eventually, I noticed Tom leaving the building. I breathed a sigh of relief. We were to be left in peace, at least for the rest of the day.

Fuck Art

by

Jack Bump

After dinner I'm ready for work. Nothing like a good meal under your belt to send you on your way to your daily task. I'm working in the meat market tonight, at an art gallery opening; sort of a high-class bouncer kind of job. I'm six-foot two, 200 pounds, and have been in more than one bare-knuckle fracas without getting too bloodied up. The gallery, Caesar's Wife, is on the north strip of Fourteenth, between Ninth and Tenth Avenues, within smelling distance of the meatpacking places, or what's left of them, now that realtors are getting $250,000 for studios. There's a big restaurant on one corner named after a shitty Belgian beer (Stella Artois), a hot no-name-out-front club (Lotus) in the middle, and a decadent, trash-for-the-rich clothing store on the other end (Jeffrey's), so the location couldn't be better.

Gallery security is usually a peaceful gig. You don't usually think of "art lovers" as society's transgressors, but they've got more than their share of prime-time assholes and obnoxious drunks. I usually work clubs and private parties; I've even bodyguarded politicians and opera stars. I know it has to do a lot with how I look. I've got dark hair and eyes, and "rugged" features (which means I've obviously had my nose broken somewhere along the line). I dress well and look clean. Most civilians eyeball me right away and say to themselves, "Don't fuck with him." Often enough there's a female or two who feels like flirting with me. I'm as susceptible as the next guy, so I try to be polite, but distant. My salary is being paid by the guy who runs the joint, so I don't fuck around on their time (usually), but every once in a while a hot tamale will make it hard, if you catch my meaning.

The owner of Caesar's Wife is Mr. Julius. I've worked for him before so I just walk in at about a quarter to six and look around. He's in a tux tonight, looking nervous, but I know that's as much part of his facade as his suit and his "So glad to see you" smile. He used to have a gallery in Soho, called Razor (the "cutting edge," right?), but he moved to Fourteenth Street halfway between the five or six years it took for the West Chelsea scene to take hold. He didn't make it up to the '20s, but he's not worried. He shows the "wacky and weird," and it's been said he's either fabulously wealthy and has the gallery as a hobby, never caring if he sells one piece, or that he's bankrolled by someone like Sir Guy Guy in "The Magic Christian," who considers the art world just another stage for his pranks. Julius's "artists" have been people who made work out of clothes dryer lint, painted with their genitals, or had "silent sound installations." Julius has been called the "Prince of Prank Art" (On Page 6 of the *New York Post*), but he pulls off lively, well-attended shows, gets reviewed, and even sells some, before moving on to the next genius in his temple of mirth.

Evidently the genius of the moment was some kind of sculptor. The first thing I noticed was a giant leather harness hanging from the center of the ceiling with the back half of a horse in it. I walked around underneath, dodging the long black tail and noting the cross-section innards (a la Damien Hirst) on the one end, and then went to the wall to look at the little white title card, which read: "Godfather Outtake." O.K., I get it. Then I noticed a tower of vibrators, like a model for some kind of modern architecture building, or a strange cactus plant. Surrounding a circular plastic tower, and sticking out at 45-degree angles, were about 40 different styled vibrators. There was a step button on the floor, near the base of the pedestal that the dildo tower sat on, so I gently put my boot on it and all the vibrators went into action. Bzz-bzz-bzzz. Some were twisting and turning, others just humming away, and a bright pink light went on inside the tower. The title card called it: "Edison's Wife Says Thanks." On another wall is what is referred to in the porn trade as "a double dong," a long, thick, black rubbery penislike object, except with a hole on each end, obviously for the gratification of two holes at the same time. It's hanging on the wall in a U-shaped position, like some kind of sex-lucky horseshoe. The title card reads: "The Worm Turns, For Dennis Rodman." Well, the artist has some kind of a sense of humor. I don't know how funny he was, but at least he was trying to be funny.

There were more transformed sex toys or original distortions on the walls but I headed for the back room, which apparently housed the show's "masterpiece." It was a lifelike, *moving* sculpture of a man and a woman fucking, doggy style. Arf-arf. Since he was coming at her from behind, you could see a lot of the good bits, and they were going at it with a nice slow, steady rutting rhythm. What's more, there were beads of sweat on their foreheads and other body parts. The tiny sweat balls (between her pendulous breasts, running down the crack of his ass, even on the soles of their feet), were a nice realistic touch. Their faces were in some sort of rictus, like they were both about to come, or shit a brick, or die from some prolonged torture. And, as if we missed the point, there were fluids emanating from the point of engagement, making a thick sucking/plopping sound where the man's penis (you never get to see the head) is plunging in and out. Red, white, and colorless liquids, sometimes sprayed, sometimes dribbled, sometimes singly, sometimes together, gushed forth in an effervescent fountain of bodily fluids. Underneath the kinetic sculpture was a shallow poop chute which collected and recycled the fluids; quite a precision mechanism. The piece was titled: "A Teenaged Duane Hanson's Wet Dream, as Imagined by Paul McCarthy, in a Conversation with Mike Kelly." Whew. Talk about referential.

I return to the main room where the reception desk is and smile at Mr. J.'s assistant, Clarice, always elegant and on top of things, whom I have a major hardon for. She's almost as tall as me, with a slim figure, short black hair, intelligent eyes, and a smile that seems to say, especially on opening nights, "I'm in on the joke too." We like each other, but there has always been this tacit understanding that it won't go any further than that, and so we feel free to parry and thrust at will, with no fear of hurt feelings or misinterpretations. I say, "And the title of this show would be—?" She offers, "The Beast With Two Backs?" I counter, "Sex For The Insane?" She rejoins, "East of Eden?" I rally with, "Porno for Pyros?" She finishes the skirmish with the definitive, "Actually it's 'Fuck Art.'" "Ah," I say, "I should have known. Lovely title, succinct. Sure to get a mention in the *Times*." We both laugh.

So then I asked her, "And who is responsible for these masturbatory masterworks?" (I always talk a little hoity-toity around Clarice). She said, "The artist is a former Capuchin monk." "Oh?" I inquire. She informs me, "Yes, his name is Brother Bumfuquaire. He's of

French descent." "Yes, I'm sure," I muse. She went on, "He lived in a monastery at Los Gatos, California, for fifteen years, and just before he took his final vows, he said he wanted out. And he's been making these things ever since." I go along with the gag and ask, "And how did he come to know about things like this if he lived for fifteen years in a monastery?" And she replied, "Well, he sort of poured himself into research once he came out." I said, "Sort of like puberty at thirty-five," and she agreed. "Something like that." I asked, "Have you met him?" And she answered, "Yes, he's very quiet and well-mannered, not at all rutty." I say, "May I ask sort of a silly question . . . ?" She reads my mind, "Actually he prefers ex-nuns." And I respond, "Don't we all?" And that's our little bit of repartee for the night, as Mr. Julius scurries up to say, "We're about ready to open," and adds, to me, "I'd like you in position."

So I go stand up against one wall in the front room, in between a flying penis, with a thorny red rose sticking out of its urethral opening (title card: "Saint Theresa's Catheter"), and two table tennis paddles lying flat on a plastic ledge, with two supposedly severed testicles sitting upon each of them (title card: "Ping-Pong Anyone?"). Mostly my job is just to stand around, like those guards in a museum. And 99 percent of the time I'm about as necessary as they are, but I think Mr. Julius likes the idea of having a "guard" for the kind of art he shows. I'm part of the gag. Of course, if someone did try to rip a "piece of art" off the wall and head for the door, it's assumed that I would be big enough and fast enough to run the person down and take it away from him. I'm like a glorified store detective, without the disguise. But you usually don't get art kleptos at these affairs. Most everyone comes for the free wine and socializing.

I see a few people I recognize from other openings. I don't acknowledge them unless they acknowledge me. Most of them don't need to fraternize with the hired help. In comes a loud group of eight or nine that looks different from the rest of the crowd. I mean loud of costumes as well as voice. Maybe they think it's Mardi Gras. They've got these colorful, puffy-armed costumes on, glitter on their faces and eyes and headdresses. I look over at Mr. J and he's smiling, so I figure he's invited them. Maybe they're some kind of dance company. He greets them effusively, and as I watch them fan out in a little circle, I notice her. La Bomba. The Latina babe with the big jugs and the broken heel, from the shoe store this afternoon, where I was getting my boots shined. I'd already had a very satisfying fantasy about her today, and now she pops up again. Hm-m-m. She's looking around, like she might be expecting to see someone in the crowd, when her eyes hit on me, and for a second she has a moment of recognition, but then it passes. She can't place me. I smile. She moves into the room with the others, as Mr. J is leading them toward the back room, and she looks again at me, quizzing herself. I point down at her feet, and finally a bell goes *ding* in her head, and she smiles back.

Later. . . .

When she opened the door she was wearing a light blue bathrobe. I could smell pot and a little incense too. Barry White was on the CD. She held the door open for me, and said as I entered, "Why don't we make ourselves comfortable?" Over by the lamp was a couch, so I sat down there and saw a half-smoked doobie on the edge of a metal ashtray. I picked it up, grabbed a green plastic lighter, and fired it up. After a hit, she asked, "Can I take your coat?" I said, "Sure," and I stood up, slipped out of it, and handed it to her. She hung it up in the closet and came back to sit down next to me. I passed her the doobie and the lighter and she fired up, took a toke and gave it to me. "You have to catch up," she said. I gave it another pull and when I offered it to her she shook her head and I placed it back on the edge of the copper tray. I could feel my eyes getting watery and a nice trill went through my body and head. I looked at her with what I knew could only be a goofy smile, and she said, "Hombre," and threw herself at me. Her momentum carried us to the back of the couch, and for a second I didn't know what to do. It came so fast and I was suddenly feeling kinda slow, so I just grabbed her with both arms and held her close to me. I kissed her, she kissed me back, and we seemed to stay like that for a while. When I opened my eyes I was dizzy, and couldn't tell how much time had passed.

I felt I needed something solid to hold on to, so I reached my hand inside the top of her bathrobe and grabbed the left one of her huge beautiful tits. I covered her nipple with my palm, and stretched out my fingers to see how much more I could hold. I have big hands, but there was no way I could cover her whole breast, and it felt as if her areola was the size of my palm. I took a breath. I have a great fondness (fetish is too small a word), for a large nipple area, and I felt like I had hit the jackpot. I rubbed my palm over her nipple and felt it get hard. I squeezed it with my thumb and fore-finger, and moved it up and down, like it was a light switch. It got bigger and harder. I took another handful and squeezed, they just were firm and heavy and natural. I was in melon heaven. I must have been making some moo-sounds, because she said, "You like?" and I said, "Yes, a lot." "Good," she said, and she closed her eyes and raised her head for me to kiss her. Our lips seemed to be a perfect fit, and she didn't force the kiss. She kissed me firmly but not des-perately, and I kissed her the same way back. It was like we'd been kissing each other for years. We stayed glued to each other, breathing easily through our noses, not feeling any need to come apart, just lick lapping like one of us was the bee and the other was the flower. It lasted for a while, I broke away first, and when I looked at her eyes I could see they were glassy. I couldn't tell if it was the kiss or the pot, but I felt like my eyes must have looked the same.

She smiled and took my left hand and put it inside her bathrobe on top of her right tit. I'd completely forgotten I had my other hand holding her left one, and she laughed and said, "Forget something?" I laughed too, then I began to cup and rub both of her breasts at the same time. She closed her eyes and said, "Oh, oh that feels good." I looked down to see what I had a hold of, and I couldn't believe how perfectly round and soft and big-nippled her breasts were. The right nipple was hard now too, popped up like a cow's udder. I rubbed and squeezed like I was Farmer John. I was working them both at the same time, and I didn't really want to move on because I could see how much she was enjoying it, plus, I was so excited to be playing with my dream titties. My dick was poking up my pants like a tent pole at a boy scout's overnighter. I felt like I was being allowed to handle two pieces of art. Like I was at the Metropolitan Museum of Art, and the curator opened up a glass case (Ancient Breastworks, The Etruscan Period, 200 B.C.) with a special key, and said, "Go ahead, feel free to fondle." It was that kind of privilege.

I went in for the suck. First I just stuck my tongue out and tickled the tip of her nipple with the tip of my tongue. She let out a little cry, and after getting the tip nice and wet and hard, I slurped it into my mouth like I was an aardvark and it was a stray bug. Then I switched over to the other one and did the same. First the tip, then the whole thing; then opening my mouth real wide so that I could take every bit of the aureola in, then pop it out. This was fun. I shoved the fingers of my left hand into her mouth and she began sucking on them, and when they were nice and wet I took them out and rubbed the nipple I wasn't sucking, so I was getting both nips equally hot, slimy wet, and hard. I stuck the fingers of both of my hands into her mouth, imagining how it would be no problem at all for her to take two dicks in that big mouth at the same time (I wished I had a spare), and after she sucked on them juicily, I sat up a little and started to play with both melons with my slippery fingers. I pulled and pinched and tweaked and rubbed, swooping in once in a while to give 'em a big fat tongue licking, trapping the entire nipple in my mouth, holding my breath like I was underwater, or like I was trying to stop time by not moving, just sucking on for dear life.

That got her. She started to grab for my dick then, and she found it poking up my pants. She put her palm down hard on the tip of it and rubbed it through the material. I didn't want her to play with me too much right then, because I knew I was so hot I would come quick. So I took her hand away and used it to spread her bathrobe, and then her legs. I put the fingers down between her legs and rubbed them up her thighs to her pussy. I rubbed them over and pushed them inside. She knew what I wanted, her juices on her fingertips. I brought her hand back up to my mouth, stuck it in and sucked real hard, licking under her long fingernails, sucking each finger at a time, like I was enjoying an order of shrimp.

She reached over to the nearby table and got a small bottle of oil and poured some on top of her chest, just above her cleavage, and let it roll between her breasts. She lay back down. Neither of us said a word. I stood up and looked down at her. She was playing with her pussy. I unbuckled my belt.

I was very careful with my pants. I kind of like the tentpost look in Armani. They should try it in some of their fashion shows, but I paid too much for this suit to let it get bent out of shape or stiffen it up with jizz stains. So I slowly took 'em off, and stood there a second with my charcoal gray jockeys pointing north. I took off my tie and unbuttoned my shirt as I watched her look at my poked out pecker head and tree trunk upper legs. (Sorry, but I've got great pins, always have. I think it's hereditary.) She reached up with her left hand, and while rubbing her tongue over her top lip, she squeezed the head of my dick with her thumb and fingers, saying, "Honk-honk," and laughed. It hurt a little, but I didn't flinch, I just said, "It's not a bicycle horn." And she replied, "It sticks out like one." So I've got to show it to her. I try to be a little teasing as I slide my thumbs into the elastic on my hips and very slowly and carefully (no sense in hurting myself) raise and then lower the top front part of my reliable jockeys. She says, "O-o-o-o-o, it's a trombone." I laugh, and she pours some more oil in her hands, rubs them together to get the oil a little warmer, reaches up with both hands and rubs it on the sides of my six inches of steel, over the head, and then, reaches underneath, cupping and rubbing my hard balls. Jesus, I almost c-c-c-came. It was the softest, hottest, oiliest handling of my equipment I'd ever experienced, and it only lasted a couple of seconds. She looked at me and smiled, because she knew she had me then.

She took hold of my dick with one hand, like she was leading a goat by the horn, and pulled me closer to the couch. She scooted down a little on the cushion and then pulled me on top of her stomach. The couch was deep enough so that I could straddle, but not squash, her and still keep my knees on the cushions. She patted my dick a couple of times, like it was the head of her pet dog. She reached her left hand underneath and began playing with my balls. She said, "Um-m, your cojones are almost as big as my tetas." She began massaging them like she was rolling a pair of billiard balls in her hand. I thought I might shoot, and she must have noticed it, because she stopped and squeezed the area where the balls hang off the rest of my body, and that stopped me. She reached her fingers back a little further, and started to pat her long-nailed fingertips on my asshole. Oh! I jumped a little, and my dick head ratcheted up another notch. As I settled my ass down again on her fingertips she began to give me a little drumroll effect, like she was playing finger bongos on my butthole. I had my eyes closed and my head was back, and she was bongoing away like some ancient hipster.

I opened my eyes, and could see she was still smiling. She liked turning me on this way. She settled in a little more, getting comfortable on the couch, while I raised myself on my knees and legs. She motioned me to come forward, and I did. My dick moved from over her belly button to above the space between her breasts. She put her hands on my thighs and pressed down; I slowly lowered myself. All the time she was looking at my dick, like a foreman at a construction site watching a crane lower a pallet of sheetrock onto the floor. I heard my knees crack. When I touched her skin with the underside of my dick she let out a soft whimper, and looked up at me and smiled. She really does like it this way, I thought. I was in heaven.

She relaxed into the cushion and my dick popped up a little. Then she took her hands and corralled her breasts from each side and folded them over it. All of a sudden my dick was gone, swallowed up by these two gorgeous mounds of warm flesh, like it was a hot dog being folded inside a loaf of Italian bread, just out of the oven. I could see my dark pubic hair, at the end nearest me, and then the two-hilled mountain through which I was trying to tunnel, and at the other end, just the tiniest hint of a dick head sticking out. There was pre-cum at the tip, so I reached down and rubbed some of it on my finger and held it up to her lips and she sucked it off. She opened her eyes then and smiled, and I realized I shouldn't have done anything, I should have just stayed perfectly still and let her hold and caress my dick between her breasts, until she wanted to do something else. But she was okay with it, she knew I wasn't being impatient or anything.

She gave me a wicked smile then, like she was the person at the Cyclone roller coaster ride on Coney Island, the last human contact before the ascent, the teenage guy who checks to make sure your safety belt is fastened down securely on your lap, before that first uphill climb, a-chucka, a-chucka, a-chucka, to the top of the first drop. Then she winked at me. I had this urge to laugh, but she started moving her breasts up and down on my dick, and there was no more laughing. I looked at her, and she wasn't smiling anymore. She was looking at me hard, as if she was trying to determine every nuance of feeling I was going through as she smoothly slid her tetas up and down my crankshaft. She was looking at me very seriously, like she was out on a lonely country road, in the moonlight, and she was on her motorcycle and she was slowly increasing the speed, turning it up, turning, a little more, turning, turning, 40–45–50 mph.

Up and down, up and down. She moved her breasts evenly on both sides and on top of my captured dick. She got into a rhythm and kept it. Oh-oh-oh. This was so good. I felt my head snap back, and wondered if it would snap off, or worse, pop my dick out of her warm oven, but it didn't. I bobbed back, like I was rising to the surface of a warm-water swimming pool. She paused. She had my full attention. She suddenly opened her breast taco and a cool breeze came from somewhere and wafted over my happy dog, and then she closed them slowly again, like one of those scenes in a James Bond movie where the two steel doors are closing to lock James Bond and the pretty girl into a dungeon they can never escape from. And I had the eerie thought, "I'll never see my dick again," and then I thought, "And I don't care."

She took her time, and let me feel that; and when she knew that I knew that I was completely in her control, and would let her do with me whatever she wanted, she started her up-and-down movements again. Up and down, up and down; very softly but very firmly. Her hot flesh baggies moved and rolled, increasing the heat and excitement in my penis. Our eyes locked. She stuck her tongue out at me and wiggled it. She laughed. She spit on me; I could feel it run down my chest hair. She started talking, quietly at first, "I want you to come on my tetas, big boy. I want a big come. No little come."

I could feel it building up in my balls. My dick was buried in soft, warm mossy earth. She was really pumping it now. Like she was revving up her Harley to 50–55–60. I heard myself say, "Yes, oh Yes, Yes." And she said, "Yes, poppy. That's it, yes, yes. Give mommy a big come." "*OH, OH, YES, YES,*" I was screaming. And then I shot my load all over her neck. Woosh. My head snapped back again, and I thought, "For sure it's going to break off this time," but I still didn't care. My dick kept pumping, I was groaning. My whole body began spasming, like I was a hooked fish, flailing in the bottom of the boat after having just been reeled in. She still held her tits tightly on top of my dick, and I thought she was doing it so I wouldn't fall off the couch and hurt myself. I was panting and gasping, trying to catch my breath, and finally I leaned over and grabbed her hands and held on. I kept saying, "Oh God, oh God, oh God."

After what seemed like a return from outer space, I opened my eyes and looked down at her. The doorway to heaven was open and my spent dick was already shrinking in size. She was rubbing the come from her neck and cleavage onto her breasts and up onto her nipples, until she had very smoothly spread it all over her tits. I could see a sticky film on her breast skin, her aureolae, and nipples. I pulled off her, stretched my legs back and lay down on top of her. She said, "Oof," but not too loud. We lay quietly, limp dick to hairy bush, my male pecs to her big, sticky tetas, and laughed at each other because we both knew she'd got me good. We kissed and tongued in our necessary cooldown. After awhile, she wriggled her way out from underneath me, pushed up to the back of the couch, grabbed her crotch, and said, "Next time I'm on top."

The Bosom Ballet

by

Annie

Sprinkle

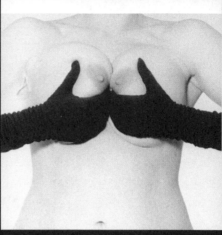

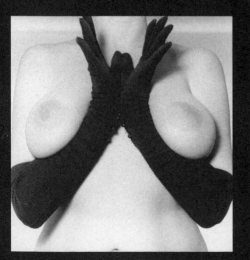
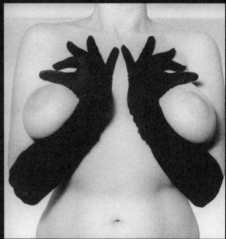

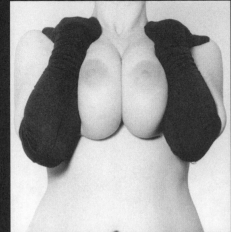

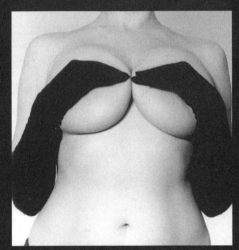

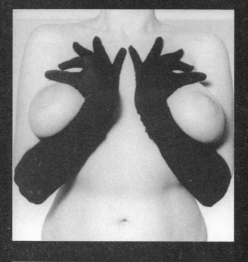

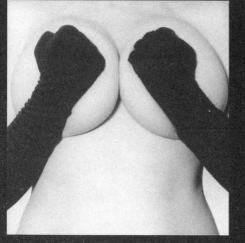
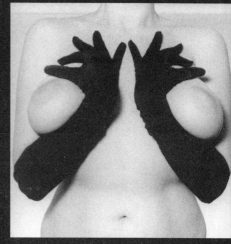

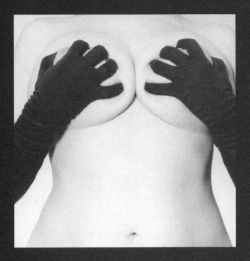

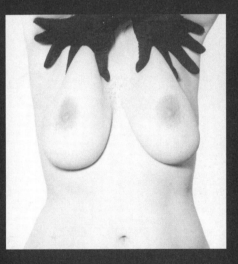
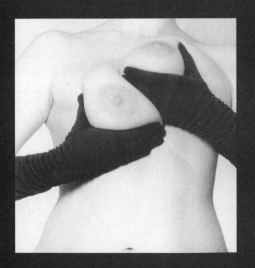
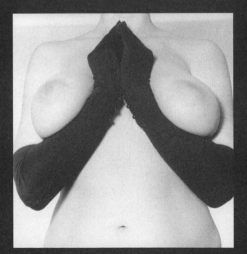

Lake Cuntry Drag King Fling

by

Diane Torr

A couple of years ago, I was invited by an English girlfriend to spend a dirty weekend in a four-star hotel in North West England—in the lake district—"I wandered lonely as a cloud" country, where William Wordsworth penned these lines, "when all at once I saw a crowd, a host of golden daffodils!" Springtime by the lake! I was excited at this treat . . . but the one proviso to this poetic and potentially erotic invitation was that we would spend the weekend as a heterosexual couple. And I would be the man.

Lake Windermere is the largest of the lakes in the Lake District. Rural, traditional, and not known for its legions of cross-dressers, I would have to be very thorough in my construction of "husband" in order to pass the scrutiny of the twinset and pearls set, and their tweedy men.

As we approached the hotel, we stopped the car in a lay-by to make the transformation. I stuck on the goatee beard, moustache, and applied a five o'clock shadow. Not an easy task, balancing cut-up bits of hair, spirit gum, stippling brush, and cream (for five o'clock shadow) and mirror on my lap, but it all added to the thrill of our subterfuge. I changed into my men clothes, ducking down into the seat as a car went past just as I was binding my breasts.

Jay and I jiggled and giggled a lot during the whole process. And then I was ready. Just what kind of a man and what were the circumstances? I had to be somewhat creative as my hair was dyed a dark burgundy shade at the time—and I wore a black shirt, Pollock-style splattered tie, and black, single-breasted, wool suit. Married to the same woman for 15 years, but indicating my sense of fun (and potential availability) with my colorful tie collection. Sound like an art school professor to you? Yes—well at least one I could think of, anyway! Jay was my art student paramour. She wore lipstick and eye makeup, a sexy, but tailored diaphanous shirt, and a black pantsuit. We were ready for our adventure as a hetero couple.

We drove along some winding country lanes and checked in to Lakeland Hotel as man and wife.

At the reception desk, eyes traveled past me, darted back to me, and then stared, as if to permeate me. I was feeling slightly disconcerted by all of this eye attention, but decided that they must think I'm either extraordinarily handsome or that I have a large penis, or both. This attitude allowed me to maintain swagger and self-assurance, which made me feel big, and thus take up a lot of space, and get in people's way. This was exactly the confirmation my "audience" was looking for, and I knew by the bland, and slightly irritated looks I got that this behavior was all too familiar. I instantly became part of the decor.

I was very courteous (in accordance with Straight Hotel expectations) with Jay, allowing her to go first into the elevator, and putting my arm protectively around her as we exited on our floor. In the hotel room, we fell on the bed laughing, rolling about, high from our first "hetero" performance, and kissing each other with delight.

"Hey MAN," Jay said. It was time to do the "manly" thing and I stood up, straddled her and took out my big dick—a long and broad strap-on. Jay pretended to be in awe of my erection, and eagerly removed garments as I towered above her. "You, yes, you— you're the one," I murmured in her ear as I entered her. We fucked and snogged and fucked and snogged until Jay suddenly stopped all activity, looked in my face, and laughed. I didn't lose my hard-on (hey, this guy is always hard), but apparently I'd lost my manliness. I stumbled into the bathroom and saw patches of dried spirit gum, and bits of flattened beard hair sticking out of them; my maleness made a mockery by lusty kisses. Time for some masculine grooming . . . and . . . *Hey presto!* there was Dave the art school professor looking back at me in the mirror! Making our way to the dining room for dinner I was aware of men checking me out. Jay is 20 years younger than I am, and quite a voluptuous siren. They'd look at her, then me, then her, then me, and some looked envious and some looked concerned. By the time we sat down for dinner, I was feeling super-confident.

The waiter deferred to me when taking the order—as if I'd know what Jay would like to eat—and there was the assumption that I would know what wine we'd like to drink. When I passed the wine menu on to Jay (she knows wine—she's a connoisseur) and she chose the wine, the waiter still offered me the glass of wine to taste. "Is this to your liking, sir?" he asked. I suggested he ask "Modom." This made the waiter break character and smile at us, as if he was in on our secret. I ignored him, and carried on with my banter with Jay—being loving, attentive, and asking about fictitious friends. We had taken on a task—a double espionage if you will—two women pretending to be a hetero couple having an affair, who were in turn pretending to be a solid married couple. This involved us in endless improv, which was fun for a couple of hours, but quickly got tedious when we were constantly under observation. It was also easy to feel paranoid, imagining that our guise was penetrated. As we left the dining room, we decided to make ground rules for ourselves. Basically, either of us could disappear to the hotel room whenever we felt uncomfortable.

But how great it was to be able to take advantage of our "heterosexuality" in this ultra-conservative British backwater. As two women publicly showing our affection for each other, we would have stuck out like an unwanted hardon. As Jay and Dave, we were invisible—that is until we started acting inappropriately.

After dinner we had a drink in an empty corner of the lounge. Cuddling on a large, many-cushioned couch, our hands roaming each other's thighs, we were so engaged that we were oblivious to the approach of strangers. We looked up to find a slightly drunk man and woman standing next to the couch and asking if they might sit with us. I was mortified as they both sat down, not waiting for a yes or no and the man immediately zeroed in on me, asking how we'd met. I realized we'd drawn attention to ourselves. Jay took this opportunity to return to the hotel room to pick up a sweater. I wanted to leave too, but I was cornered. I pushed my American accent, muttering something about New York and the Staten Island ferry. The question about how we met was just an opener for him, because what he really wanted to talk about was *football*. And he wanted to talk about it with me. Again, I emphasized an American drawl, and told him I knew nothing about "soccer." Undaunted, he was off and running with what looked like a very long story. His home team, Liverpool, had just won an important match and he was super-excited and wanted to retell in great detail every aspect of the game. Can you imagine? It let me off the hook as I didn't have to talk much—just look engaged.

His wife listened but was not really included. I was relieved when Jay returned. I jumped up from the couch and said, "We're going for a walk in the moonlight," and took her arm. My new male friend was midstream, ". . . then Robbie Fowler dribbled the ball and passed it to Owen. . . ." He was dumbfounded. "Oh, all right well, meet us in the bar later, won't you?" he asked, as we were leaving. "I think we might be busy, but if not . . . sure," I replied, giving him a man-to-man nod. Phew—the promise of sex rules!

Jay and I escaped to the lake and took a walk along the shore. We sat down on a bench and got lost in kissin and huggin. Then I suddenly realized my goatee had disappeared. As this was an essential signifier in my particular male identity, I felt kind of bereft. I was immediately anxious and wanted to return to the hotel room right away. Jay didn't, and she didn't want to be told what to do, or where to go either. This was our first squabble. We went inside the hotel, me to the hotel room, and she for a drink at the bar. I kept my head down and my chin tucked under my scarf, in order to conceal my lack. I checked out my reflection in the mirror in the elevator, and I looked absurdly contrived, and yet, still manly. Walking out of the elevator with my chin tucked in like that, I saw in the hotel mirror a character akin to the Three Stooges, but without their zaniness and without their rationale for akimbo-ness . . . . Gawd, I was lucky to have a woman at all.

It took maybe two minutes to apply the goatee—and I was back downstairs in the bar, reclaiming my playmate. She liked my speediness. Fortunately football-man was deeply engaged in conversation with another guy at the bar and his wife didn't notice us. I enticed Jay to our hotel room. I did not want to be in a public space where we could be targets for boors. It was her that I wanted!! Our role-play continued in the bedroom and Jay was behaving like a sulky mistress, so I went along with that. I seduced her with my tongue, licking her neck, ear, lips, closed eyelids, and I pressed the whole weight of my body on her, pinning her down and tickling her into surrender.

The following morning, reapplying my facial hair, I'd forgotten exactly the length of the sideburns and the thickness of the moustache, and I hoped none of the other guests would have better memories and notice the difference. As I walked along the buffet breakfast table, helping myself to cereal, eggs and home fries, I was aware of being looked at, but I kept moving. I sat down and Jay told me that the men at the next table had stared fixedly at me as I collected my breakfast. Then one had turned to another, leaned in, and said conclusively, "Well, he's got women's hair." I wanted to laugh out loud, but had to repress that spontaneous impulse, not yet having mastered the impersonation of this particular male's laughter. During breakfast, Jay and I tried hard to emulate the subdued behavior of the breakfast crowd, but when I looked in my bowl of cereal, and found part of my moustache floating in the milk, I couldn't contain my horror/distress. I let out a shriek. All eyes on us. Fortunately, people assumed that sound had come from Jay, and they smiled and returned to eating. It was time to get out of there. We decided to take a boat trip across the lake.

We took the boat from the dock beside the hotel and sat on the top deck where the wind blew fiercely (resulting in more beard hair depletion). The other seats were occupied by couples in purple and green fleece jackets, with all the females huddled up close to their protective men. I imitated the men and threw my arm around Jay, but being smaller than her, it was awkward to hold on to her as my arm only reached halfway across Jay's back. But I imagined I looked valiant, and this created in me a strong sense of self. The wind became calmer toward the middle of the lake and we could relax a bit and look out from under our jacket hoods. Land on either side of the lake slipped past us, and the clouds moved in tandem with the boat. I had a sensation of speed and suspension that was out of my control—kind of like being at the funfair sitting on a ride, with my babe at my side. . . . *Yessss!* We reached a harbor that was overrun with tourists, where the boat docked. We walked for a mile and came to a ferry which took us across to an island with a hill. On top of the island was a castle.

That's where the drag king took his princess—on a long, long hike up winding paths, past Roman ruins, and tunnels and old oak trees—to the castle in the sky and there he enchanted her with his magic. All drag kings are magicians. We both gave our thanks to the elements and bowed to the North, South, East, and West and played like boys at peeing standing up. David used his "pisser"* and Jay needed no pretend penis. She has a mighty skill. She simply takes off her underpants, spreads her legs and pees into the earth, and well, once she has those panties off . . . it's an open invitation. The hill's hips moved under us.

With thanks to Jane C. for her impeccable taste in weekend fun, and Lakeland Hotels, thanks also to Paul Langland for his immaculate perception.—Diane torr

*The pisser is a rubber mold, designed by London artist Svar, shaped almost like a small clog with a curled end that hooks into the vagina. If you hold it firmly in place, the piss collects in the pisser and arcs out of a penis-shaped bell end. This is an indispensable (and pocket-sized) item for all drag kings, and it fulfills the passage of pissing in a urinal as a basic human right.

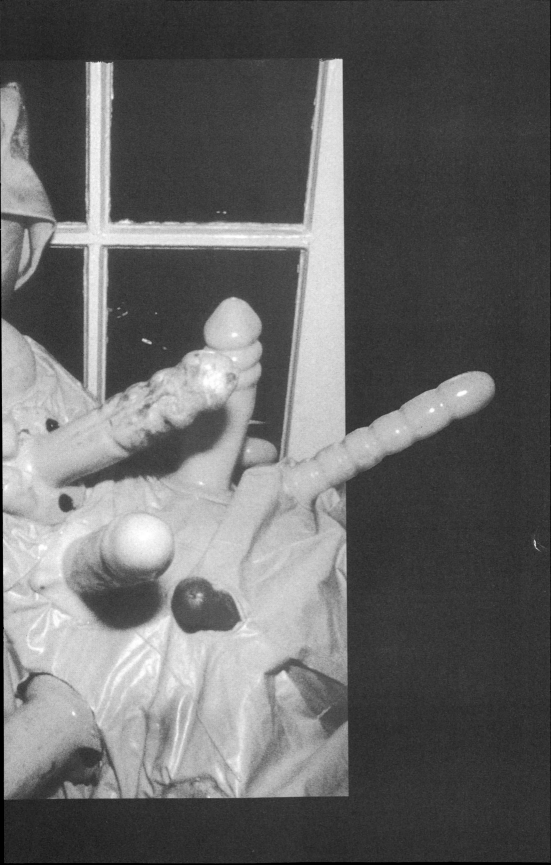

Eargasm

by

Saint

Reverend Jen

I t is February, and my beloved landlord has failed to fix the frozen boiler, which has not been replaced or repaired since 1892. I am swathed in several pairs of footy pajamas, there are icicles forming on my nipples, and my vagina is frostbitten. My freaky-freezy-clad hand trembles as it lifts a 24-ounce Budweiser to my blue-tinged lips but I find comfort in knowing that all 24 ounces will stay cold by the time I finish consuming them. I glance around my squalor-laden home and notice that my baby sea monkeys have all died from the frost. Their lifeless bodies float like pond scum in their "Magical Micro-Vue" Aquarium.

Valentine's Day is around the corner, and not only do I not have a boyfriend, I no longer even have the companionship of my pet crustaceans. There won't be any candy hearts, Whitman's Samplers, or "doing it" for me this year. I'll be spending the fourteenth alone, watching reruns of *Sabrina the Teenage Witch* and warming my hands over a cup of ramen noodles. Yet, despite these Dickensian hardships, I will do my best to enrich the lives of readers everywhere by making light of my own pain and loneliness.

My original plan to write a treatise on the vulva quickly changed when I was forced to bury my own under 40 pounds of flannel. Instead, I have decided to pay homage to the most under-appreciated, most easily accessed phallus of all time: the Cotton Swab.

In *Trainspotting*, Irvine Welsh wrote, "Take your best orgasm, multiply it by a thousand, and you're still miles off the place." I've never tried heroin, but I have little trouble relating to Welsh's junkie protagonist. The arousal experienced upon inserting cotton swabs into one's ear canal is perhaps one of the most addictive sensations known to man.

Being the most prolific artist of the 21st century means that I don't have time for dating, courtly love, or even sex. However, once a year, I find time to pay a visit to Duane Reade where for only 99 cents, I purchase 525 generic cotton swabs. ("Q-Tips" are better, but they're out of my price range.) And, I know that upon purchasing those crisp, new cotton swabs, that I will have 525 pleasurable experiences.

Earwax removal, or "tipping," as I like to call it, is unlike sex in that it's almost never disappointing. There's no morning breath, ass-hair or ball-sac odor. It is unlikely that your cotton swab will have abandonment issues or an inferiority complex, and you don't have to listen to your cotton swab while it talks for hours about its latest visionary screenplay. Best of all, once you finally abandon your cotton swab, it won't stalk you.

This does not mean that all "tipping" experiences are magical. Occasionally, a "tipping addict" like myself may find that they have difficulty extracting any wax at all, and when this happens, earwax removal becomes more like an archaeological dig than a sensual pastime. When this happens do not plunge your swab deep into the canal, searching for the lost city of earwax. You will only end up wearing a hearing aid by the age of 30. Do, however, reach into your medicine cabinet and pull out a bottle of hydrogen peroxide. A capful of peroxide loosens the wax so that even the most hardened tipper can extract a little something. (Please note: This is the "tippers" version of mainlining. When you find yourself reaching for the hydro, you might want to cool out on the tips for a while. Also, please note: I am not a doctor and I am not recommending that you try this. I have heard that "tipping" is dangerous, but I am too far gone in my addiction to take heed. If you have never tipped, don't start now! And, if you do head for the hydro, and you permanently damage your ears, don't sue me!)

I feel a slight tingle travel down my spine as I remember my first hydrogen peroxide/cotton swab-induced "Eargasm." I recently penned a song, which recounts this experience, and which also expresses my frustration at my inability to get a handle on my addiction. What follows are some choice lyrics:

(Please Note: The following should be sung as though one were singing a Judas Priest song.)

I plunge my swab into the canal,
Who said that hygiene was banal?
Eargasm, eargasm.
Doctor, I can't hear, cuz I can't stop cleanin' my ears.
And, no rehab group will have me,
cuz I'm not your average junky.
Who needs liquor or hard drugs?
All I need are my cotton swabs!
Who needs a man?
My tiny phallus throbs inside me,
cleanin' my ears of all that's grimy . . .

While "Eargasm" may never be a Top-40 hit, I felt it was important for me to debunk the myth that cotton swabs are only used in
our culture as tools with which to extract earwax. Quite the contrary, people don't tip because they're obsessed with keeping their
ears clean. They do it because it's the fastest, cheapest, most guilt-
free form of pleasure in the world. People do it because it feels good.

Answer Me

by

Annie

Sprinkle

Was our relationship something special?
Or was it the same kind of thing?
Was it ever a 'relationship'?
Or simply a passionate fling?

Yes your love was so amusing,
But overwhelmingly confusing.
Why did you lead me on,
Knowing you'd feel put upon?

How did the stress of our romance get so repetitive,
And our lover's games get so competitive?
Who could build the pedestal the highest?
Who could knock it down?
Who was too good for the other?
Who was the better lover?
Who was under whose spell?
I could never tell.
Who taught who more?
Who got the higher score?
Whose world was better at the core?
Who was more of a whore?

Why was the sex so fucking hot?
Did we enjoy it, or did we not?
Why was it so satisfying,
When it was so frustrating?

How could we communicate so deeply,
When we could not communicate at all?

Why did you lie to me?
Or did I lie to myself?
Did we ever really trust each other?
Or did we trust each other too much?
Was the truth ever spoken?
Or was the truth always changing?
Aren't you astonished,
How it got so dishonest?

Were you a very wise woman?
Or were you really dumb?
Were you a calculating cruel pest?
Or were you really trying your best?

Why did it end so quickly?
How did it last so long?
Who ended it?
Did it end?
Did it ever really start?
How'd it get so dramatic?
What made it so traumatic?

Didn't we make such a handsome pair?
People would even stop and stare.
You gave my life such a boon.
Are we giving up on a good thing too soon?

Did you wound me deeply forever?
Or did you heal my life?

Who will make the next move?
Will it worsen or improve?
Why does our passion make us nauseous?
Who has a better reason to be cautious?
Why do you act like nothing happened,
When everything has changed?

Why do you continue to invite me,
When you really want to spite me?
Why do we still see each other?
When we're so relieved when we don't?
Wouldn't it be better for us to stay apart?
Or is getting together the way to mend our heart?
It seems to have ended and we're both glad,
But why do we feel so damned sad?

Is it better for me to stay angry?
Or will forgiveness set me free?
Will you ever make amends?
Can we possibly be just friends?

Why did you just kiss me so intensely?
Do you really love me so immensely?

What else can I say
That's not a bad cliché?
Will we end up full of hate?
Or is loving each other eternally our fate?

Please write your answers here:

_____
_____
_____
_____
_____
_____
_____
_____
_____
_____
_____
_____
_____
_____
_____

Continue on the back.

Physical Love

by

Lizbeth

Hasse

When he died, Harold was my oldest friend, both in age and in duration. My more aged friend Mindy had died the year before. Mindy was 95 when she went, and she had been part of my daily life for about a dozen years.

It was the week of my birthday. Mindy had been confined to bed for the first time since the time she had broken a hip a decade earlier. She called me over to celebrate my day. We toasted each other with champagne in her bedroom. We laughed and discussed our usual topics: men, particular men, sex, art, art and sex, politics, politics and sex (she remembered for sure that every president but one in her lifetime had an extramarital affair; but which one was the one). The 50 years difference between Mindy and me was an irrelevance except in the very large way in which this was a friendship without any agenda but itself, and, thus, unconditional.

Then she brought up what she hated to discuss, but the subject that now most affected her existence: her "ailments." She refused to let herself become them. But in a very few weeks, she had lost her ability to care for herself, to walk to the Safeway, to cook her own meals, to take herself to the hairdresser, to bathe without assistance, to feel independent. The loss was irritating to her. The irritation was constant and unacceptable. She toasted to all the fun we'd had, to our great love, and announced that she had decided, her last act of independence, that she'd had enough. She had decided to die and would do that. No crying allowed. She would do it by stopping eating. I wanted to crawl into her bed, to hold her, to give her a physical affection that I thought might show the extent of my love. I didn't. She seemed so fragile. I thought about my inadequacy for wanting to express my love in the flesh when she had transcended it, and I felt my inadequacy for not crawling into bed and doing it.

Our celebration was the last time we spoke. The next day she was in a coma. A doctor friend told me that Mindy could live another couple of weeks even without food. But it was only a little more than a day before she died in her bed. She was a woman who knew what she wanted and was strong-willed about getting it.

Harold was less ready to go. Ten years Mindy's junior, he was robust and active. He was caring for MaryElizabeth, his invalid wife of 60 years, when he was told he had a leukemia that would take his life in a few weeks. He called me in San Francisco from his room at Yale–New Haven Hospital and asked me to come help him put his "affairs in order." I was, after all, the only lawyer in his life.

I reflected on the plane to Hartford about just how much more intimate and confidential being a lawyer can permit one's friendships to become. There is one other kind of conversation that can take place. One of gravitas, of a different significance and tone, a new space of communication that friends can enter by virtue of this other relationship.

Harold and I discussed his will. We talked about MaryElizabeth. We also talked about the arms race and global warming, science and environmentalism, politics and rational thinking, time and cosmology. Harold was a physicist and mathematician, and it was the larger particles in the universe, the immense in size and duration, that grounded his commitments and his beliefs about the relative significance and insignificance of humans in a larger world. A scientist who had worked on nuclear submarines, he became a very effective and informed organizer of the nuclear freeze movement in Connecticut.

Harold was my longest friend because he and MaryLiz had lived next door when I was growing up, from nursery school until high school. They were childless and perhaps only a curious and active child could really appreciate Harold's many projects and activities. Year after year, Harold took me bluefishing. Together we dredged the neighborhood creek and planted fruit trees. When he paved his driveway, it was my little handprint that was pressed into the concrete. When he built his garage, I put together the time capsule to bury in the foundation. We launched his canoe on the pond. We made a pair of long stilts to walk through the pond to the little beaver island in the center. The stilts stuck in the mud and Harold was stuck there in the middle of the pond on them, sinking. Together we capsized the canoe as I tried to effect a rescue. Every Christmas we made a large batch of peanut brittle—our specialty— and each year with equal anticipation, we watched that simmering pot of sugar syrup approach the hard crack stage and ran outside in the cold to stretch the hardening mass over a smooth marble slab in the snow. Everything was always exciting and fun with Harold, and usually funny too, as if he had in mind all the time the miniscule nature of the time and space we occupied in the cosmology he studied, and grasped a pure pleasure in making something of it.

Harold's room at Yale–New Haven, if not for the IV and monitoring equipment, was more monastic than medical. He had set up a writing table, and the windowsill was stacked with books about astronomy and scientific theory. I wanted to tell Harold how handsome he looked, how irresistible his eyes and smile. I wanted to crawl into his bed and show him the depths of my love. "I've been trying to reach a good friend to say good-bye," he said. "I think you can help." Did I remember the young boy Scott who had come to stay with him and MaryLiz one summer? It was Scott's mother he wanted to contact. He asked me about Scott with that usual Harold giggle and wink. Yes, I remembered Scott.

Scott was my youngest and first love. I was six when Scott had arrived next door. He was a few months older. Harold introduced us. I was to be the kid who would provide Scott with a companion during his summerlong visit with this childless couple in Connecticut, his mother's friends.

I led Scott to the creek, showed him the best place to catch salamanders and bullfrogs, to the stone path and the best rock to turn over for earthworms. The flat irregular stones the size of dinner plates provided several possible worlds. You could pick up one to find a squirming mass of nightcrawlers in the pebbly earth they had digested. Pick up the neighboring stone and millions of yellow ants, each carrying a translucent white ricelike egg, farmed their exposed dusty tunnels. Another upturned stone revealed a primordial world of centipedal and hairy organisms worthy of the darkest imagination. Sometimes those weird creatures coexisted with papery-winged termites; other times they ruled a patch of earth that no lesser-footed creature dared to enter.

Scott and I made up contests and ceremonies. Which universe would the lifting of which rock reveal. We solemnly appointed one of ourselves to raise the rock, the other to make the formal pronouncement of who had been right and who not about what lay beneath.

We climbed the apple trees and looked for resinous sap to stick our fingers into, for holes in the crotches of limbs hiding nests and spiders, for fruit with wormholes that went in one side and not out another. We found a secret, surrounded place to crawl into, a small room made of a close circle of firs in which, in whispers, we would create our own universe. In there on the pine needles we performed ceremonies for the removal of clothes, sometimes the shoes first, sometimes last. Scott's little sandals, my tomboy Keds. The needles clung to our smooth damp bottoms and made a random mass of crisscrosses in the child-smooth flesh. We traced the trajectory of each of the thousand lines on the other's skin. Our liberated toes were soldiers one day, teacher and students the next. One of us became the ringmaster of a three-ringed circus, two pink nipples flat against rippling ribs provided the spot for miniature trained tigers to perform. Fingers traced a navel, fitting site from which to monitor the movements of battalions of armed forces over the expanse of an abdomen and the slope of a small rounded thigh. The deeper folds in the discovered differences between our thighs became the headquarters of generals and the hiding places of secret spies.

The war games and maneuvers lasted hours, whole humid days. After rushing the dinner hour, we would escape from our respective kitchens to return to the pine-needled spot and resume the last interrupted action. Into the evening until it became too chilly and mosquitoey not to reclothe ourselves and part reluctantly until the next day. The salamanders were still interesting, catching frogs had some allure, guessing what lay under the rocks was not wholly abandoned, but almost always those amusements were suggestive of the more private, richer, and fertile place between the trees where we spent some part of almost every day. I wondered if Harold felt abandoned on those days when his fishing companion disappeared all day long with his young visitor. Scott left to return to California before the school year began, and I spent the rest of the summer day-dreaming about 3-ring circuses, battalions in motion, and infiltrating spies. Luckily, the bluefish run that September was plentiful and kept Harold and me very occupied with each other.

"See if you can locate Scott M__. and have him contact his

mother for me," Harold said. "I think he's mayor or councilman in this small northern California mining town."

I returned to San Francisco. Scott and I would be in the same time zone when I tried to reach him. I called the mayor's office in that small town. I was directed to the fire department. Their mayor was also their fire chief. I called the fire station. No, the chief was at home sleeping. He had worked the night shift. I explained myself a bit, my mission, and was told I could call his home. His wife would be awake. Her name? "Cynthia."

I called. A pleasant, slightly tired, I thought, but sunny female voice answered. It was Cynthia. I told her my name, that I was making a call for Harold N__. "Oh, Liz," she replied with depths of recognition, and laughed, happily. Was it stories of 3-ring circuses she was recalling, or of exposed termite tunnels, hidden salamanders, or headquartered commanders? I didn't ask. She promised to give Harold's message to Scott and her mother-in-law. We both hesitated a moment and then said good-bye.

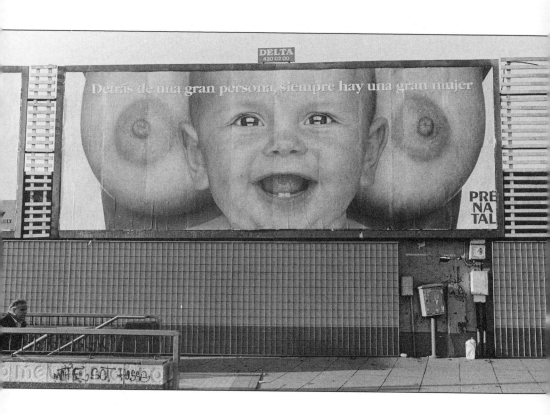

Of Breasts and Transhistories
and
Bald, Impotent, and Depressed

by

Jonathan

Ames

Of Breasts and Transhistories

In the late 80s and early 90s I was obsessed with women's breasts to an appalling degree. Every woman I saw I wanted to nurse on. This obsessive state of mind, which I've since outgrown (now I want to go down on all women—much healthier, I think), was very painful. The world was filled with boobs I couldn't have! I was like that desolate baby chick from the children's book, who, accidentally ejected from his nest, staggers about in a Beckettian landscape looking for his mommy.

I was living in Princeton, New Jersey, during this difficult period and had a lovely girlfriend, but her breasts—for the idiot I was at that time—were too small. The poor girl, a wonderful artist, sensed intuitively my condition—I had the decency to never say anything about it, but women are emotional tuning forks, they pick up everything—and she painted this large canvas of a stupendously endowed woman rising out of the sea. She hung it over my bed, perhaps for me to look at while I mounted her, which now that I think of it is like the remedy that Dr. Richard von Krafft-Ebing, the famous 19th-century German psychiatrist, recommended for a shoe fetishist: His wife's high heel was to be nailed to the wall over their conjugal bed so that he could peer at it and be aroused sufficiently to perform his marital duties.

I didn't like my condition and I thought of contacting the Kinsey Institute and asking to be allowed to nurse on 100 women lined up in a gymnasium. I thought that might heal me once and for all; the idea being to demystify the breast, to get my fill. Later, I did attempt such a cure on my own when I moved to New York in 1992 and frequented the suckling booths of a peep show on Forty-third Street, though I was often concerned about getting TB from the nipples of those women. They didn't seem to wash their boobs between clients, but I never developed a bad cough, and I think the cure worked on my breast problem. By 1993, after just a few months of steady nursing, I was interested in all parts of the female anatomy, including the penis. Turns out that right next to the peep show on Forty-third Street was a legendary tranny bar, Sally's. So I cured myself of my bosom condition and then right next door, I developed another problem, which took me years to get over. But this is one of the strengths of my character: When it comes to sexual fetishes, I can't be pigeonholed! I'm always changing, always growing!

Anyway, I've digressed, let me go back in time to late October of 1990, when I was still that wandering chick looking for the perfect nipple. I was flying back from Los Angeles and a friend picked me up at the airport in Philadelphia. It was around 10:00 P.M. and I was tired, but on our way back to Princeton my friend, an older man, wanted to stop at a gay bar in New Hope, Pennsylvania—the Provincetown of the Keystone State.

So into this gay bar, called the Cartwheel, we ventured. Being straightish, I didn't feel entirely at ease as we penetrated the establishment, which is often my reaction to gay bars. It's like how I, as a Conservative Jew, feel in Orthodox synagogues—I almost belong, but not quite. So I was very pleased when immediately on approaching the large circular, cartwheelish bar, a gorgeous, older blond woman said to me, "Where have you been my whole life, baby? Look at those blond eyelashes!"

She was sitting on a barstool and right away gathered me into her arms. She was a big woman, about six feet tall in a low-cut blouse and stylish skirt—and she began to make love to me, in the old-fashioned sense, that is.

She looked to be in her late forties, had a beautiful smile, bed-room eyes which ate you up, glamorous long legs, and very important to the young, 26-year-old Jonathan—an ample, delicious bosom. Her breasts were as big as the ones my girlfriend had put in that painting! It was just about the quickest pickup of my life. She held me against her lovely, comforting chest, and we chatted happily and spontaneously. We were kindred spirits: she wanted to mother and I wanted to be mothered.

Well, our barside lovemaking went on for about an hour and then my friend, who brought me there, wanted to get back to

Princeton. I kissed my new lady friend good-bye and she gave me her number, written on a Cartwheel napkin, and we promised each other that we would get together—a promise tinged with erotic possibility.

During the car ride home, my friend expressed his wonderment at my ability to pick up—or rather to be picked up by—the only woman in the bar. I was also impressed with myself, but guilty, too; my girlfriend the artist was waiting for me at home! I was a cad. But how could I have resisted?

Over the next two weeks, this older woman and I had two or three quasi-erotic phone conversations. She lived a few towns away from Princeton and was acting in a local theater company—she had gone to the bar with some gay members of her troupe. We talked about getting together, but I kept postponing this: I was scared about cheating on my girlfriend.

I felt unfaithful, though, just by possessing that Cartwheel napkin, it seemed to burn inside my desk drawer where I had it hidden beneath unpaid bills. I would often look at that napkin, with its hastily scribbled name and phone number, and become guiltily excited—should I call or not call? Should I arrange an encounter? But then; in what felt like a heroic moment after a therapy session, I threw the number away! For all my faults, I loved my artist girl, and I never again saw or spoke to the woman from the bar.

Now let's fast-forward. The girl and I broke up two years later and I moved to New York, as I said, in 1992. I took my cure at the peep show and picked up my new fetish condition at Sally's. Over the next several years, I wrote a novel, which was very much inspired by my tenure as a Sally's barfly. The book, *The Extra Man*, came out in 1998 and since that time, I've often been solicited to provide blurbs for books with sexual content. For example, a few months ago, I was contacted, via e-mail, by a publicist for Temple University Press, who was hoping that I might read and blurb one of Temple's forthcoming books—the memoir of a transsexual. I happily assented and the book, in galley form, was sent to me—*The Woman I Was Not Born to Be: A Transsexual Journey*, by Aleshia Brevard.

I loved the book and found it absolutely fascinating and it inspired me to read several other transsexual memoirs. These personal histories, like Ms. Brevard's, are very similar in structure to that classic literary model—the bildungsroman, the coming-of-age novel. In fact, there is such a wealth now of transsexual memoirs that they are deserving of their own category, maybe "transhistory" or "transromance" or "genitomemoir." Well, I'll leave it to the Ph.D.s, but I think I will go with my first suggestion.

The basic outline of the *Transhistory* is as follows: boys or girls very early on in life feel terribly uncomfortable in their gender role and there is a sense that some terrible mistake has occurred, that they were meant to be the other sex. Attempts are made—by parents or society—to reform them and they learn to repress as much as possible their instincts. Eventually—like the protagonist of the bildungsroman—they leave the home, their small world, and venture out, usually to a big city. There they begin to privately or publicly masquerade as the other sex, until eventually the masquerade goes beyond costume and posture and becomes permanent—especially in the latter part of the twentieth century with the advent of synthetic hormones and plastic and sex-change surgeries.

The third act to transhistories—first act: gender-dysphoric childhood; second act: the move to the big city and the transformation—is the aftermath of the sex-change. In most of the books I've read, whether it be female-to-male or male-to-female transsexuals, the writer will not proclaim that great happiness has been found or that all their problems are solved, but they all do seem to express this feeling that *they've done all they can* (penises removed, breasts implanted; penises constructed, breasts removed; myriad other surgeries; great physical and psychological suffering) and they have come, finally, to a place of self-acceptance and peace. These are the success stories, though, and it takes a lot of courage to write them, but what of the transsexuals for whom gender reassignment doesn't work? To tell their story would take even more courage, if they even had the will to pen such a tale.

Aleshia Brevard's memoir follows this basic transhistory model and I'm happy to say that her tale is one of the success stories, and is one of the most amazing memoirs—transsexual or otherwise—I've ever read. Here's the Hollywood plot summary: Born in the late 30s on a farm in the south, as Alfred Brevard Crenshaw, but called Buddy; quits the farm and runs away to the West Coast, landing eventually in San Francisco where he becomes a drag queen at the famous Finocchio's; performing as Lee Shaw in the late fifties, Buddy is perhaps the first Marilyn Monroe impersonator and achieves such a level of fame that MM herself comes to his show;

during this time he meets the love of his life, a man named Hank, and so that they may be married, Buddy undergoes in 1962, at age 23, a sex-change operation; as Aleshia the relationship with Hank sadly falls apart, but she goes to college, studies drama, and is twice voted "Actress of the Year"; after college there's a brief marriage, then a move to Los Angeles and a career as a B-movie and soap-opera actress and Playboy bunny—becoming the first transsexual Hollywood starlet, but all the while never revealing to Tinseltown her previous life as Buddy Crenshaw; there's also a second marriage and the role of mother to three stepsons.

This life story, which I've summarized with the barest-bone details, is told with incredible wit and grace and feeling. Especially moving is her portrait of her mother, Mozelle, this Southern woman who never stopped loving and supporting her child. Here's an incredible example of her mother's devotion (the day after the surgery):

> I was curious about the appearance of my vagina. I'd never seen one—and now I had my own. In fact, I had a brand-new one! I'd bought the darn thing sight unseen. I wanted to see exactly what it looked like.
>
> The day after surgery, I asked for a hand mirror and tenderly positioned myself for my first peek at a vagina.
>
> "Good God!" I shrieked, "what have they done to me? This looks like something you'd hang in your smokehouse . . . after a hog killing."
>
> I'd never seen anything so gross. It was swollen, red and WRINKLED . . . This thing needed to be ironed. . . . I started to cry, which only made matters worse.
>
> Mother rang for the nurse.
>
> "You're perfectly normal," they both reassured me. "That's how you're supposed to look."
>
> Who did they think they were fooling? I was having none of it.
>
> "Like *this*?" I keened . . . This thing had

folds! I was suddenly reminded of that unattractive rear view as I herded home the cows.

I was truly upset.

"We'll show you," my mother volunteered. My mother and the Westlake Clinic's charge nurse both lifted their skirts, presenting me a view of not one but two naturally born vaginas. By golly, they did have folds. There were four outer labial folds on each vagina. Satisfied that I was normal, I drifted off to sleep.

Well, I absolutely adored this book and all the while as I read it I kept wondering why the name Aleshia Brevard was so familiar to me. I had this vague feeling that maybe I had spoken to Aleshia on a phone-sex line or something; it was kind of haunting. And I kept looking at her sexy pictures in the middle of the book and I found her, as Hollywood casting agents had, very beautiful—that's the other aspect of transhistories: incredible before-and-after photos. Then I got to the end of the memoir and there was a brief mention of having been in a small theater company in Princeton. She was the woman—though I couldn't quite recall the name, was it Aleshia Brevard?—whom I had met at the Cartwheel! I promptly e-mailed the publicist at Temple University Press: "I love the book and will happily give it a blurb. But there's something curious going on—I think I've met Aleshia. Can you ask her if she remembers meeting me at a bar in New Hope, Pennsylvania, ten years ago?"

A few hours later the publicist forwarded an E-mail to me from Aleshia Brevard. It was one line long: "Where have you been, baby?"

Bald, Impotent, and Depressed

I used to be a breast man, but now I'm an ass man.

I still like to nurse on breasts, but it's more fun to nurse on the buttocks. They're like really large breasts. Also they have such a beautiful curvature, especially if you can get your lady friend to bend her knees while lying on her stomach. Then the ass is in the air and quite firm and delicious. The ass crack is also very nice, like a cleavage from heaven. So, in essence, if I am to be honest with myself, I must still be a breast man. I now simply pretend that the buttocks are breasts. There is the nipple problem, though. No nipples down there. That's why I haven't given up on the breast entirely. Regardless, it's all madness. I should be out discovering vaccines, doing something decent with my life, but instead all I care about is sex and my financial problems. And what about my soul? I hardly think of it. I need to pray more.

My problem is that I am surrounded by like-minded people—individuals who are obsessed with their genitals. For example, a few nights ago, I was at a dinner party in a dimly lit Tribeca loft. Halfway through the meal, my good friend Spencer, a therapist-in-training, announced with pride that he had used Viagra. The conversation up until that point had naturally been about sexual intercourse—why women like to have their hair pulled had just been covered—but this Viagra confession shocked all of us.

"Why?" we all asked Spencer. After all, he's a young, healthy vital man with a full head of hair and a good-standing membership at a sophisticated gymnasium.

"Well, it was the first night with someone and that's often difficult for me. I get stagefright. So the Viagra ensured a good performance."

"It worked?" I asked.

"Oh, yeah," he said. "Nothing out of the ordinary, but it was very solid. No jitters. Viagra removed the anxiety."

"Won't you want to use it again? Might you not become dependent?" asked a woman at the table, a licensed therapist, who was pulling rank on Spencer, only a therapist-in-training.

"No," said Spencer, holding his ground. "I will only use it for opening nights when the critics are there. That's the only time when I might have problems. And now with this new woman I have established my capabilities as a lover. Not having to prove anything the second night if I had been lousy the first night, which would make the second night worst than the first night . . . So I advocate Viagra use . . . but only for the first night. Unless, of course, there's an emergency, and then one can keep the pill in a glass case and break it open like a fireman."

"Any side effects?" I asked.

"A headache. But who doesn't have a headache after sex?" Spencer lifted his eyebrow, indicating his utterance of a bad joke. And everyone found all of this amusing, except me. I felt betrayed by my friend. The whole world was going on Viagra. But I never will. I am against all pills and medications, anything unnatural. I have smoked crack cocaine, but I won't take antibiotics.

"This is terrible," I said to my dinner companions. "I won't go on Rogaine or any hair pills. And I won't take Viagra. I am a natural person. But I am going to be the only bald and impotent man in New York. I'll be completely alone."

"And depressed since you won't go on Prozac," said another friend of mine, a sculptor, and he laughed loudly as he said it, and everyone at the table joined him. My artistic friend knew well my legendary stance against Prozac despite my years of depressive episodes and suicidal ideation and compulsive masturbation.

"My God," I said, "I'll be the only bald, impotent, and depressed man in New York. I'll have to hang out in vegan restaurants. Only organically minded women will like me. I may become an acronym—a BID man."

After that there was a general discussion of who at the table had actually suffered from impotence. All of the men confessed to having had this problem at least once, though I've never really had this problem that I can recall, and needing to regain some stature with the ladies at the table, I said, "My problem isn't impotence, at least not yet. My problem is too many erections caused by too many things."

"What do you mean?" asked the woman therapist, putting me on the spot.

"He's polymorphously perverse," said Spencer, showing his superior that he has the goods.

"That's right," I said, "I've tried every perversion and none of them have stuck. I am now working on my soul."

Then the CD player went haywire, everyone made comments about CDs, and then the wineglasses were refilled, except mine since I only drink temperance beverages. The evening wound down without further incident.

I walked home with Spencer. "I can see the future," I said. "I am going to need a woman who won't care that I can't get erections."

"There's no such woman," he said.

"I know one," I said, and I told him the tale of this lover I had on the Upper East Side in 1993. She was 15 years my elder and we met in Carl Shurz Park sitting beside each other on a bench. There was a sympathy in our worldviews and a two-month affair ensued. But she had a tremendous paranoia about venereal diseases, AIDS in particular, so she wouldn't engage in intercourse with me; she didn't trust condoms. She only liked to do one thing: to sit on my face and suffocate me for about an hour. She was a tiny dark woman of Greek heritage and very demure, but she loved this dominant position. She said it made her feel like a queen on a throne. She wouldn't even move that much while I flickered my tongue and struggled for air. She even faced away from my penis, not very interested in it, and so without her looking at it I could play with myself if I wanted. To her it was immaterial. After about an hour of just sitting there like a hen, she would have an orgasm. And the whole thing was so exotic and unusual that I enjoyed it.

This one time, though, there was a problem. She shifted her weight and my nose, which was buried, seemed to make a cracking noise. Then I thought I was having a bloody nose. I've been prone to bloody noses almost all my life. When I was seven years old a mildly retarded, violent boy, who was eventually removed from his home and put in some kind of training facility, attacked me and smashed me in the nose and I've had a weak vessel in my left nostril ever since. It's been cauterized many times, most notably when I really punctured the thing while nosepicking as a teenager and almost bled to death.

Anyway, while my Greek lady friend was sitting on my face that one time when my nose cracked I thought I was having a nosebleed inside of her. I began to panic. If this was the case, she would go insane. Bleeding inside her would be worse than coming inside her. Her AIDS paranoia was extremely severe. What to do? We were only about 30 minutes into our sitting. Naturally, I couldn't see what was going on. I was deprived of almost all my senses. It was an incredible predicament; I knew of no one else who had suffered a nosebleed during oral sex. And I didn't dare disturb my queen on her throne. It was a terribly long half hour that ensued. When her orgasm came and she removed herself, I ran to the bathroom hiding my face from her. I studied myself in the mirror and to my considerable relief there was no blood coming from my left nostril, or the right. I had imagined the whole scary thing.

Spencer was quite impressed with this story, and I added that I was thinking of looking that woman back up. His therapeutic side emerged. "Listen," he said, "you can do better than a woman who just sits on you for an hour." Then he told me that a pretty woman at the dinner party, whom I didn't know very well, found me attractive.

"But I'm going bald," I said.

He ignored me and gave me her number. I called her and one thing led to another and by the second date I was in bed with her. And once our clothes were off, I immediately became overwhelmed with gas. I don't have erection problems the first time I'm in bed with a woman—I have gas problems. My nervousness produces flatulence. This woman was kissing me tenderly and I was trying to hold in farts. I excused myself from her bed to go to the bathroom. Luckily for me the toilet had a fan, so there was no chance that she could hear what I was doing in there. I farted in safety.

I returned to her bed. A new fart needed to be held in. This was torture. Then the woman said, "I have condoms." The call of the wild. I tried to put a positive spin on things: I thought that my bloated abdomen might rub against her in a favorable way. I rolled on the condom, went to mount her, almost farted, and lost my erection. I rolled off her and removed the defeated condom.

"It's all this talk about Viagra these days," I said. "It must be subliminal marketing; it has destroyed my confidence. Please forgive me. This is my first experience with erection loss. With mild impotence." She was sweet and understanding. I let a fart slowly leak out. It didn't smell. To rally myself, I crawled downward and nursed on her buttocks. With my hand, I reached under her and tried to find the clitoris, but I couldn't locate it. I haven't been able to find one in years. But I was rubbing against the bed and an erection announced itself. I quickly put on a new condom. I mounted her from behind and was so nervous about the whole thing that I had a premature ejaculation. I tried to fake a few thrusts, but my spirit was crushed and the flesh was unwilling.

I rolled off. We lay there silently. Then I said, "My new book is coming out soon." I had to show her that I had some worth. She smiled at me in the darkness. Women are quite kind to men.

I didn't spend the night. I went home around 2:00 A.M. and called Spencer. He's an insomniac and can be reached at indecent hours.

"What happened?" he asked.

"She invited me up and I had gas. I got an erection but lost it. Then got another one, but I had premature ejaculation. My only recourse was to brag that my book was coming out."

The other end of the phone was silent. The study of object relations had not prepared him for this. Perhaps if he was a Freudian, he might have been equipped to help me. Finally, he spoke. "I can't think of anything consoling to say."

"I'm going to call the woman on the Upper East Side."

"Good idea," he said.

Contributors

This is the first time Michael Alago will be showing work from his upcoming book entitled *Rough Gods*. Better known for his work in the music industry as a top executive producer, working with the likes of Metallica and Nina Simone.

Jonathan Ames is the author of the novels *I Pass Like Night* and *The Extra Man,* and the memoir *What's Not to Love?: The Adventures of a Mildly Perverted Young Writer.*

Art Club 2000 was formed in 1992 in cooperation with Colin de Land (current members include: Will Rollins, Craig Wadlin, Shannon Pultz, Daniel McDonald, Gillian Havatani and Patterson Beckwith). A retrospective of the work was shown at Museo de Arte Carillo Gil, Mexico City, Mexico.

Leslie Baze, a teacher and psychic counselor from San Diego, recently completed an MFA in Poetry. Current projects include a collection of poems and performance monologues for the stage.

Downtown New York City playwright Jack Bump is the "Alter Libido" of performance artist Alien Comic. His first play, *Whores on the Range,* was published in 1998 by Sock Monkey Press. His second, *Sport-Fuckers,* was produced at Theater for the New City in June and October 2000.

Paul Ciotti is a Los Angeles writer of books and magazine articles. He specializes in covering the more raggedy edges of the ongoing paradigm shift.

e m curley: studied architecture in London, film and photography at the SF Art Institute, and is currently working with digital technologies at the SF Academy of Art. A passion for black and white photography.

Walking installation piece, Vaginal Davis for almost two decades has been known as a per-

forming and visual arts treasure. Her medium is the indefinite nature of her own whimsy.

Photographer f-stop Fitzgerald has documented subjects ranging from fishing to punk rock. He collaborated with horror writer Stephen King on the bestselling volume *Nightmares in the Sky* and his photographs have been exhibited around the world at museums and galleries. His work has appeared in over 100 periodicals and newspapers.

Mary Gaitskill is the author of 2 previous collections of stories, *Bad Behavior* and *Because They Wanted To; Two Girls, Fat and Thin,* and numerous stories and articles.

Charles Gatewood has been "family photographer of America's erotic underground" for nearly forty years. His books include *Sidtripping* (with William S. Burroughs), *Forbidden Photographs, The Body and Beyond, Primitives, True Blood,* and *Badlands.* www.charlesgatewood.com

Jessica Hagedorn poet, performer, artist and the author of the critically acclaimed *Dogeaters.*

Lizbeth Hasse is an entertainment and intellectual property attorney with an international practice based in San Francisco. She frequently writes and lectures on issues in the media, constitutional and intellectual property law fields.

Tom Healy lives in New York City and Miami. One of the first art dealers in Chelsea, he is starting a new literary magazine called *Translation.*

Richard Hell is the author of the novel *Go Now* /Scribner, 1996. His newest book is a collection of his essays, notebooks, poems, drawings, collaborations, and fiction called *Hot and Cold* from powerHouse Books.

bell hooks, feminist scholar, poet, memorist and social critic. She is the author of numerous books including *Bone Black: Memories of Girlhood.*

Ishmael Houston-Jones is a writer and choreographer living and making work in New York City. His fiction, essays, and performance texts have been anthologized in several books, including *Best Gay Erotica, 2000* and *Footnotes: six choreographers inscribe the page.*

Tessa Hughes-Freeland is a British born film-maker and writer who lives in New York City. Her films have been shown internationally, in venerable museums and seedy bars. Her writing has appeared in numerous magazines as well as in several books.

The poetry, memoirs, and short fiction of Kathe Izzo have been published in many journals and anthologies including *The Outlaw Bible of American Poetry/* Thunder's Mouth Press, *Best Lesbian Erotica 1998–2000 /*Cleis Press and *Blood and Tears/*Painted Leaf Press. She is currently working on the novel *Hummer.*

Richard Kern is a filmmaker and photographer. His book of photography is titled *New York Girls.* He lives in New York City.

Eric Kroll is considered to be one of the classic photographers in the genre of fetish, bizarre and erotic photography. His books include *Fetish Girls* and *Beauty Parade.*

Tony Labat's work has taken many different forms, performance, installation, video, photography, and sculpture. Labat has presented his work internationally, has received numerous grants and awards and his work is included in many private and public collections. He is a professor at the San Francisco Art Institute, and has taught in the New Genres department since 1985. Tony Labat lives and works in San Francisco.

Adam Levy is a writer and filmmaker. He has made three documentary films for the BBC, has co-authored a book, and is working on another.

Marilyn Jaye Lewis' short stories and novellas have been widely anthologized. Author of the critically praised erotic fiction collection, *Neptune & Surf,* she is winner of the Erotic Writer of the Year in England award.

Richard Lewis has spun his anxieties into a compelling art form both as a performer and writer. Often compared to Lenny Bruce for his fearlessness, he landed on *GQ* magazine's list of the '20th Century's Most Influential Humorists.'

Lydia Lunch is a multimedia art terrorist who refuses to be pigeonholed by definition.

Dona Ann McAdams is an internationally exhibited and published photographer. Her work has been shown at, among other places, the Whitney Museum of American Art and the Musuem of Modern Art. Her book, *Caught in the Act,* was published by Aperture.

I was born in Australia in 1971. My writing has appeared in *Boy Meets Boy, James White Review,* and in the forthcoming *Best Gay Erotica 2002.*—Alistair McCartney

Carlo McCormick is Senior Editor of *Paper* magazine in New York.

Hailed for its humor and passion, Tim Miller's solo performances have been presented all over the world. He is the author of the book *Shirts & Skins.*

Linda Montano, performance artist, is a graduate of College of New Rochelle, Villa Schifanoia where she received an MA in Sculpture, University of Wisconsin, Madison, MFA Sculpture, Hobart Welding School, and was a Novice at the Maryknoll Sisters for two years. She has performed her dreams, fears, concepts since 1965 so that she could prepare herself for the Ecstasy of Silence.

Magdalen Pierrakos lives in New York City. Her work, which includes performance, video, film, installation, and painting has been shown at the Kitchen, P. S. 122, Anthology Film Archive, and 80 Langton.

Jack Pierson exhibits his photography and installations internationally.

Mark Russell is the Executive Director of Performance Space 122, the infamous arts center in the East Village of New York City. He edited *Out of Character, Rants Raves and Monologues from Today*s Top Performance Artists* published by Bantam in 1997.

Saint Rev Jen is a poet, preacher, painter, performer, prophet, literary giant, upcoming celebrity/personality, Patron Saint of the Uncool and Voice of the Downtrodden and Tired.

Sarah Schulman is the author of seven novels and two nonfiction books. Most recently *Shimmer* (Avon) and *Stagestruck Theater, AIDS and the Marketing of Gay America* (Duke University Press/ American Library Association Book Award). Her play, *Carson McCullers,* will open at Playwrights Horizons in NYC in 2002, directed by Marion McClinton.

Lori E. Seid has worked in theatre, film, TV, and rock-n-roll as a producer, lighting designer, technical director, and road manager.

I was born in 1928. Have yet to die . . . irrevocably. I am a fiction writer. I am short, skinny, and funny-looking. I am a virgin.—Hubert Selby, Jr.

Wallace Shawn is the author of *The Designated Mourner and Four Plays,* both published by Farrar, Straus and Giroux. With Andre Gregory, he wrote *My Dinner With Andre.*

Annie Sprinkle is the prostitute/porn star turned transmedia artist/sex guru. Recently she earned her doctorate and is now officially "Dr. Sprinkle," sexologist. She lives by the sea with her butch mermaid girlfriend.

Jerry Stahl is the author of the narcotic memoir, *Permanent Midnight,* along with the novels *Perv: A Love Story* and *Plainclothes Naked.*

Internationally claimed drag king, Diane Torr has pioneered and presented drag king workshops throughout the U.S. Canada and Europe. Her performances have focussed on feminism and transgender issues for over 20 years.

Movie director John Waters was born and lives in Baltimore, Maryland. He has exhibited his photography at American Fine Arts, Co., in New York, since his first show in 1995. Stating that he avoids viewing any film a second time, his photo montages are taken directly from the TV screen and redirected in the form of photographic storyboards. John Waters critically acclaimed exhibitions have been shown internationally. A book of his photographs, *Director's Cut,* was published by Scalo books in 1996, and his *Twelve Assholes and a Dirty Foot,* was published by Little Cockroach in 1999.

Self-taught performance artist Johanna Went is infamous for splattering chaotic and visceral imagery and jagged sound across the music stages and art venues of underground America. She is also a recording artist and has acted in several films.

Tim Wildin is theatre artist and attends New York University.

Acknowledgments

Jim Ellison for his editing skills, Michelle Rosenfield for her assistance, Paul Paddock for his design, Maria Fernandez for production, Linda Kosarin for her art direction. Dan O'Connor, Ghadah Alrawi, Catheline Jean Francois, and Neil Ortenberg for his generosity and encouragement in making this book happen. And everyone at Avalon.

—*Karen Finley*

We gratefully acknowledge all those who gave permission for their work to appear in this book. We have made every effort to trace and contact copyright holders. If an error or omission is brought to our notice we will be pleased to remedy the situation in future editions of this book. For further information, please contact the publisher.

Aroused by Karen Finley. Copyright © 2001 by Karen Finley. Used by permission of the author. ❖ *Writing Sex* by Richard Hell. Copyright © 2001 by Richard Hell. ❖ An excerpt from "Little Trophy" from *Perv—A Love Story* by Jerry Stahl, published by William Morrow. Reprinted by permission of the author. ❖ *The Mewling* (abridged) by Kathe Izzo. Copyright © 2001 by Kathe Izzo. Used by permission of the author. ❖ *The Boy is Peeling* by Alistair McCartney. Copyright © 2001 by Alistair McCartney. Used by permission of the author. ❖ *First Love* by Hubert Selby, Jr. Copyright © 2001 by Hubert Selby, Jr. Used by permission of the author. ❖ *Night on Twelfth Street* by Marilyn Jaye Lewis. Copyright © 2001 by Marilyn Jaye Lewis. Used by permission of the author. ❖ "The Youth Hostel" from "A Thought in Three Parts" from *Four Plays* by Wallace Shawn. Copyright © 1997 by Wallace Shawn. Reprinted by permission of Farrarr, Straus and Giroux, LLC. ❖ "12 Assholes and a Dirty Foot" by John Waters. Copyright © 1999 by John Waters. Artist's work appears courtesy of American Fine Arts Co., New York. ❖ *Folksong 1999* by Mary Gaitskill. Copyright © 1999 by Mary Gaitskill. Used by permission of the author. Originally appeared on *nerve.com*, April 2000. ❖ *Analgesic* by Lydia Lunch. Copyright © 2001 by Lydia Lunch. Used by permission of the author. ❖ *Cumming to the Conclusion: An Erotic Trilogy from Hell* by Richard Lewis. Copyright © 2001 by Richard Lewis. Used by permission of the author. ❖ *Miss Anne* by Lori E. Seid. Copyright © 2001 by Lori E. Seid. Used by permission of the author. ❖ *A Wedding Day* by Tim Miller. Copyright © 2001 by Tim Miller. Used by permission of the author. ❖ *He Delivers! A Straight Woman Looks at Gay Male Porn* by Karen Finley. Copyright © 2001 by Karen Finley. Used by permission of the author. First appeared in the *Village Voice*, 2001. ❖ *Songs of Experience* by Tom Healy. Copyright © 2001 by Tom Healy. Used by permission of the author. ❖ *Slither* by Mark Russell. Copyright ©